神奇的 **自然拼读**

Amazing PHONICS

WORKBOOK

Vol. **1**

SHORT VOWEL
SOUNDS

My Writing Note

Step 1

Write the words

You can practise writing words from the Student Book.

Step 2

Trace & write the sentences

You can practise tracing and writing sentences from the Student Book.

Step 3

Make your own sentences

Using the words you learned, you can make your own sentences!

Step 4

Write your own sentences!

Write your own sentences and read them out loud!

AMAZING PHONICS **WORKBOOK**
Vol.1 Short Vowel Sounds

CONTENTS

Step 1

Look and write the right word.

- dad - sad - cat - can - sat
- man - mat - bad - fan

1

dad

2

3

4

5

6

7

8

9

1

A cat sat on a mat.

A cat sat on a mat.

2

A man has a bad fan.

A man has a bad fan.

1

A cat sat on a mat.

2

A man has a bad fan.

bad

dad

sad

fan

can

man

sat

cat

mat

★ **New Sight Words** ★

a, on, has

Let's Practise!

1 **A bad cat.**

A bad cat.

2 **A man has a fan.**

A man has a fan.

3 **A cat sat on a mat.**

A cat sat on a mat.

Write your own sentence.

★ **Phonics Word Bank** ★

bad, dad, sad, can, fan, man, cat, mat, sat,

★ *Sight Word Bank* ★

a, on, has

1   RECORD   PLAY

2   RECORD   PLAY

3   RECORD   PLAY

4   RECORD   PLAY

5   RECORD   PLAY

UNIT 2 ag, am, ap

Step 1 **Look and write the right word.**

·jam · ham · nap · wag · ram
·map · tag · bag · cap

1

jam

2

3

4

5

6

7

8

9

Trace the sentence.

1

I see a tag on a bag.

I see a tag on a bag.

2

I see a ram on a map.

I see a ram on a map.

Write the sentence.

1

I see a tag on a bag.

2

I see a ram on a map.

bag

tag

wag

ham

jam

ram

cap

nap

map

★ **New Sight Words** ★

I, see

🐰 **Let's Practise!**

1 **I see a ham.**

I see a ham.

2 **I see a ram on a map.**

I see a ram on a map.

Advanced
3 Use the words that you know.

A man has a bag.

A man has a bag.

Write your own sentence.

★ **Phonics Word Bank** ★

Unit 2

bag, tag, wag, ham, jam, ram, cap, map, nap,

★ *Sight Word Bank* ★

a, on, has, I, see

1 _____ RECORD PLAY

2 _____ RECORD PLAY

3 _____ RECORD PLAY

4 _____ RECORD PLAY

5 _____ RECORD PLAY

UNIT 3 ed, eg

Look and write the right word.

·red	·Meg	·wed	·beg
·bed	·leg	·egg	·Ted

1

red

2

3

4

5

6

7

8

Have fun!

Trace the Sentence.

1

This is a red bed.

This is a red bed.

2

Ted weds Meg.

Ted weds Meg.

Write the Sentence.

1

This is a red bed.

2

Ted weds Meg.

bed

red

wed

Ted

beg

egg

leg

Meg

★ **New Sight Words** ★

this, is

🐰 **Let's Practise!**

1 **This is Ted.**

This is Ted.

2 **This is a red bed.**

This is a red bed.

Advanced

3 Use the words that you know.

Meg has red jam.

Meg has red jam.

Write your own sentence.

★ **Phonics Word Bank** ★

bed, red, Ted, wed, beg, egg, leg, Meg

★ **Sight Word Bank** ★

a, on, has, I, see, this, is

1 _____ RECORD PLAY

2 _____ RECORD PLAY

3 _____ RECORD PLAY

4 _____ RECORD PLAY

5 _____ RECORD PLAY

UNIT 4 en, et

Look and write the right word.

· wet	· pen	· jet	· ten
· hen	· men	· net	· pet

1

———————
wet

2

3

4

5

6

7

8

Have fun!

Step 2-1 *Trace the Sentence.*

1
There are men on a jet.

There are men on a jet.

2
There is a hen in a net.

There is a hen in a net.

Step 2-2 *Write the Sentence.*

1
There are men on a jet.

2
There is a hen in a net.

Make your own sentence.

hen

men

pen

ten

jet

net

pet

wet

★ **New Sight Words** ★

there, are, in

🐰 **Let's Practise!**

1 **There are ten men.**

There are ten men.

2 **There is a hen in a net.**

There is a hen in a net.

Advanced

3 Use the words that you know.

Ted has ten eggs.

Ted has ten eggs.

Write your own sentence.

★ **Phonics Word Bank** ★

hen, men, pen, ten, jet, net, pet, wet

★ **Sight Word Bank** ★

a, on, has, I, see, this, is, there, are, in

1 _____
RECORD PLAY

2 _____
RECORD PLAY

3 _____
RECORD PLAY

4 _____
RECORD PLAY

5 _____
RECORD PLAY

UNIT 5 id, ig, in

Step 1 Look and write the right word.

·fin	·dig	·win	·hid	·kid
·pig	·bin	·lid	·big	

1

fin

2

3

4

5

6

7

8

9

1

A man hid a lid.

A man hid a lid.

2

A pig digs to find a lid.

A pig digs to find a lid.

1

A man hid a lid.

2

A pig digs to find a lid.

hid

kid

lid

big

dig

pig

bin

fin

win

★ **New Sight Words** ★

can, find

🐰 **Let's Practise!**

1 **I can find a bin.**

I can find a bin.

2 **A kid hid a lid.**

A kid hid a lid.

Advanced

3 Use the words that you know.

I see a big fin.

I see a big fin.

Write your own sentence.

Unit 5

★ **Phonics Word Bank** ★

hid, kid, lid, big, dig, pig, bin, fin, win

★ **Sight Word Bank** ★

a, on, has, I, see, this, is, there, are, in, can, find

1 _____ RECORD PLAY

2 _____ RECORD PLAY

3 _____ RECORD PLAY

4 _____ RECORD PLAY

5 _____ RECORD PLAY

Step 1 Look and write the right word.

· zip · hit · fix · hip · kit
· mix · dip · sit · six

1

zip

2

3

4

5

6

7

8

9

Step 2-1 *Trace the sentence.*

1
Dad can fix the zip.
Dad can fix the zip.

2
The six men sit.
The six men sit.

Step 2-2 *Write the sentence.*

1
Dad can fix the zip.

2
The six men sit.

Make your own sentence.

dip

hip

zip

kit

hit

sit

fix

mix

six

★ **New Sight Word** ★

the

🐰 **Let's Practise!**

1 I see the kit.

I see the kit.

2 I can fix the zip.

I can fix the zip.

Advanced

3 Use the words that you know.

Dad can fix the kit.

Dad can fix the kit.

Write your own sentence.

★ *Phonics Word Bank* ★

dip, hip, zip, kit, hit, sit, fix, mix, six

★ *Sight Word Bank* ★

a, on, has, I, see, this, is, there, are, in, can, find, the

1

RECORD PLAY

2

RECORD PLAY

3

RECORD PLAY

4

RECORD PLAY

5

RECORD PLAY

UNIT 7 og, op

Look and write the right word.

·log	·top	·fog	·pop
·dog	·mop	·hop	·jog

1

log

2

3

4

5

6

7

8

Have fun!

Trace the Sentence.

1

He is on a log.

He is on a log.

2

He can see a mop.

He can see a mop.

Step 2-2 **Write the Sentence.**

1

He is on a log.

2

He can see a mop.

Make your own sentence.

dog

fog

jog

log

hop

mop

pop

top

★ New Sight Word ★

he

🐰 **Let's Practise!**

1 **There is a dog.**

There is a dog.

2 **He can see a mop.**

He can see a mop.

Advanced

3 Use the words that you know.

There is a dog in a bag.

There is a dog in a bag.

Step 4 *Write your own sentence.*

★ *Phonics Word Bank* ★

dog, fog, jog, log, hop, mop, pop, top

★ *Sight Word Bank* ★

a, on, has, I, see, this, is, there, are, in, can, find, the, he

1

2

3

4

5

RECORD PLAY

Look and write the right word.

· cod · nod · pod · dot · hot
· pot · box · fox · ox

1

box

2

3

4

5

6

7

8

9

Trace the sentence.

1

It is a hot pot.

It is a hot pot.

2

The fox is in the box.

The fox is in the box.

Step 2-2 *Write the sentence.*

1

It is a hot pot.

2

The fox is in the box.

Make your own sentence.

cod

nod

pod

dot

hot

pot

box

fox

ox

★ New Sight Word ★

it

🐰 **Let's Practise!**

1 It is a cod.

It is a cod.

2 It is a hot pot.

It is a hot pot.

Advanced

3 Use the words that you know.

I can see a red dot.

I can see a red dot.

Unit 8

★ *Phonics Word Bank* ★

cod, nod, pod, dot, hot, pot, box, fox, ox

★ *Sight Word Bank* ★

a, on, has, I, see, this, is, there, are, in, can, find, the, he, it

1 _____

RECORD   PLAY

2 _____

RECORD   PLAY

3 _____

RECORD   PLAY

4 _____

RECORD   PLAY

5 _____

RECORD   PLAY

Step 1 — Look and write the right word.

·mug   ·up   ·rub   ·cup   ·hug
·tub   ·bug   ·cub   ·pup

1

cup

2

3

4

5

6

7

8

9

Trace the sentence.

1

She hugs a wet pup.

She hugs a wet pup.

2

She rubs a hot mug.

She rubs a hot mug.

Step 2-2 **Write the sentence.**

1

She hugs a wet pup.

2

She rubs a hot mug.

cub

rub

tub

bug

hug

mug

cup

pup

up

★ New Sight Word ★

she

🐰 **Let's Practise!**

1 **She has a mug.**

She has a mug.

2 **She hugs a pup.**

She hugs a pup.

Advanced

3 Use the words that you know.

Dad has a bug in a cup.

Dad has a bug in a cup.

★ **Phonics Word Bank** ★

Unit 9

cub, rub, tub, bug, hug, mug, cup, pup, up

★ **Sight Word Bank** ★

a, on, has, I, see, this, is, there, are, in, can, find, the, he, it, she

1 _____
RECORD PLAY

2 _____
RECORD PLAY

3 _____
RECORD PLAY

4 _____
RECORD PLAY

5 _____
RECORD PLAY

Step 1 *Look and write the right word.*

·mud ·sun ·cut ·hut ·run
·bud ·nut ·bun ·cud

1

sun

2

3

4

5

6

7

8

9

1

She can run in the mud.

She can run in the mud.

2

There is a hut in the sun.

There is a hut in the sun.

1

She can run in the mud.

2

There is a hut in the sun.

Make your own sentence.

bud

cud

mud

bun

sun

run

cut

hut

nut

★ **New Sight Words** ★

look, at

Let's Practise!

1 **Look at the mud.**

Look at the mud.

2 **There is a hut in the sun.**

There is a hut in the sun.

Advanced

3 Use the words that you know.

Look at the nut in a bag.

Look at the nut in a bag.

Step 4 *Write your own sentence.*

★ **Phonics Word Bank** ★

bud, cud, mud, bun, sun, run, cut, hut, nut

★ **Sight Word Bank** ★

a, on, has, I, see, this, is, there, are, in, can, find, the, he, it, is, she, look, at

1 _____ RECORD PLAY

2 _____ RECORD PLAY

3 _____ RECORD PLAY

4 _____ RECORD PLAY

5 _____ RECORD PLAY

ANSWER KEY

★ **Unit 01**
pp.22-23

★ **Unit 02**
pp.32-33

★ **Unit 03**
pp.44-45

★ Unit 04 pp.54-55

★ Unit 05 pp.66-67

★ Unit 06 pp.76-77

ANSWER KEY

★ Unit 07
pp.88-89

REVIEW

Well done!

Check Up 01

1. Listen and check the right picture.

✓ (popcorn)

2. Listen and check the right word.

mop | ✓ jog | top

Check Up 02

1. Read the sentence and write the right number.

a. **2** He can hop.
b. **1** There is a dog on a log.
c. **3** There is a top.

2. Read the sentence and circle the right word.

1. (He) She has a cat.
2. I can see a (mop) hop .
3. He can top (hop)
4. He can log (jog)

★ Unit 08
pp.98-99

REVIEW

Well done!

Check Up 01

1. Listen and check the right picture.

✓ (cow)

2. Listen and check the right word.

fox | hot | ✓ nod

Check Up 02

1. Read the sentence and write the right number.

a. **2** There is a fox in the box.
b. **1** He can nod.
c. **3** It is a pod.

2. Read the sentence and circle the right word.

1. It (is) has hot.
2. A pod has pots (dots)
3. It is a nod (cod)
4. The (fox) ox is in the box.

★ Unit 09
pp.110-111

REVIEW

Well done!

Check Up 01

1. Listen and check the right picture.

✓ (grasshopper)

2. Listen and check the right word.

cup | hug | ✓ pup

Check Up 02

1. Read the sentence and write the right number.

a. **2** She has a mug.
b. **1** She hugs a wet pup.
c. **3** She rubs a hot mug.

2. Read the sentence and circle the right word.

1. He (She) has a cup.
2. She hugs a wet (pup) cup .
3. She has a hub (mug)
4. She cubs (rubs) a hot mug.

★ Unit 10
pp.120-121

★ Final Review 01
pp.122-123

★ Final Review 02
pp.124-125

神奇的 自然拼读

Amazing PHONiCs

WORKBOOK

Vol. **2**

LONG VOWEL
SOUNDS

My Writing Note

Step 1

Write the words

You can practise writing words from the Student Book.

Step 2

Trace & write the sentences

You can practise tracing and writing sentences from the Student Book.

Step 3

Make your own sentences

Using the words you learned, you can make your own sentences!

Step 4

Write your own sentences!

Write your own sentences and read them out loud!

AMAZING PHONICS WORKBOOK
Vol.2 Long Vowel Sounds

CONTENTS

a

e

i

o

u

UNIT 1 magic 'e', a_e

Step 1 *Look and write the right word.*

- man   - gate   - tap   - bake
- face   - mane   - tape   - cake

1

tape

2

_____

3

_____

4

_____

5

_____

6

_____

7

_____

8

_____

Have fun!

Trace the Sentence.

1

He can bake a big cake.

He can bake a big cake.

2

The gate is big.

The gate is big.

Write the Sentence.

1

He can bake a big cake.

2

The gate is big.

man

mane

tap

tape

cake

gate

bake

face

★ **New Sight Words** ★

big, little

Let's Practise!

1 **It is a big cake.**

It is a big cake.

2 **There is a little tape.**

There is a little tape.

Advanced

3 Use the words that you know.

He has a big cake.

He has a big cake.

★ *Phonics Word Bank* ★

man, mane, tap, tape
bake, cake, face, gate

★ *Sight Word Bank* ★

big, little

1 _____ RECORD PLAY

2 _____ RECORD PLAY

3 _____ RECORD PLAY

4 _____ RECORD PLAY

5 _____ RECORD PLAY

UNIT 2 a, ai, ay

Look and write the right word.

> · rain · acorn · say · paper · baby
> · hay · tail · mail · day

1

acorn

2

Hi

3

4

5

6

7

8

9

Trace the sentence.

1

It is a nice day.

It is a nice day.

2

A tail!

He can say "A tail!"

He can say "A tail!"

Write the sentence.

1

It is a nice day.

2

A tail!

He can say "A tail!"

Make your own sentence.

acorn

baby

paper

mail

rain

tail

day

hay

say

★ **New Sight Word** ★

my

🐰 **Let's Practise!**

1 **My baby can see the dog.**

My baby can see the dog.

2 **My baby can say "Mail!"**

My baby can say "Mail!"

Advanced

3 Use the words that you know.

There is my baby.

There is my baby.

★ Phonics Word Bank ★

Unit 2

acorn, baby, paper, mail, rain, tail, day, hay, say

★ Sight Word Bank ★

big, little, my

1

RECORD   PLAY

2

RECORD   PLAY

3

RECORD   PLAY

4

RECORD   PLAY

5

RECORD   PLAY

Step 1 **Look and write the right word.**

▪ me	▪ city	▪ we	▪ eve	▪ Steve
▪ here	▪ body	▪ he	▪ tiny	

1

city

2

3

4

5

6

7

8

9

Step 2-1 *Trace the sentence.*

1

It is a big city.

It is a big city.

2

We look tiny here.

We look tiny here.

Step 2-2 *Write the sentence.*

1

It is a big city.

2

We look tiny here.

he

me

we

eve

here

Steve

body

city

tiny

★ New Sight Word ★

come

🐰 **Let's Practise!**

1 **Come here, Steve.**

Come here, Steve.

2 **We come to the city.**

We come to the city.

Advanced

3 Use the words that you know.

Look! She comes to me.

Look! She comes to me.

Write your own sentence.

★ *Phonics Word Bank* ★

Unit 3

he, me, we, eve, here, Steve, body, city, tiny

★ *Sight Word Bank* ★

big, little, my, come

1

RECORD PLAY

2

RECORD PLAY

3

RECORD PLAY

4

RECORD PLAY

5

RECORD PLAY

Step 1 *Look and write the right word.*

- eat
- tree
- pea
- bee
- weak
- need
- seed
- leaf

1 weak

2

3

4

5

6

7

8

Have fun!

Trace the Sentence.

1

I need to eat peas.

I need to eat peas.

2

There are three bees in the tree.

There are three bees in the tree.

Write the Sentence.

1

I need to eat peas.

2

There are three bees in the tree.

eat

leaf

pea

weak

bee

need

seed

tree

★ **New Sight Words** ★

one, two, three

🐰 **Let's Practise!**

1 I see one leaf.

I see one leaf.

2 I eat three peas.

I eat three peas.

Advanced

3 Use the words that you know.

I can find three seeds.

I can find three seeds.

Write your own sentence.

★ *Phonics Word Bank* ★

eat, leaf, pea, weak, bee, need, seed, tree

★ *Sight Word Bank* ★

big, little, my, come, one, two, three

1 _____ RECORD PLAY

2 _____ RECORD PLAY

3 _____ RECORD PLAY

4 _____ RECORD PLAY

5 _____ RECORD PLAY

Look and write the right word.

- iris
- tire
- pilot
- bike
- tiger
- ride
- size
- iron

1

size

2

3

4

5

6

7

8

Have fun!

Step 2-1 *Trace the Sentence.*

1

I have a bike.

I have a bike.

2

I can ride my bike.

I can ride my bike.

Step 2-2 *Write the Sentence.*

1

I have a bike.

2

I can ride my bike.

iris

iron

pilot

tiger

bike

ride

size

tire

★ New Sight Word ★

like

🐰 Let's Practise!

1 **I like tigers.**

I like tigers.

2 **I like to ride a bike.**

I like to ride a bike.

Advanced

3 Use the words that you know.

Ted likes the irises.

Ted likes the irises.

Write your own sentence.

★ **Phonics Word Bank** ★

iris, iron, pilot, tiger
bike, ride, size, tire

★ **Sight Word Bank** ★

big, little, my, come,
one, two, three, like

1 _____ RECORD PLAY

2 _____ RECORD PLAY

3 _____ RECORD PLAY

4 _____ RECORD PLAY

5 _____ RECORD PLAY

Look and write the right word.

·dry	·night	·cry	·lie	·pie
·high	·tie	·fly	·sigh	

1

sigh

2

3

4

5

6

7

8

9

Trace the sentence.

1

I can fly high at night.

I can fly high at night.

2

I am wet! I sigh.

I am wet! I sigh.

Write the sentence.

1

I can fly high at night.

2

I am wet! I sigh.

night

sigh

lie

pie

tie

cry

dry

fly

★ **New Sight Words** ★

want, to

🐰 **Let's Practise!**

1 I want to fly high.

I want to fly high.

2 I want to cry.

I want to cry.

Advanced

3 Use the words that you know.

Steve wants to be a pilot.

Steve wants to be a pilot.

★ *Phonics Word Bank* ★

high, night, sigh, lie, pie, tie, cry, dry, fly

Unit 6

★ *Sight Word Bank* ★

big, little, my, come, one, two, three, like, **want**, **to**

1

RECORD PLAY

2

RECORD PLAY

3

RECORD PLAY

4

RECORD PLAY

5

RECORD PLAY

Step 1
Look and write the right word.

·go	·rose	·piano	·home
·cone	·robot	·note	·no

1

robot

2

3

4

5

6

7

8

Have fun!

Trace the Sentence.

1

I love my piano.

I love my piano.

2

Do you have a note?

Do you have a note?

Write the Sentence.

1

I love my piano.

2

Do you have a note?

go

no

piano

robot

cone

home

note

rose

★ **New Sight Words** ★

do, you

🐰 **Let's Practise!**

1 **Do you have a robot?**

Do you have a robot?

2 **Yes, I do.**

Yes, I do.

Advanced

3 Use the words that you know.

Do you want a big pet?

Do you want a big pet?

Write your own sentence.

★ *Phonics Word Bank* ★

Unit 7

go, no, piano, robot, cone, home, note, rose

★ *Sight Word Bank* ★

big, little, my, come, one, two, three, like, want, to, do, you

1 _____

RECORD PLAY

2 _____

RECORD PLAY

3 _____

RECORD PLAY

4 _____

RECORD PLAY

5 _____

RECORD PLAY

UNIT 8 oa, ow, oe

Step 1 **Look and write the right word.**

- toe - road - soap - slow - row
- bow - boat - hoe - Joe

1 toe

2

3

4

5

6

7

8

9

Trace the sentence.

1

He can row the boat.

He can row the boat.

2

He likes to play with a boat.

He likes to play with a boat.

Write the sentence.

1

He can row the boat.

2

He likes to play with a boat.

Make your own sentence.

boat

road

soap

bow

row

slow

Joe

hoe

toe

★ New Sight Word ★

play

🐰 **Let's Practise!**

1 **Little Joe likes to play.**

Little Joe likes to play.

2 **Joe plays with soap.**

Joe plays with soap.

Advanced

3 Use the words that you know.

I like to play with soap.

I like to play with soap.

Unit 8

★ *Phonics Word Bank* ★

boat, road, soap, bow, row, slow, Joe, hoe, toe

★ *Sight Word Bank* ★

big, little, my, come, one, two, three, like, want, to, do, you, play

1

RECORD   PLAY

2

RECORD   PLAY

3

RECORD   PLAY

4

RECORD   PLAY

5

RECORD   PLAY

Step 1 *Look and write the right word.*

- new   · music   · tube   · cute   · huge
- unicorn   · chew   · few   · cupid

1

cute

2

NEW

3

4

5

6

7

BRAND

8

9

Trace the sentence.

1

The cupid is cute.

The cupid is cute.

2

He can play music.

He can play music.

Step 2-2 *Write the sentence.*

1

The cupid is cute.

2

He can play music.

cupid

music

unicorn

cute

huge

tube

chew

few

new

★ **New Sight Words** ★

on, under

Let's Practise!

1 **I am under a huge tree.**

I am under a huge tree.

2 **He is on a unicorn.**

He is on a unicorn.

Advanced
3 Use the words that you know.

There is a tiny acorn on the mat.

There is a tiny acorn on the mat.

Write your own sentence.

★ *Phonics Word Bank* ★

cupid, music, unicorn, cute, huge, tube, chew, few, new

★ *Sight Word Bank* ★

big, little, my, come, one, two, three, like, want, to, do, you, play, on, under

1 _____ RECORD PLAY

2 _____ RECORD PLAY

3 _____ RECORD PLAY

4 _____ RECORD PLAY

5 _____ RECORD PLAY

Step 1 Look and write the right word.

·Sue	·food	·clue	·pool
·blue	·moon	·glue	·cool

1

pool

2

Sue

3

4

5

6

7

8

Have fun!

Trace the Sentence.

1

Sue can see food.

Sue can see food.

2

The pool is blue.

The pool is blue.

Write the Sentence.

1

Sue can see food.

2

The pool is blue.

Step 3 *Make your own sentence.*

cool

food

moon

pool

blue

clue

glue

Sue

★ New Sight Word ★

yellow

🐰 **Let's Practise!**

1 The moon is yellow.

The moon is yellow.

2 A banana is a yellow food.

A banana is a yellow food.

Advanced 3 Use the words that you know.

I can see a yellow bug on a leaf.

I can see a yellow bug on a leaf.

Step 4 *Write your own sentence.*

★ **Phonics Word Bank** ★

cool, food, moon, pool, blue, clue, glue, Sue

★ **Sight Word Bank** ★

big, little, my, come, one, two, three, like, want, to, do, you, play, on, under, yellow

1 _____ RECORD PLAY

2 _____ RECORD PLAY

3 _____ RECORD PLAY

4 _____ RECORD PLAY

5 _____ RECORD PLAY

ANSWER KEY

★ **Unit 01**
pp.22-23

★ **Unit 02**
pp.32-33

★ **Unit 03**
pp.44-45

Unit 01

REVIEW

Check Up 01

1. Listen and check the right picture.

2. Listen and check the right word.

tape | face | tap ✔

Check Up 02

1. Complete the word puzzle.

1. c / t a p / k / g a t e
2. m / m a n / n / t a p e

2. Check the box with the right sentence for the picture.

1. ✔ I see a mane. / I see a name.
2. I can bake a lake. / ✔ I can bake a cake.
3. I see a little gate. / ✔ I see a big gate.
4. There is a tap. / ✔ There is a tape.

Unit 02

REVIEW

Check Up 01

1. Listen and check the right picture.

2. Listen and check the right word.

baby | rain ✔ | say

Check Up 02

1. Complete the word puzzle.

1. b / s a y / b / d a y
2. r / p a p e r / i / n

2. Check the box with the right sentence for the picture.

1. My baby can see a rail. / ✔ My baby can see a tail.
2. ✔ This is my hay. / This is my bay.
3. Look at the mail. / ✔ Look at the rain.
4. ✔ This is my paper. / This is my acorn.

Unit 03

REVIEW

Check Up 01

1. Listen and check the right picture.

2. Listen and check the right word.

tiny | here ✔ | body

Check Up 02

1. Complete the word puzzle.

1. m / w / h e r e
2. t / i / n / b o d y

2. Check the box with the right sentence for the picture.

1. He is here. / ✔ We are here.
2. ✔ Come here, Steve. / Come here, Eve.
3. We look big here. / ✔ We look tiny here.
4. ✔ There is a city map. / There is a tiny map.

★ Unit 04 pp.54-55

★ Unit 05 pp.66-67

★ Unit 06 pp.76-77

ANSWER KEY

★ Unit 07
pp.88-89

REVIEW

Well done!

For answer keys, go to p.46, workbook

Check Up 01

1. Listen and check the right picture.

2. Listen and check the right word.

home | **note** ✓ | no ✓

Check Up 02

1. Complete the word puzzle.

2. Check the box with the right sentence for the picture.

1. ☐ I love my cone. / ✓ I love my piano.
2. ✓ Do you have a rose? / ☐ Do you have a note?
3. ☐ I have a robot at rose. / ✓ I have a robot at home.
4. ☐ I no home. / ✓ I go home.

★ Unit 08
pp.98-99

REVIEW

Well done!

For answer keys, go to p.46, workbook

Check Up 01

1. Listen and check the right picture.

2. Listen and check the right word.

slow | road ✓ | bow ✓

Check Up 02

1. Complete the word puzzle.

2. Check the box with the right sentence for the picture.

1. ☐ I play with my boat. / ✓ I play with my soap.
2. ☐ Look at hoe! / ✓ Look at Joe!
3. ✓ Wow! A boat! / ☐ Wow! A road!
4. ✓ I play with my toes. / ☐ I play with my Joes.

★ Unit 09
pp.110-111

REVIEW

Well done!

For answer keys, go to p.46, workbook

Check Up 01

1. Listen and check the right picture.

2. Listen and check the right word.

new | cupid | few ✓

Check Up 02

1. Complete the word puzzle.

2. Check the box with the right sentence for the picture.

1. ✓ It is on the piano. / ☐ It is under the piano.
2. ✓ It is under the boat. / ☐ It is on the boat.
3. ✓ Look at the cute cupid! / ☐ Look at the huge cupid!
4. ✓ I can chew it. / ☐ I can few it.

★ **Unit 10**
   pp.120-121

★ **Final Review 01**
   pp.122-123

★ **Final Review 02**
   pp.124-125

神奇的 自然拼读

Amazing PHONiCs

WORKBOOK

Vol. **3**

**CONSONANT
BLENDS & DIGRAPHS**

My Writing Note

Step 1

Write the words

You can practise writing words from the Student Book.

Step 2

Trace & write the sentences

You can practise tracing and writing sentences from the Student Book.

Step 3

Make your own sentences

Using the words you learned, you can make your own sentences!

Step 4

Write your own sentences!

Write your own sentences and read them out loud!

AMAZING PHONICS WORKBOOK
Vol.3 Consonant Blends & Digraphs

CONTENTS

Step 1 Look and write the right word.

> · cliff · flag · blouse · flame · block
> · fly · clock · clap · black

1. flame

2.

3.

4.

5.

6.

7.

8.

9.

Step 2-1 *Trace the sentence.*

1

I am a black fly.

I am a black fly.

2

It is next to a big clock.

It is next to a big clock.

Step 2-2 *Write the sentence.*

1

I am a black fly.

2

It is next to a big clock.

black

block

blouse

clap

cliff

clock

flag

fly

flame

★ **New Sight Word** ★

next

🐰 **Let's Practise!**

1 **I am next to a flag.**

I am next to a flag.

2 **There is a clock next to you.**

There is a clock next to you.

Advanced

3 Use the words that you know.

I see my blouse next to the bed.

I see my blouse next to the bed.

Write your own sentence.

★ *Phonics Word Bank* ★

black, block, blouse, clap, cliff, clock, flag, flame, fly

★ *Sight Word Bank* ★

next

1 RECORD PLAY

2 RECORD PLAY

3 RECORD PLAY

4 RECORD PLAY

5 RECORD PLAY

UNIT 2 gl, pl, sl

Look and write the right word.

- slide   - plate   - glass   - plant   - sleep
- globe   - plug   - glow   - slow

1 slide

2

3

4

5

6

7

8

9

Step 2-1 *Trace the sentence.*

1
I have a glass globe.

I have a glass globe.

2
I plug in the globe.

I plug in the globe.

Step 2-2 *Write the sentence.*

1
I have a glass globe.

2
I plug in the globe.

globe

glass

glow

plant

plate

plug

sleep

slide

slow

★ New Sight Word ★

when

🐰 **Let's Practise!**

1 **When do you go to sleep?**

When do you go to sleep?

2 **I like it when it glows.**

I like it when it glows.

Advanced

3 Use the words that you know.

When I am sad, I go to sleep.

When I am sad, I go to sleep.

Unit 2

★ *Phonics Word Bank* ★

globe, glass, glow, plant, plate, plug, sleep, slide, slow

★ *Sight Word Bank* ★

next, when

1 _____ RECORD PLAY

2 _____ RECORD PLAY

3 _____ RECORD PLAY

4 _____ RECORD PLAY

5 _____ RECORD PLAY

UNIT 3 br, cr, dr

Look and write the right word.

· cross · dress · bride · drum · bread
· dragon · cream · crow · bridge

1

cream

2

3

4

5

6

7

8

9

Trace the sentence.

1

I am a bride.

I am a bride.

2

I cross the bridge in my dress.

I cross the bridge in my dress.

Write the sentence.

1

I am a bride.

2

I cross the bridge in my dress.

Step 3 *Make your own sentence.*

bread

bride

bridge

cream

cross

crow

dragon

dress

drum

★ **New Sight Word** ★

put

🐰 **Let's Practise!**

1 **I put on my dress.**

I put on my dress.

2 **I put cream on bread.**

I put cream on bread.

Advanced

3 Use the words that you know.

The bride puts cream on bread.

The bride puts cream on bread.

Unit 3

★ *Phonics Word Bank* ★

bread, bride, bridge, cream, cross, crow, dragon, dress, drum

★ *Sight Word Bank* ★

next, when, put

1   RECORD   PLAY

2   RECORD   PLAY

3   RECORD   PLAY

4   RECORD   PLAY

5   RECORD   PLAY

UNIT 4 fr, gr, tr

Step 1 **Look and write the right word.**

· tree	· frog	· grass	· green	· trip
· fruit	· friend	· grape	· train	

1

train

2

3

4

5

6

7

8

9

Step 2-1 *Trace the sentence.*

1

I go on a trip.

I go on a trip.

2

I see green grass.

I see green grass.

Step 2-2 *Write the sentence.*

1

I go on a trip.

2

I see green grass.

friend

frog

fruit

grape

grass

green

train

tree

trip

★ New Sight Word ★

get

🐰 **Let's Practise!**

1 **I get on a bike.**

I get on a bike.

2 **I get some grapes.**

I get some grapes.

Advanced

3 Use the words that you know.

I get on the train with my friends.

I get on the train with my friends.

★ Phonics Word Bank ★

Unit 4

friend, frog, fruit, grape, grass, green, train, tree, trip

★ Sight Word Bank ★

next, when, put, get

1 _____
RECORD PLAY

2 _____
RECORD PLAY

3 _____
RECORD PLAY

4 _____
RECORD PLAY

5 _____
RECORD PLAY

UNIT 5 sn, sp, st

Step 1

Look and write the right word.

· spider · snack · space · stop · spin
· snake · snail · stone · star

1

2

STOP

3

4

5

6

7

8

CHIPS

9

Step 2-1 *Trace the sentence.*

1

I find a snake on a stone.

I find a snake on a stone.

2

He can see many stars.

He can see many stars.

Step 2-2 *Write the sentence.*

1

I find a snake on a stone.

2

He can see many stars.

snack

snake

snail

space

spider

spin

star

stone

stop

★ **New Sight Word** ★

many

Let's Practise!

1 **There are many stars.**

There are many stars.

2 **I see many stones.**

I see many stones.

Advanced

3 Use the words that you know.

I have many stones.

I have many stones.

Write your own sentence.

Unit 5

★ *Phonics Word Bank* ★

snack, snake, snail, space, spider, spin, star, stone, stop

★ *Sight Word Bank* ★

next, when, put, get, many

1   RECORD   PLAY

2   RECORD   PLAY

3   RECORD   PLAY

4   RECORD   PLAY

5   RECORD   PLAY

Step 1   *Look and write the right word.*

- swan
- small
- ski
- sky
- sweet
- skate
- smell
- smile
- swim

1 small

2

3

4

5

6

7

8

9

1

We walk to a small lake.

We walk to a small lake.

2

"It smells sweet!"

"It smells sweet!"

1

We walk to a small lake.

2

"It smells sweet!"

skate

ski

sky

small

smell

smile

swan

sweet

swim

★ **New Sight Word** ★

walk

🐰 **Let's Practise!**

1 **I walk to see swans.**

I walk to see swans.

2 **I walk my small dog.**

I walk my small dog.

Advanced

3 Use the words that you know.

I can smell food here when I walk.

I can smell food here when I walk.

Write your own sentence.

★ **Phonics Word Bank** ★

skate, ski, sky, small, smell, smile, swan, sweet, swim

★ **Sight Word Bank** ★

next, when, put, get, many, walk

Unit 6

1 _____
RECORD   PLAY

2 _____
RECORD   PLAY

3 _____
RECORD   PLAY

4 _____
RECORD   PLAY

5 _____
RECORD   PLAY

UNIT 7 ch-, sh-

Look and write the right word.

· chop	· shape	· cherry	· shirt
· cheese	· shake	· sheep	· chin

1 sheep

2

3

4

5

6

7

8

Have fun!

Trace the sentence.

1

There are some sheep.

There are some sheep.

2

I chop up the cheeses.

I chop up the cheeses.

Write the sentence.

1

There are some sheep.

2

I chop up the cheeses.

cheese

cherry

chin

chop

shake

shape

sheep

shirt

★ **New Sight Word** ★

some

🐰 **Let's Practise!**

1 **I want some cheese.**

I want some cheese.

2 **I need some new shirts.**

I need some new shirts.

^{Advanced}
3 Use the words that you know.

I can chop up some cheese.

I can chop up some cheese.

Write your own sentence.

★ *Phonics Word Bank* ★

Unit 7

cheese, cherry, chin, chop, shake, shape, sheep, shirt

★ *Sight Word Bank* ★

next, when, put, get, many, walk, some

1 _____ RECORD PLAY

2 _____ RECORD PLAY

3 _____ RECORD PLAY

4 _____ RECORD PLAY

5 _____ RECORD PLAY

UNIT 8 wh-, ph-, th-

Step 1 **Look and write the right word.**

· phonics · that · whale · think · photo
· white · what · phone · thin

1 thin

2

3

4

5

6

7

8

9

Trace the sentence.

1

This is a white phone.

This is a white phone.

2

They are whales.

They are whales.

Write the sentence.

1

This is a white phone.

2

They are whales.

whale
what
white
phone
phonics
photo

that
thin
think

★ New Sight Word ★

they

🐰 **Let's Practise!**

1 **What are they?**

What are they?

2 **They have phones.**

They have phones.

Advanced

3 Use the words that you know.

Look! They are white whales!

Look! They are white whales!

Write your own sentence.

★ *Phonics Word Bank* ★

whale, what, white, phone, phonics, photo, that, thin, think

★ *Sight Word Bank* ★

next, when, put, get, many, walk, some, they

1   RECORD   PLAY

2   RECORD   PLAY

3   RECORD   PLAY

4   RECORD   PLAY

5   RECORD   PLAY

UNIT 9 -ch, -sh

Step 1 **Look and write the right word.**

· lunch	· dish	· beach	· fish
· wish	· cash	· bench	· each

1

cash

2

3

4

5

6

7

8

Have fun!

Trace the sentence.

1

I have some cash.

I have some cash.

2

I want to eat a fish dish.

I want to eat a fish dish.

Write the sentence.

1

I have some cash.

2

I want to eat a fish dish.

beach
bench
each
lunch
cash
dish

fish
wish

★ **New Sight Word** ★

let's

🐰 **Let's Practise!**

1 **Let's eat some lunch.**

Let's eat some lunch.

2 **Let's make a wish.**

Let's make a wish.

Advanced

3 Use the words that you know.

Let's go get some fish.

Let's go get some fish.

Write your own sentence.

Unit 9

★ *Phonics Word Bank* ★

beach, bench, each, lunch, cash, dish, fish, wish

★ *Sight Word Bank* ★

next, when, put, get, many, walk, some, they, let's

1   RECORD   PLAY

2   RECORD   PLAY

3   RECORD   PLAY

4   RECORD   PLAY

5   RECORD   PLAY

Step 1
Look and write the right word.

· long	· kick	· cloth	· duck	· smooth
· ring	· wing	· neck	· with	

1 neck

2

3

4

5

6

7

8

9

Trace the sentence.

1

There is a duck with long wings.

There is a duck with long wings.

2

He kicks it under a tree.

He kicks it under a tree.

Write the sentence.

1

There is a duck with long wings.

2

He kicks it under a tree.

Make your own sentence.

duck

kick

neck

cloth

smooth

with

long

ring

wing

★ New Sight Word ★

too

🐰 Let's Practise!

1 **I want to swim like a duck, too.**

I want to swim like a duck, too.

2 **I want to eat fish, too.**

I want to eat fish, too.

Advanced

3 Use the words that you know.

Ducks have two wings, too.

Ducks have two wings, too.

★ **Phonics Word Bank** ★

Unit 10

duck, kick, neck, cloth, smooth, with, long, ring, wing

★ *Sight Word Bank* ★

next, when, put, get, many, walk, some, they, let's, too

1 _____

RECORD   PLAY

2 _____

RECORD   PLAY

3 _____

RECORD   PLAY

4 _____

RECORD   PLAY

5 _____

RECORD   PLAY

ANSWER KEY

★ **Unit 01**
pp.22-23

★ **Unit 02**
pp.32-33

★ **Unit 03**
pp.44-45

REVIEW — *Well done!*

Check Up 01

1. Listen and check the right picture.
   - ✓ (fly) | (blot) | (flag)

2. Listen and check the right word.
   - block | ✓ clock | clap

Check Up 02

1. Look and circle the right blend for the picture.
   1. cl / **fl**
   2. fl / **bl**
   3. **cl** / bl

2. Circle the right word to complete the sentence.
   1. I am a _____ fly.
      a. block **b. black** c. blouse
   2. It is _____ to a big clock.
      a. want b. are **c. next**
   3. I like my new _____.
      a. blouse b. cliff c. flame
   4. I want to play with my _____.
      a. cliff **b. blocks** c. flame

REVIEW — *Well done!*

Check Up 01

1. Listen and check the right picture.
   - (globe) | ✓ (turtle) | (light)

2. Listen and check the right word.
   - slide | plate | ✓ plant

Check Up 02

1. Look and circle the right blend for the picture.
   1. **sl** / gl
   2. **gl** / pl
   3. sl / **pl**

2. Circle the right word to complete the sentence.
   1. I have a _____ globe.
      a. plate **b. glass** c. plant
   2. I plug in the globe _____ I go to bed.
      a. next **b. when** c. sleep
   3. At night, I go to _____.
      a. sleep b. slide c. globe
   4. I see a _____ next to a plant.
      a. slide b. glow c. slow

REVIEW — *Well done!*

Check Up 01

1. Listen and check the right picture.
   - ✓ (crow) | (bridge) | (dragon)

2. Listen and check the right word.
   - dress | bridge | ✓ bride

Check Up 02

1. Look and circle the right blend for the picture.
   1. **cr** / br
   2. dr / **br**
   3. cr / **dr**

2. Circle the right word to complete the sentence.
   1. I put on a _____.
      a. dragon b. drum **c. dress**
   2. I _____ the bridge.
      a. cross b. cream c. crow
   3. I like to eat cream _____.
      a. bride **b. bread** c. bridge
   4. I can play the _____.
      a. drums b. cross c. bread

★ **Unit 04**
pp.54-55

★ **Unit 05**
pp.66-67

★ **Unit 06**
pp.76-77

ANSWER KEY

★ Unit 07 pp.88-89

REVIEW — Well done!

Check Up 01

1. Listen and check the right picture.
(second picture checked ✓)

2. Listen and check the right word.
shake ✓ | shirt | shape

Check Up 02

1. Look and circle the right digraph for the picture.
1. ch (sh) | 2. ch (sh) | 3. (ch) sh

2. Circle the right word to complete the sentence.

1. I _____ up some cheeses.
a. cherry b. shake **c. chop**

2. _____ eat grass.
a. Shirt **b. Sheep** c. Cheese

3. There are many _____.
a. shapes b. chop c. shake

4. I want to eat some _____.
a. chin **b. cherries** c. shape

★ Unit 08 pp.98-99

REVIEW — Well done!

Check Up 01

1. Listen and check the right picture.
(first picture checked ✓)

2. Listen and check the right word.
thin | phone | **phonics** ✓

Check Up 02

1. Look and circle the right digraph for the picture.
1. (ph) th | 2. (wh) ph | 3. (th) wh

2. Circle the right word to complete the sentence.

1. _____ is this?
a. White **b. What** c. That

2. Look! It is a white _____.
a. whale b. what c. that

3. ABC~ I like _____!
a. phonics b. thin c. what

4. I like the color _____.
a. phonics b. thin **c. white**

★ Unit 09 pp.110-111

REVIEW — Well done!

Check Up 01

1. Listen and check the right picture.
(first picture checked ✓)

2. Listen and check the right word.
wish | **dish** ✓ | fish

Check Up 02

1. Look and circle the right digraph for the picture.
1. -ch (-sh) | 2. -ch (-sh) | 3. (-ch) -sh

2. Circle the right word to complete the sentence.

1. I make a _____.
a. fish b. each **c. wish**

2. _____ sit on a bench.
a. Let's b. See c. Some

3. I want to eat a _____ dish.
a. wish b. cash **c. fish**

4. Let's eat some _____.
a. each **b. lunch** c. beach

★ **Unit 10**
pp.120-121

REVIEW

Check Up 01

1. Listen and check the right picture.

2. Listen and check the right word.

with   ✔ wing   long

Check Up 02

1. Look and circle the right digraph for the picture.

1 (-th) -ng   2 -ng (-ck)   3 (-th) -ck

2. Circle the right word to complete the sentence.

1 A duck has two _____.
   a. kick   (b. wings)   c. rings

2 I am _____ my family.
   a. long   b. wing   (c. with)

3 Look at the yellow _____.
   (a. ducks)   b. kick   c. smooth

4 A giraffe has a long _____.
   (a. neck)   b. cloth   c. wing

★ **Final Review 01**
pp.122-123

FINAL REVIEW 01

1. Listen and circle the right picture.

2. Listen and circle the right blend for the word.

a (cl)   cr   b gl   (gr)

c sm   (sn)   (sp)   st

3. Look and complete the word.

a t h ink   b benc h

c f l ame   d s l ide

4. Read the sentence and circle the right word.

a I am a block/(black)/fly.

b I see (green) grape grass.

c I find a snail (snake) on a stone.

d I want to eat a cash (fish) dish.

★ **Final Review 02**
pp.124-125

FINAL REVIEW 02

1. Listen and circle the right picture.

2. Listen and circle the right blend for the word.

a bl   br   sm   (sw)

b (sh)   ch   (ng)   wh

3. Look and complete the word.

a g l obe   b d r ess

c smoo t h   d w h ale

4. Read the sentence and circle the right word.

a I put (cream) cross on the bread.

b "Swim (swan) sweet, swim!"

c They are white (whales).

d He puts the long (ring) on a wing.

神奇的 自然拼读

Amazing PHONiCs

WORKBOOK

Vol. **4**

ADVANCED
VOWELS
& SILENT LETTERS

My Writing Note

Step 1

Write the words
You can practise writing words from the Student Book.

Step 2

Trace & write the sentences
You can practise tracing and writing sentences from the Student Book.

Step 3

Make your own sentences
Using the words you learned, you can make your own sentences!

Step 4

Write your own sentences!
Write your own sentences and read them out loud!

AMAZING PHONICS **WORKBOOK**
Vol.4 Advanced Vowels & Silent Letters

CONTENTS

Step 1 *Look and write the right word.*

- girl
- car
- bird
- party
- card
- third
- garden
- birthday

1

party

2

3

4

5

6

7

8

Have fun!

Trace the sentence.

1

It is her third birthday.

It is her third birthday.

2

The party will be in a garden.

The party will be in a garden.

Write the sentence.

1

It is her third birthday.

2

The party will be in a garden.

Make your own sentence.

car
card
garden
party
bird
third

birthday
girl

★ **New Sight Word** ★

will

🐰 **Let's Practise!**

1 It will be my car.

It will be my car.

2 I will give her the card.

I will give her the card.

Advanced
3 Use the words that you know.

My garden will be like this.

My garden will be like this.

Write your own sentence.

★ **Phonics Word Bank** ★

car, card, garden, party, bird, birthday, girl, third

★ **Sight Word Bank** ★

will

1 ———————————————————— RECORD PLAY

2 ———————————————————— RECORD PLAY

3 ———————————————————— RECORD PLAY

4 ———————————————————— RECORD PLAY

5 ———————————————————— RECORD PLAY

UNIT 2 er, or, ur

Step 1 *Look and write the right word.*

·fork	·burn	·water	·turn	·dinner
·surf	·actor	·pork	·finger	

1

burn

2

3

4

5

6

7

8

9

Step 2-1 *Trace the sentence.*

1

Can I have my fork?

Can I have my fork?

2

It's dinner time!

It's dinner time!

Step 2-2 *Write the sentence.*

1

Can I have my fork?

2

It's dinner time!

dinner
finger
water
actor
fork
pork

burn
surf
turn

★ **New Sight Word** ★

and

🐰 **Let's Practise!**

1 **I like turkey and pork.**

I like turkey and pork.

2 **Wash it with soap and water.**

Wash it with soap and water.

Advanced

3 Use the words that you know.

I want to eat dinner and surf.

I want to eat dinner and surf.

Write your own sentence.

Unit 2

★ *Phonics Word Bank* ★

dinner, finger, water, actor, fork, pork, burn, surf, turn

★ *Sight Word Bank* ★

will, and

1   RECORD   PLAY

2   RECORD   PLAY

3   RECORD   PLAY

4   RECORD   PLAY

5   RECORD   PLAY

UNIT 3 au, aw

Step 1 **Look and write the right word.**

- Laura
- saw
- awful
- author
- Paul
- awesome
- prawn
- autumn

1 autumn

2

3

4

5 Paul

6

7

8 My name is Laura

Have fun!

Trace the sentence.

1

Laura and Paul are friends.

Laura and Paul are friends.

2

Laura loves the autumn.

Laura loves the autumn.

Write the sentence.

1

Laura and Paul are friends.

2

Laura loves the autumn.

Step 3 *Make your own sentence.*

author

autumn

Laura

Paul

awesome

awful

prawn

saw

★ New Sight Word ★

about

🐰 Let's Practise!

1 **Autumn is about to start.**

Autumn is about to start.

2 **I know all about Laura.**

I know all about Laura.

Advanced

3 Use the words that you know.

I think about my yellow dog.

I think about my yellow dog.

Step 4   *Write your own sentence.*

★ *Phonics Word Bank* ★

author, autumn, Laura, Paul, awesome, awful, prawn, saw

★ *Sight Word Bank* ★

will, and, about

1 _____   RECORD PLAY

2 _____   RECORD PLAY

3 _____   RECORD PLAY

4 _____   RECORD PLAY

5 _____   RECORD PLAY

Step 1 *Look and write the right word.*

point	boy	toy	oink
soy	noise	coin	joy

1

point

2

3

4

5

6

7

8

Have fun!

Trace the sentence.

1

My boy has a toy pig.

My boy has a toy pig.

2

It looks like a coin!

It looks like a coin!

Write the sentence.

1

My boy has a toy pig.

2

It looks like a coin!

coin

oink

noise

point

boy

joy

soy

toy

★ New Sight Word ★

enjoy

🐰 **Let's Practise!**

1 **I enjoy making noise.**

I enjoy making noise.

2 **He enjoys lunch.**

He enjoys lunch.

Advanced

3 Use the words that you know.

I enjoy eating soy beans.

I enjoy eating soy beans.

★ *Phonics Word Bank* ★

coin, oink, noise, point, boy, joy, soy, toy

★ *Sight Word Bank* ★

will, and, about, enjoy

1   RECORD PLAY

2   RECORD PLAY

3   RECORD PLAY

4   RECORD PLAY

5   RECORD PLAY

Step 1 *Look and write the right word.*

· around · cloud · house · mountain
· cow · brown · flower · town

1 brown

2

3

4

5

6

7

8

Have fun!

Trace the sentence.

1

I have a small house.

I have a small house.

2

You can see big clouds.

You can see big clouds.

Write the sentence.

1

I have a small house.

2

You can see big clouds.

around

cloud

house

mountain

brown

cow

flower

town

★ **New Sight Word** ★

down

🐰 **Let's Practise!**

1 I go down the mountain.

I go down the mountain.

2 Put down the flowers.

Put down the flowers.

Advanced

3 Use the words that you know.

I can see a cow down there.

I can see a cow down there.

Write your own sentence.

★ *Phonics Word Bank* ★

around, cloud, house, mountain, cow, brown, flower, town

Unit 5

★ *Sight Word Bank* ★

will, and, about, enjoy, down

1 _____ RECORD PLAY

2 _____ RECORD PLAY

3 _____ RECORD PLAY

4 _____ RECORD PLAY

5 _____ RECORD PLAY

UNIT 6 al, wa

Look and write the right word.

· wall   · call   · wand   · talk
· tall   · waffle   · was   · always

1 talk

2

3

4

5

6

7

8 24/7

Have fun!

Trace the sentence.

1

I always call you.

I always call you.

2

Because I like talking.

Because I like talking.

Write the sentence.

1

I always call you.

2

Because I like talking.

always
call
tall
talk
wand
was

wall
waffle

★ New Sight Word ★

because

🐰 **Let's Practise!**

1 **Because he is tall.**

Because he is tall.

2 **Because I smell waffles.**

Because I smell waffles.

Advanced
3 Use the words that you know.

There is no waffle because I had it.

There is no waffle because I had it.

Write your own sentence.

Unit 6

★ **Phonics Word Bank** ★

always, call, tall, talk, wand, was, wall, waffle

★ **Sight Word Bank** ★

will, and, about, enjoy, down, **because**

1 _____ RECORD PLAY

2 _____ RECORD PLAY

3 _____ RECORD PLAY

4 _____ RECORD PLAY

5 _____ RECORD PLAY

UNIT 7 air, are, ear

Step 1 — *Look and write the right word.*

> · bear   · hair   · wear   · hare   · stair
> · pear   · square   · chair   · stare

1

hare

2

3

4

5

6

7

8

9

Trace the sentence.

1

I come up the stairs.

I come up the stairs.

2

He eats a pear.

He eats a pear.

Write the sentence.

1

I come up the stairs.

2

He eats a pear.

Make your own sentence.

chair

hair

stair

stare

hare

square

bear

pear

wear

★ New Sight Word ★

her

🐰 **Let's Practise!**

1 It is her chair.

It is her chair.

2 A bear eats her pear.

A bear eats her pear.

Advanced
3 Use the words that you know.

I stare at her black hair.

I stare at her black hair.

★ **Phonics Word Bank** ★

chair, hair, stair, hare, square, stare, bear, pear, wear

Unit 7

★ **Sight Word Bank** ★

will, and, about, enjoy, down, because, her

1 _____   RECORD PLAY

2 _____   RECORD PLAY

3 _____   RECORD PLAY

4 _____   RECORD PLAY

5 _____   RECORD PLAY

UNIT 8 ear, eer, ere

Step 1 **Look and write the right word.**

> ·here ·deer ·hear ·adhere ·near
> ·ear ·steer ·cheer ·sphere

1

near

2

3

4

5

6

7

8

9

Step 2-1 *Trace the sentence.*

1. I hear a noise in my ear.

   I hear a noise in my ear.

2. A baby deer!

   A baby deer!

Step 2-2 *Write the sentence.*

1. I hear a noise in my ear.

2. A baby deer!

ear

hear

near

cheer

deer

steer

adhere

here

sphere

★ New Sight Word ★

something

🐰 **Let's Practise!**

1 **I hear something.**

I hear something.

2 **Something is in my ear.**

Something is in my ear.

Advanced

3 Use the words that you know.

I see something big here.

I see something big here.

Write your own sentence.

★ Phonics Word Bank ★

ear, hear, near, cheer, deer, steer, adhere, here, sphere

★ Sight Word Bank ★

will, and, about, enjoy, down, because, her, something

1 _____ RECORD PLAY

2 _____ RECORD PLAY

3 _____ RECORD PLAY

4 _____ RECORD PLAY

5 _____ RECORD PLAY

Step 1 Look and write the right word.

> · lamb · knee · wrap · knock · wrist
> · climb · write · knife · thumb

1. knee
2.
3.
4.
5.
6.
7.
8.
9.

1

Look at my knees.

Look at my knees.

2

I use a pen to write.

I use a pen to write.

1

Look at my knees.

2

I use a pen to write.

knee
knife
knock
wrap
wrist
write

climb
lamb
thumb

★ New Sight Word ★

use

🐰 **Let's Practise!**

1 **I use a knife to eat.**

I use a knife to eat.

2 **I use my wrist to knock.**

I use my wrist to knock.

Advanced
3 Use the words that you know.

I use my knees to walk.

I use my knees to walk.

Write your own sentence.

★ **Phonics Word Bank** ★

knee, knife, knock, wrap, wrist, write, climb, lamb, thumb

★ **Sight Word Bank** ★

will, and, about, enjoy, down, because, her, something, use

1 _____ RECORD PLAY

2 _____ RECORD PLAY

3 _____ RECORD PLAY

4 _____ RECORD PLAY

5 _____ RECORD PLAY

UNIT 10 g, h, t

Look and write the right word.

· design · eight · sigh · hour · ghost
· school · castle · listen · watch

1

hour

2

3

4

5

6

7

8

9

Step 2-1　*Trace the sentence.*

1

My school is a design school.

My school is a design school.

2

Do you like your school?

Do you like your school?

Step 2-2　*Write the sentence.*

1

My school is a design school.

2

Do you like your school?

design eight

sigh hour

ghost school

castle listen

watch

★ **New Sight Word** ★

your

🐰 **Let's Practise!**

1 I like your design.

I like your design.

2 Is it your castle?

Is it your castle?

Advanced

3 Use the words that you know.

I can see your school.

I can see your school.

Step 4 *Write your own sentence.*

★ Phonics Word Bank ★

📎 **Unit 10**

design, eight, sigh, hour, ghost, school, castle, listen, watch

★ Sight Word Bank ★

will, and, about, enjoy, down, because, her, something, use, **your**

1   RECORD   PLAY

2   RECORD   PLAY

3   RECORD   PLAY

4   RECORD   PLAY

5   RECORD   PLAY

ANSWER KEY

★ Unit 01 pp.22-23

REVIEW

Well done!

Check Up 01

1. Listen and check the right picture.

✓

2. Listen and check the right word.

✓ girl | bird | third

Check Up 02

1. Look and circle the right word for the picture.

1. thild / thard / (third)
2. cal / (car) / cir
3. (bird) / bard / bild
4. gardon / girden / (garden)

2. Read the sentence. Look in the word bank. Write the right word for each sentence.

Word Bank
1. car   2. third
3. party   4. bird

1. It is my baby's __third__ birthday.
2. I have a yellow __car__.
3. My __bird__ can sing very well.
4. It is my baby's birthday __party__.

★ Unit 02 pp.32-33

REVIEW

Well done!

Check Up 01

1. Listen and check the right picture.

✓

2. Listen and check the right word.

pork | ✓ fork | actor

Check Up 02

1. Look and circle the right word for the picture.

1. wator / (water) / watur
2. (pork) / perk / purk
3. (dinner) / dinnor / dinnur
4. actur / acter / (actor)

2. Read the sentence. Look in the word bank. Write the right word for each sentence.

Word Bank
1. Dinner   2. Turn
3. fingers   4. pork

1. I like turkey and __pork__.
2. __Dinner__ is ready!
3. __Turn__ on the tap and wash your hands.
4. I have ten __fingers__.

★ Unit 03 pp.44-45

REVIEW

Well done!

Check Up 01

1. Listen and check the right picture.

✓

2. Listen and check the right word.

autumn | Laura | ✓ author

Check Up 02

1. Look and circle the right word for the picture.

1. (Paul) / Pawl / Parl
2. arful / auful / (awful)
3. artumn / awtumn / (autumn)
4. (prawn) / praun / pram

2. Read the sentence. Look in the word bank. Write the right word for each sentence.

Word Bank
1. Laura   2. autumn
3. awesome   4. about

1. I write __about__ autumn.
2. __Laura__ and Paul are friends.
3. Look at the __awesome__ car!
4. Paul loves the __autumn__.

★ **Unit 04**
pp.54-55

REVIEW

Well done!

🎧 🔵 **Check Up 01**

1. Listen and check the right picture.

2. Listen and check the right word.

✓ oink   point   coin

📖 🅰 **Check Up 02**

1. Look and circle the right word for the picture.

1. soi / **soy** / saw
2. **point** / poynt / paunt
3. coyn / **coin** / caun
4. baw / boi / **boy**

2. Read the sentence. Look in the word bank.
Write the right word for each sentence.

Word Bank
1. oink   2. toy
3. noise   4. boy

1 I play with my ___toy___.

2 What is the ___noise___?

3 A pig says "___oink___"!

4 Look at the ___boy___.

★ **Unit 05**
pp.66-67

REVIEW

Well done!

🎧 🔵 **Check Up 01**

1. Listen and check the right picture.

2. Listen and check the right word.

flower   around   ✓ cloud

📖 🅰 **Check Up 02**

1. Look and circle the right word for the picture.

1. hause / howse / **house**
2. cau / **cow** / cou
3. braun / broun / **brown**
4. **mountain** / mowntain / mountain

2. Read the sentence. Look in the word bank.
Write the right word for each sentence.

Word Bank
1. around   2. flowers
3. town   4. clouds

1 I live in a small ___town___.

2 I like red ___flowers___.

3 There are some ___clouds___ in the sky.

4 I walk ___around___ my house.

★ **Unit 06**
pp.76-77

REVIEW

Well done!

🎧 🔵 **Check Up 01**

1. Listen and check the right picture.

2. Listen and check the right word.

✓ was   waffle   wand

📖 🅰 **Check Up 02**

1. Look and circle the right word for the picture.

1. carr / call / **wall**
2. **wand** / was / waffle
3. tall / **talk** / walk
4. wand / **waffle** / wall

2. Read the sentence. Look in the word bank.
Write the right word for each sentence.

Word Bank
1. waffles   2. call
3. wand   4. tall

1 I like to eat ___waffles___.

2 He is very ___tall___.

3 I have a magic ___wand___.

4 I will ___call___ you.

ANSWER KEY

★ Unit 07 pp.88-89

REVIEW

Well done!

Check Up 01
1. Listen and check the right picture.
2. Listen and check the right word.

bear | pear | wear ✓

Check Up 02
1. Look and circle the right word for the picture.

1. hair / (hare) / hear
2. bare / (bear) / bair
3. (stare) / staire / stear
4. chare / (chair) / chear

2. Read the sentence. Look in the word bank.
Write the right word for each sentence.

Word Bank
1. bear 2. chair
3. hair 4. square

1 I see a big brown __bear__ .

2 I want to sit on a __chair__ .

3 It is a __square__ .

4 You have long __hair__ .

★ Unit 08 pp.98-99

REVIEW

Well done!

Check Up 01
1. Listen and check the right picture.
2. Listen and check the right word.

ear | hear | near ✓

Check Up 02
1. Look and circle the right word for the picture.

1. heer / (hear) / here
2. chear / (cheer) / chere
3. dear / (deer) / dere
4. are / eer / (ear)

2. Read the sentence. Look in the word bank.
Write the right word for each sentence.

Word Bank
1. here 2. deer
3. hear 4. ears

1 I __hear__ a noise.

2 I have two __ears__ .

3 We are __here__ .

4 A __deer__ is near me.

★ Unit 09 pp.110-111

REVIEW

Well done!

Check Up 01
1. Listen and check the right picture.
2. Listen and check the right word.

climb | lamb | thumb ✓

Check Up 02
1. Look and circle the right word for the picture.

1. (lamb) / lam / lab
2. (knock) / knoc / knok
3. clib / clim / (climb)
4. (wrist) / wist / rist

2. Read the sentence. Look in the word bank.
Write the right word for each sentence.

Word Bank
1. knife 2. knees
3. climb 4. lambs

1 I have two __knees__ .

2 I see many __lambs__ in the grass.

3 I can __climb__ up the mountain.

4 I see a fork and a __knife__ .

★ **Unit 10**
pp.120-121

REVIEW

Check Up 01

1. Listen and check the right picture.

2. Listen and check the right word.

design   **eight** ✓   sigh

Check Up 02

1. Look and circle the right word for the picture.

1. shool / **school** / scool
2. wauch / **watch** / wach
3. gost / **ghost** / goust
4. desain / desin / **design**

2. Read the sentence. Look in the word bank. Write the right word for each sentence.

Word Bank
1. eight   2. castle
3. ghost   4. watch

1. I go to school at **eight** o'clock.
2. There is a **ghost** here.
3. I see a big **castle** .
4. I need a new **watch** .

★ **Final Review 01**
pp.122-123

FINAL REVIEW 01

1. Listen and circle the right picture.

2. Listen and circle the right word.

coin   **toy**   **steer**   stair
autumn   awful   deer   **here**

3. Look and complete the word.

a. g**h**ost   b. pa**r**ty
c. ch**air**   d. bo**y**

4. Read the sentence and circle the right word.

- Do you like your scool / **school** ?
- There are turkey and pork / **fork** .
- My boy has a soy / **toy** pig.
- I smell **waffles** / flowers .

★ **Final Review 02**
pp.124-125

FINAL REVIEW 02

1. Listen and circle the right picture.

2. Listen and circle the right word.

burn   **dinner**   **bear**   hare
sphere   **hear**   author   **awesome**

3. Look and complete the word.

a. ar**ou**nd   b. no**i**se
c. cl**i**mb   d. pe**ar**

4. Read the sentence and circle the right word.

- I come up the chairs / **stairs** .
- You can see big around / **clouds** .
- It is her third **birthday** / garden .
- Laura loves the author / **autumn** .

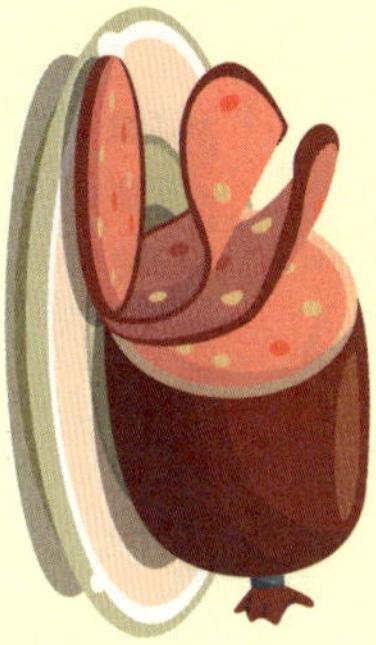
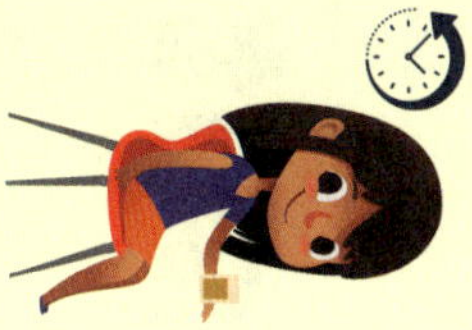
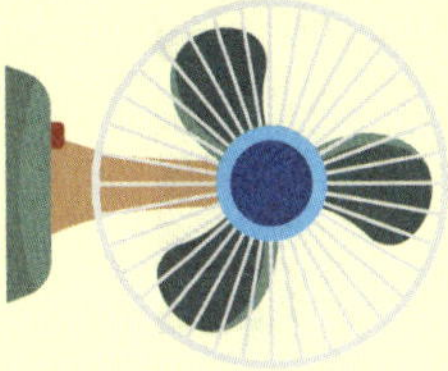

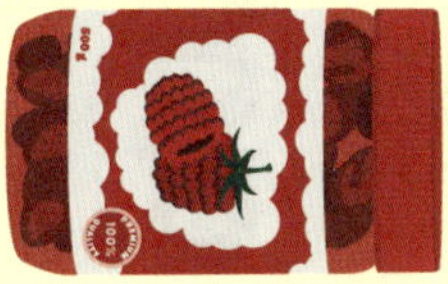
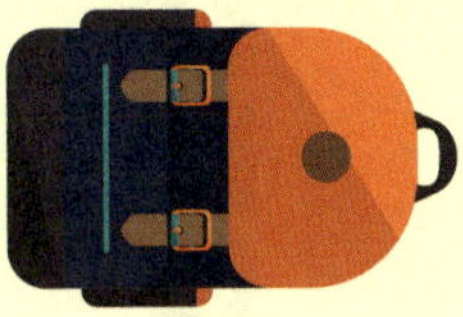
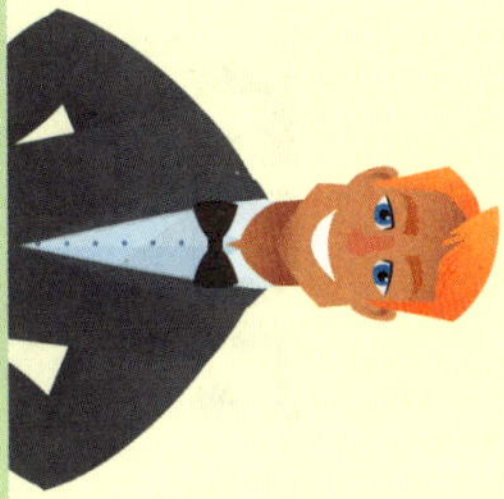
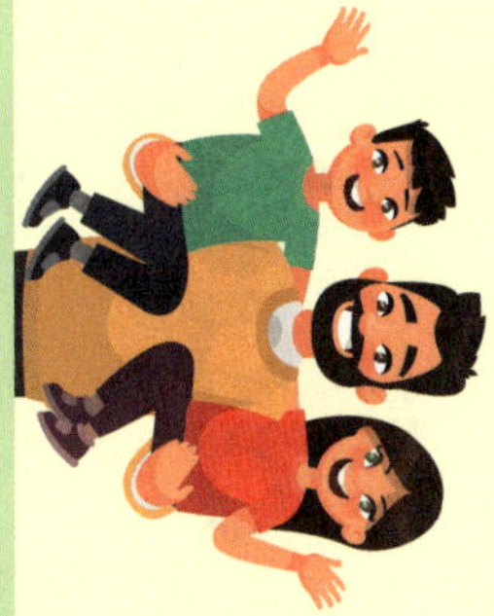
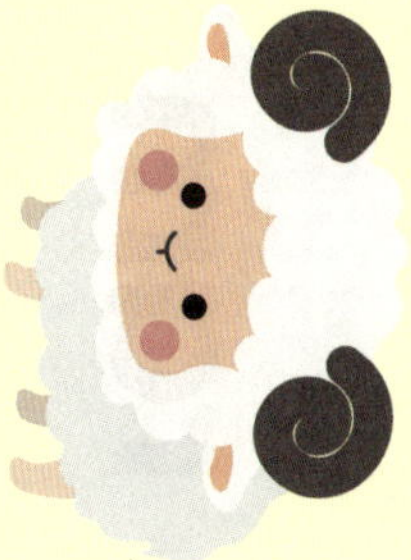
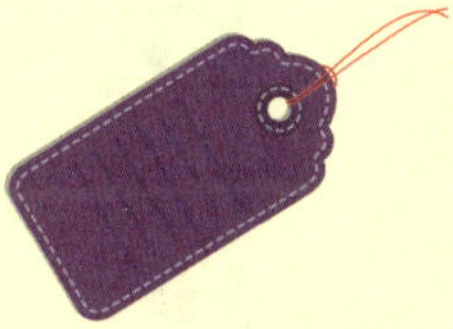
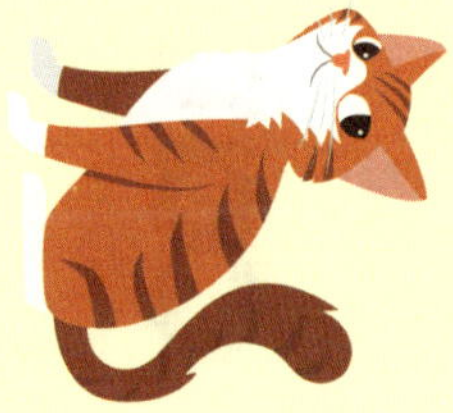
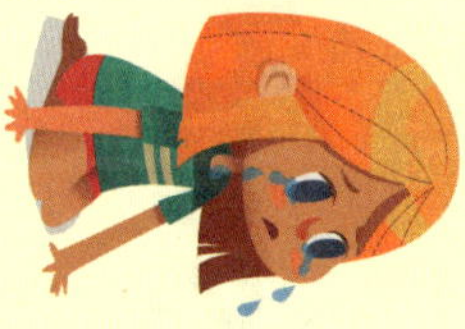
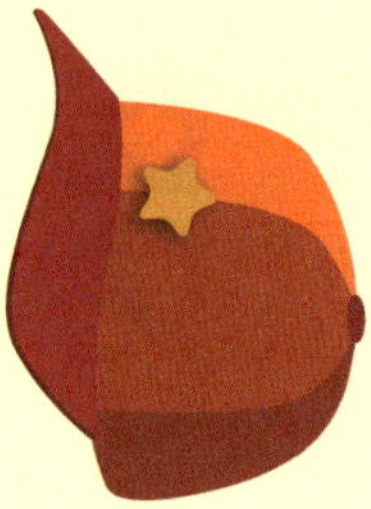
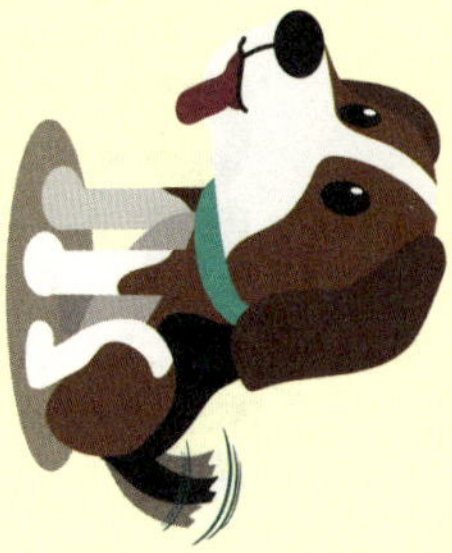
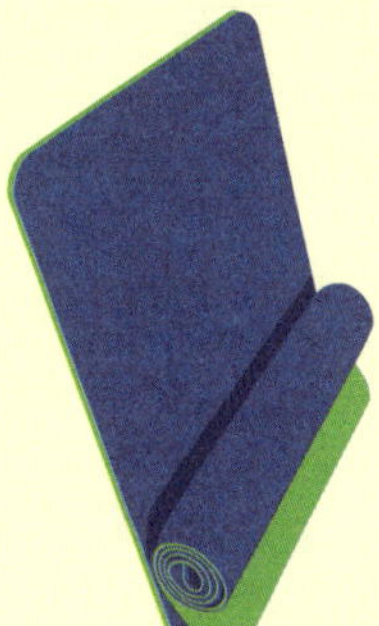
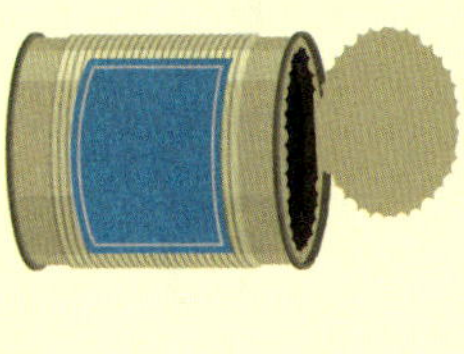

bad	fan	sat	ham
dad	man	bag	jam
sad	cat	tag	ram
can	mat	wag	cap

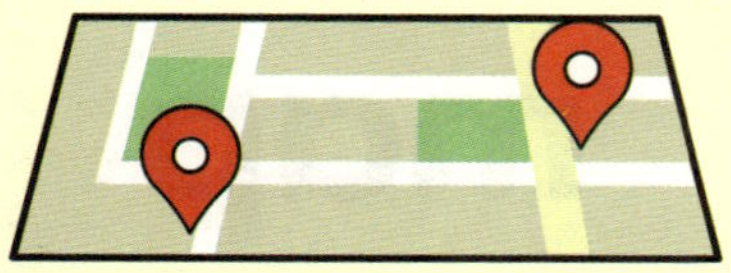
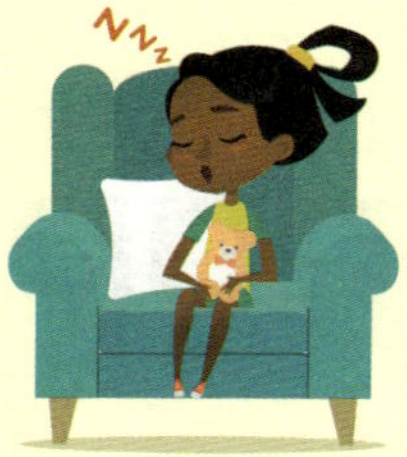
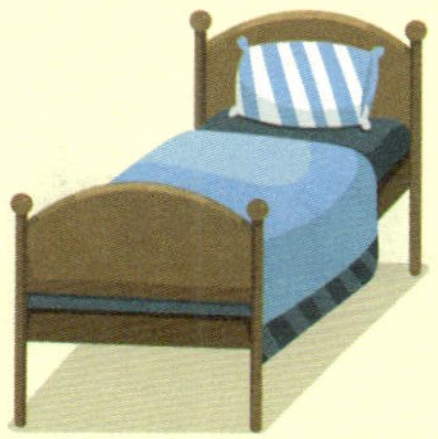
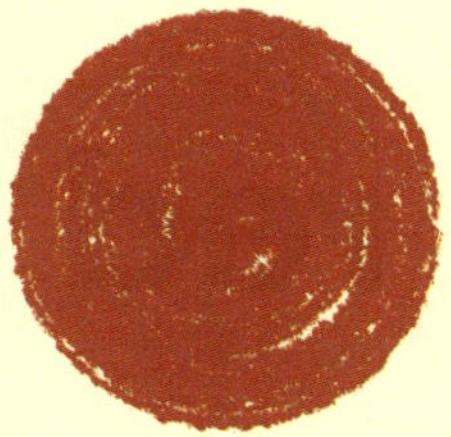
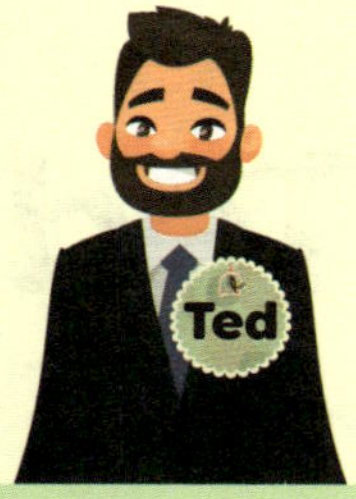
Ted
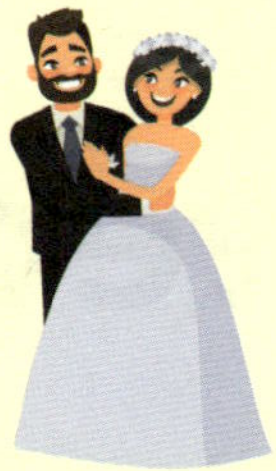
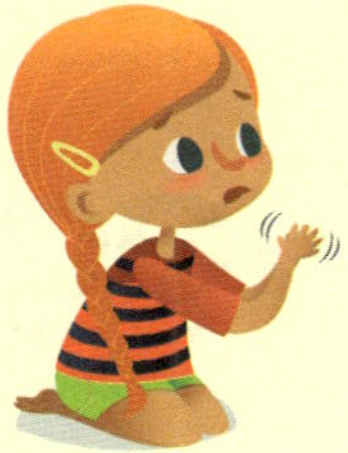
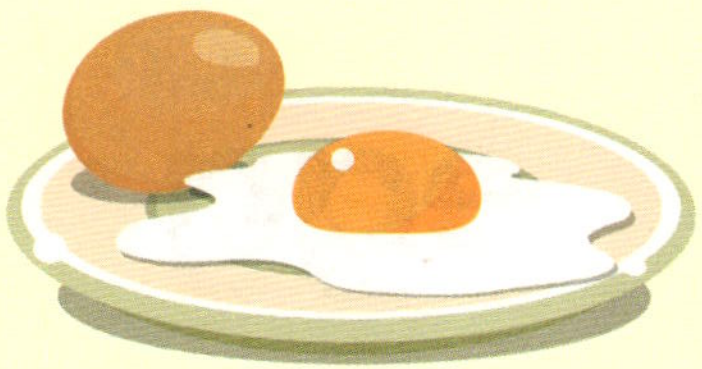
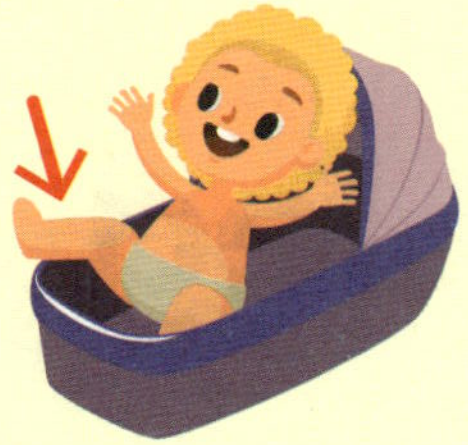
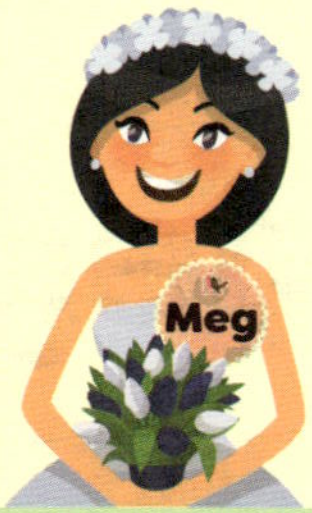
Meg
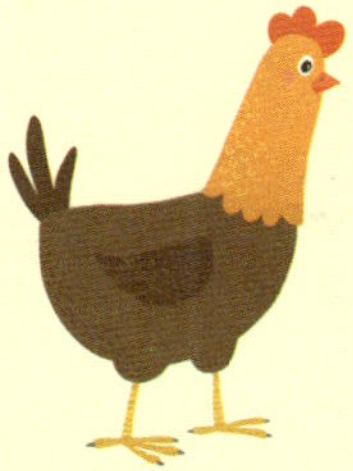
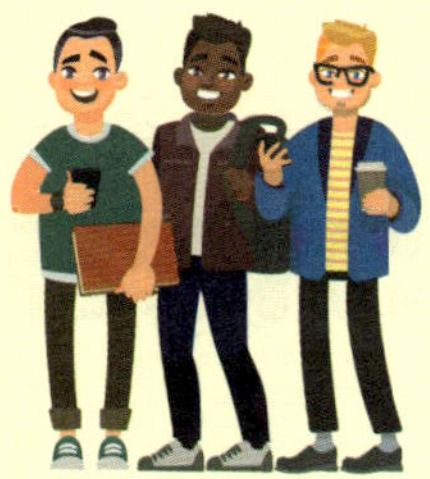
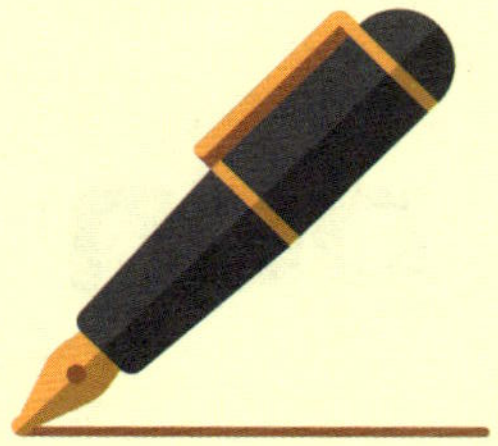
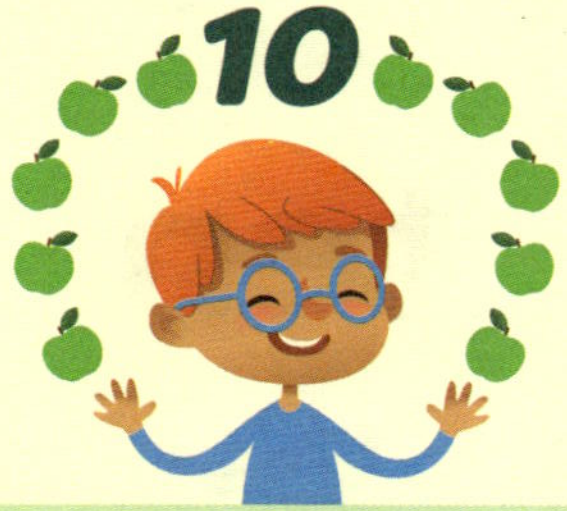
10
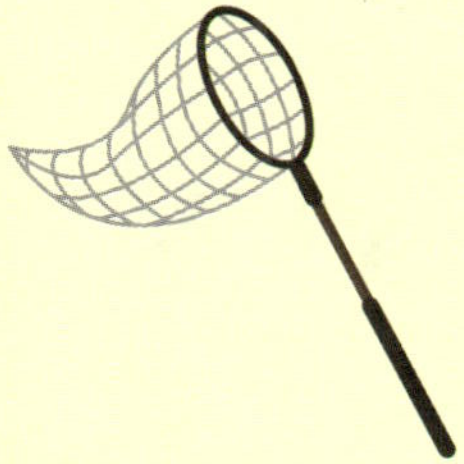
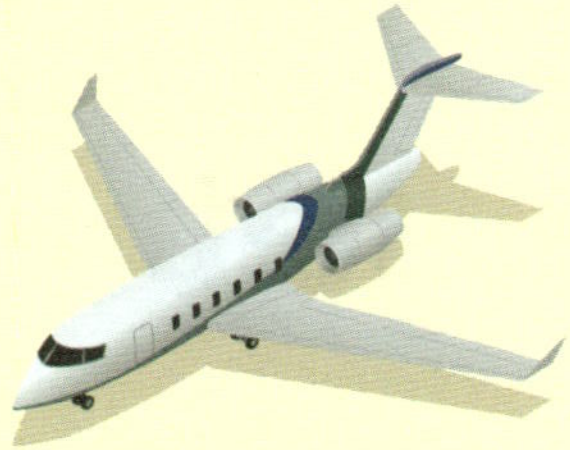

map	Ted	leg	pen
nap	wed	Meg	ten
bed	beg	hen	net
red	egg	men	jet

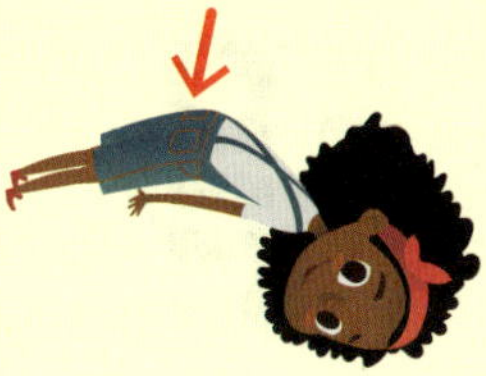
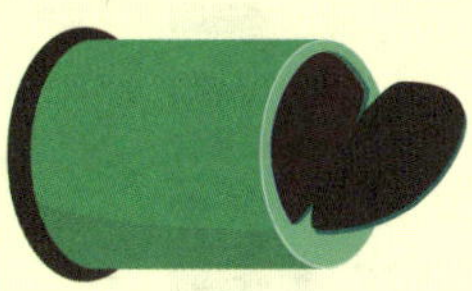
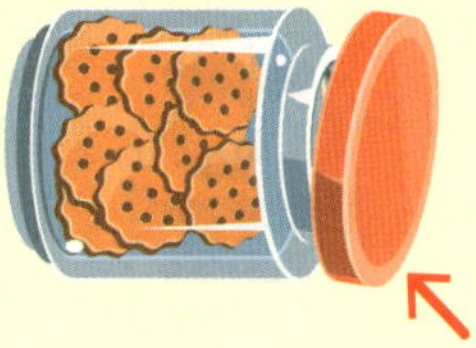
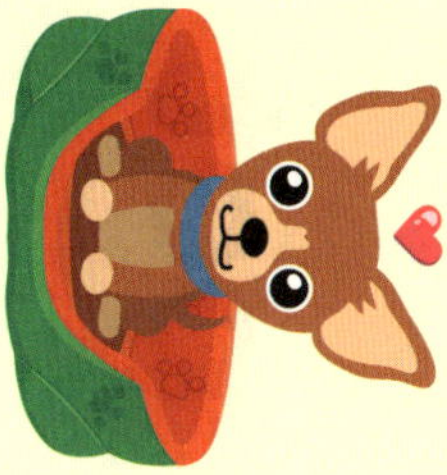
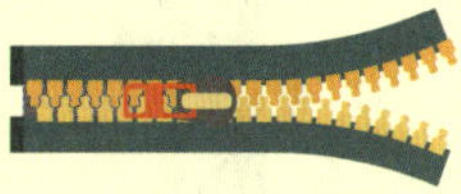
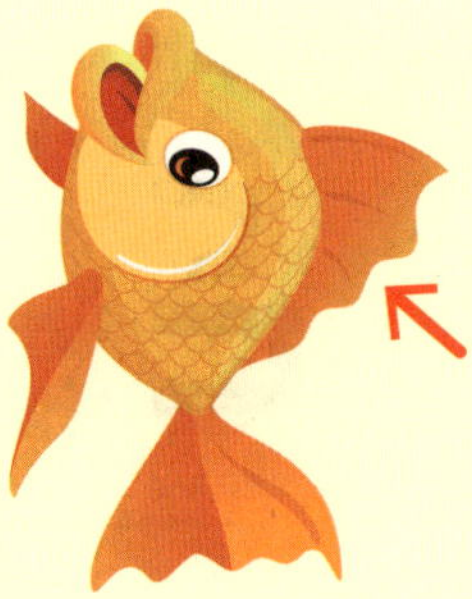
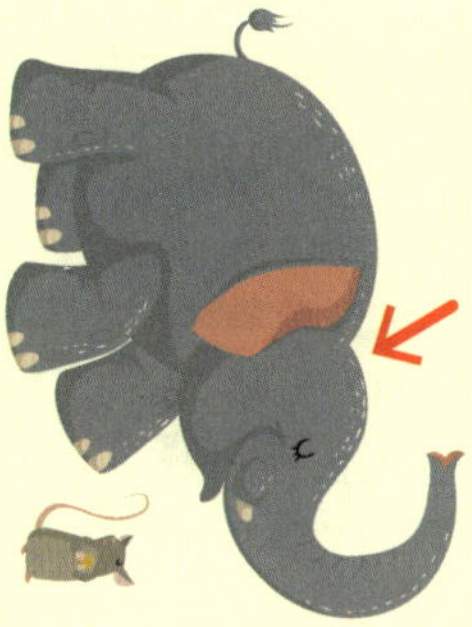
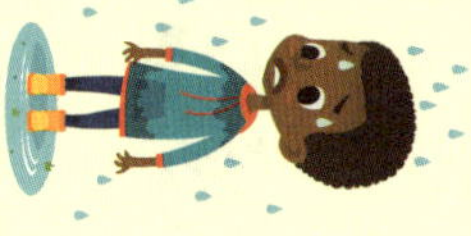
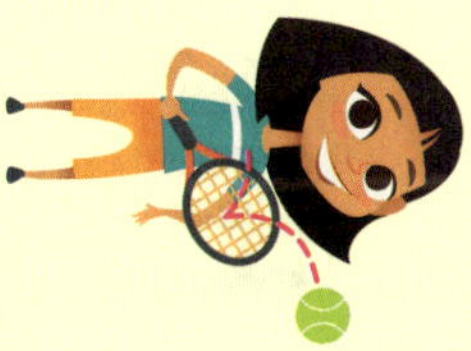
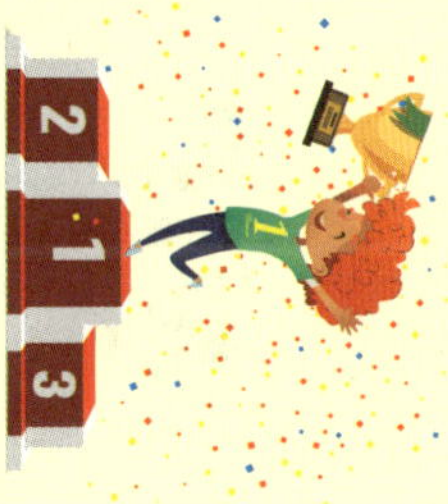
2
1
3
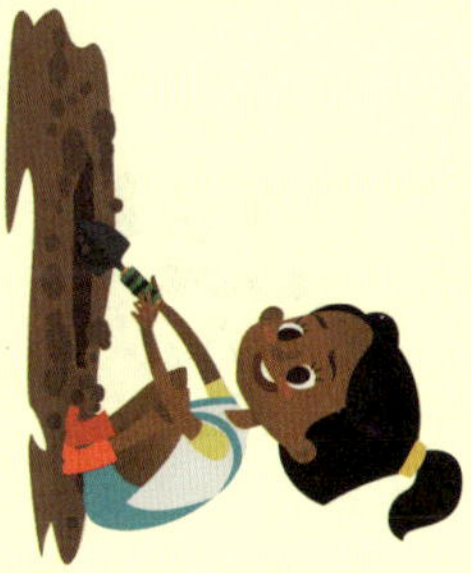
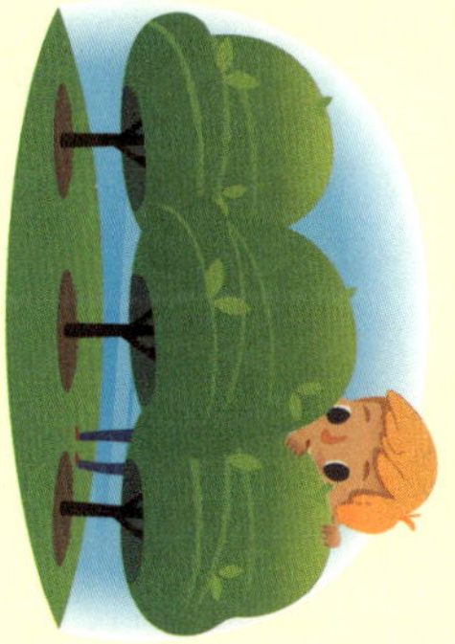
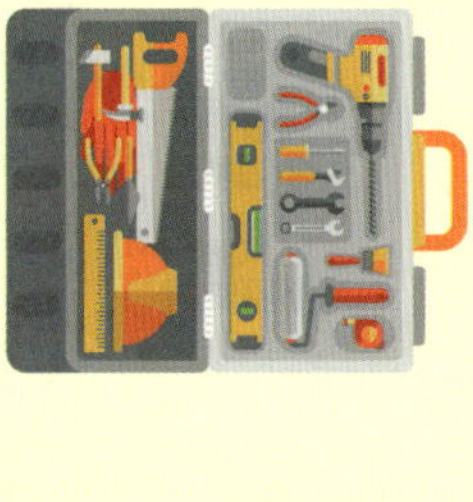
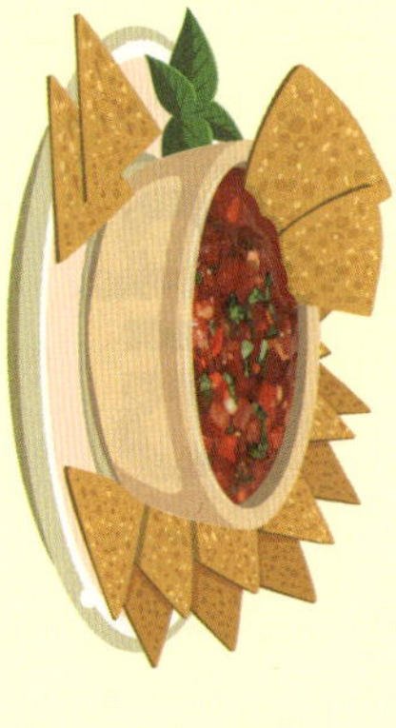
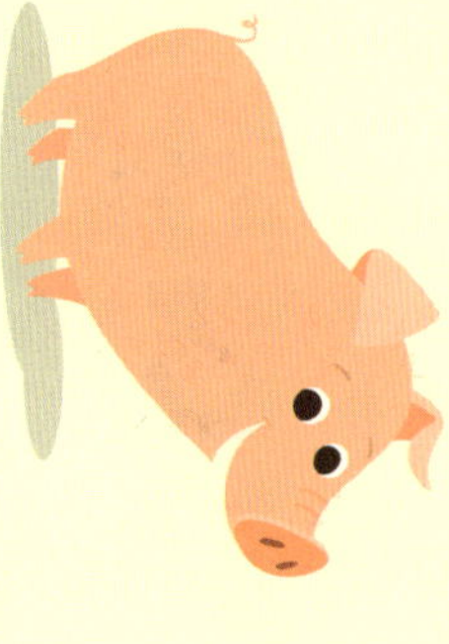
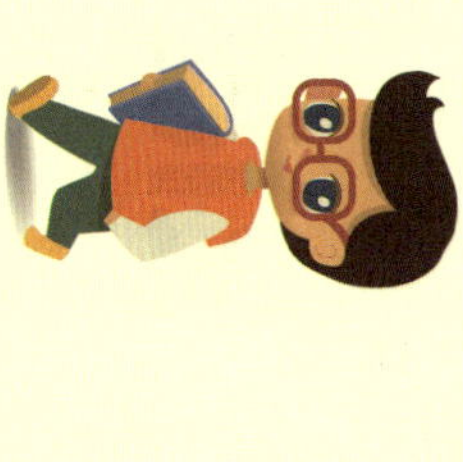

pet	lid	bin	hip
wet	big	fin	zip
hid	dig	win	hit
kid	pig	dip	kit

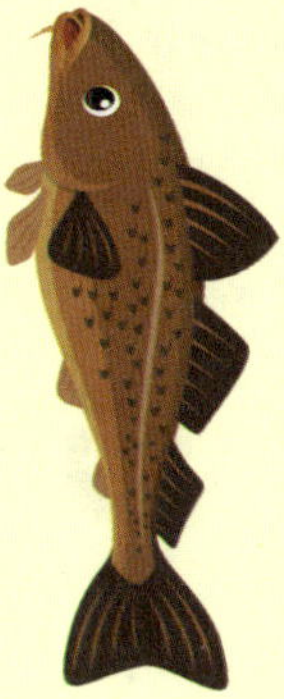
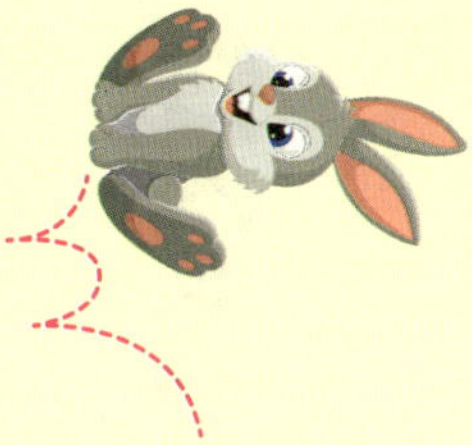
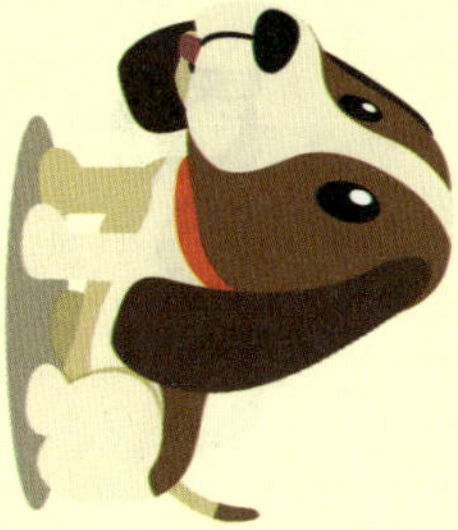
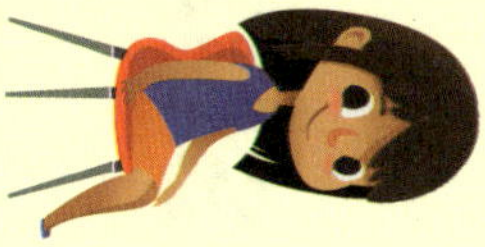
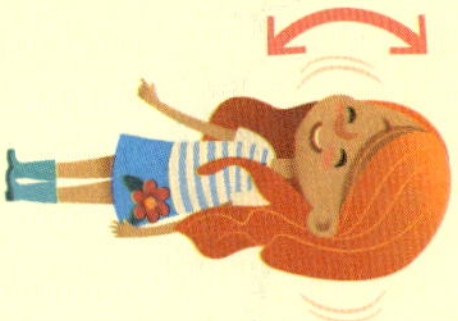
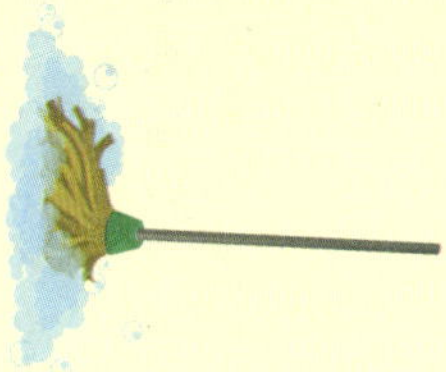
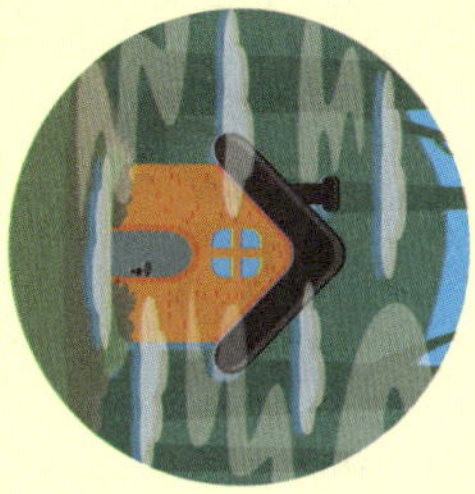
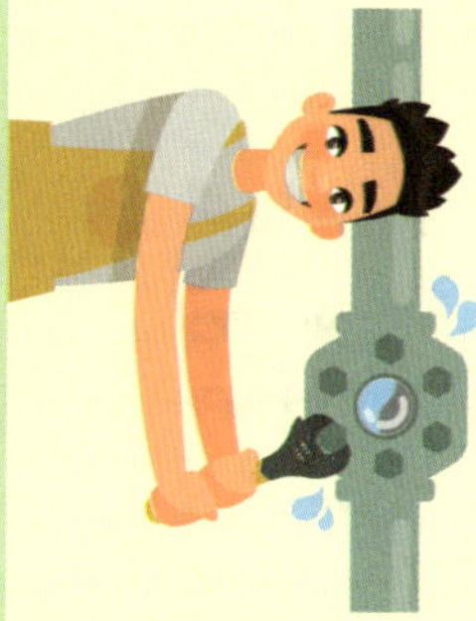
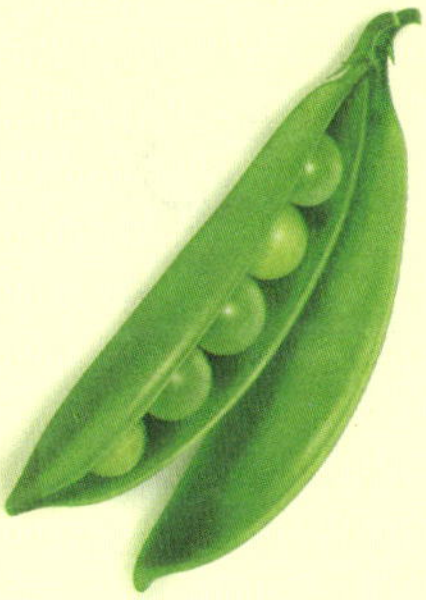
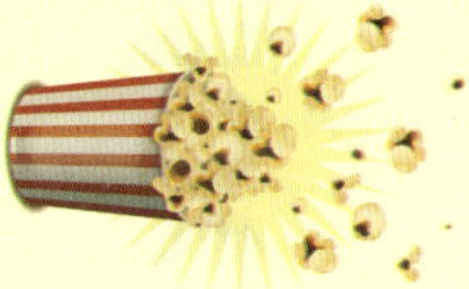
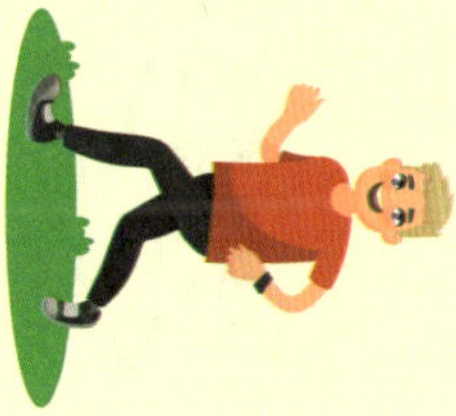
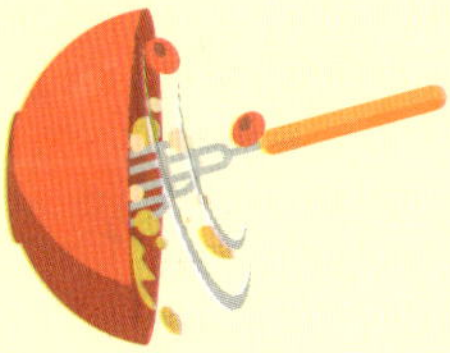

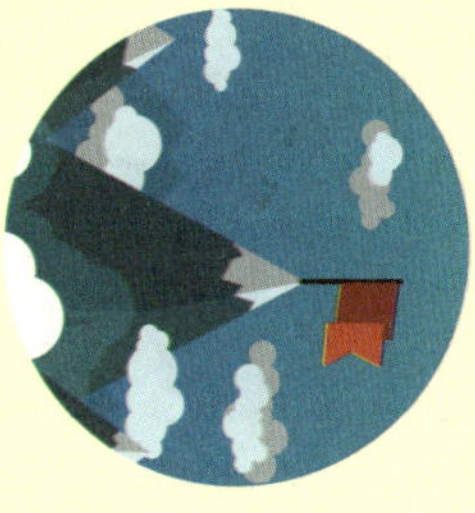
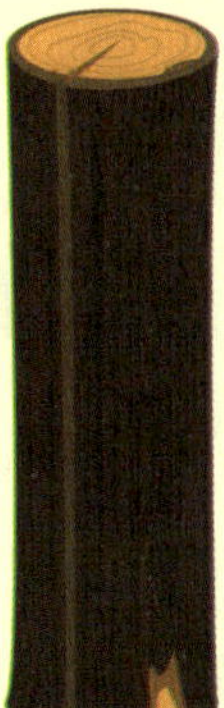
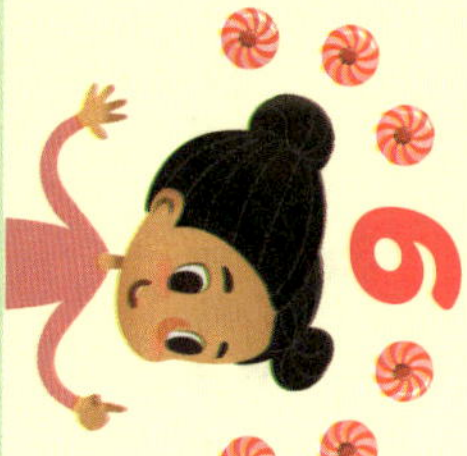

sit	dog	hop	cod
fix	fog	mop	nod
mix	jog	pop	pod
six	log	top	dot

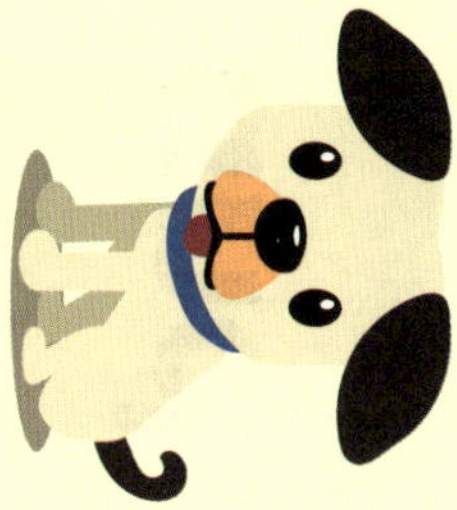
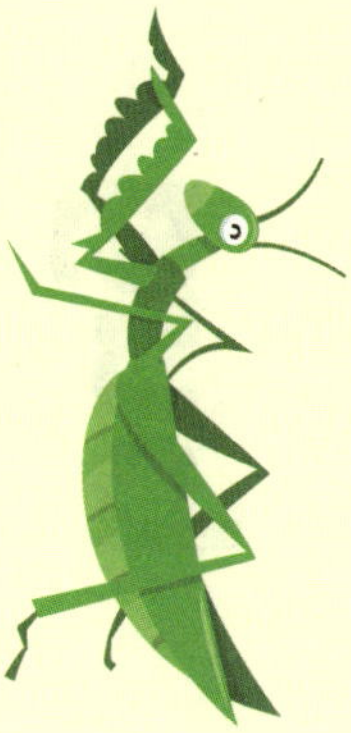
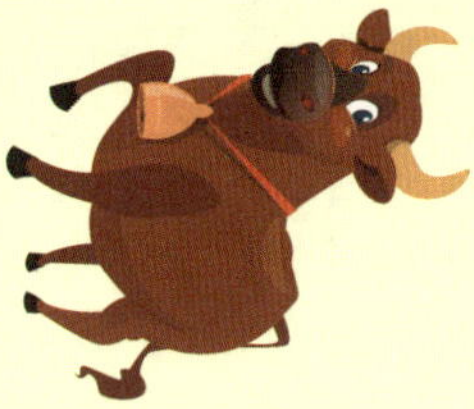
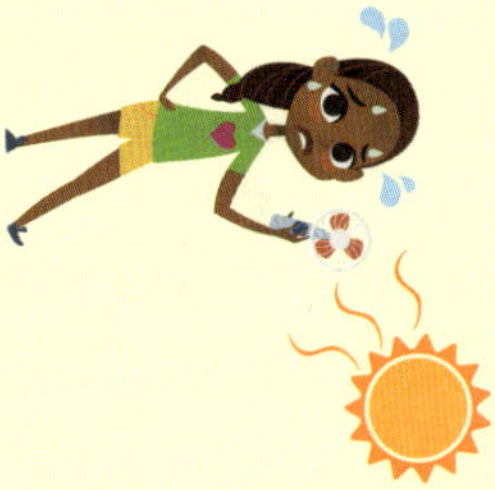
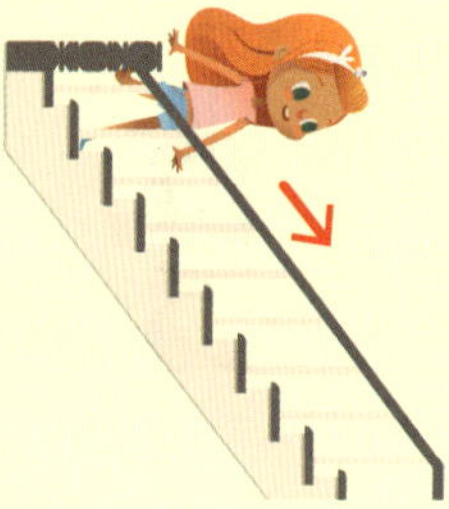
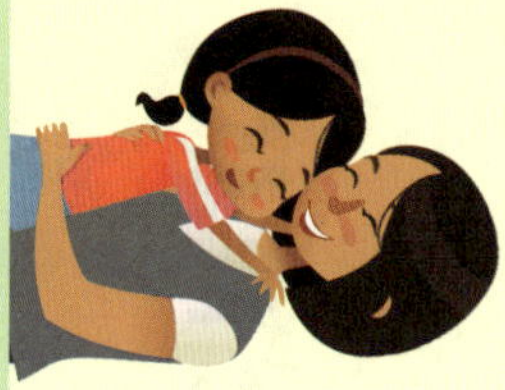
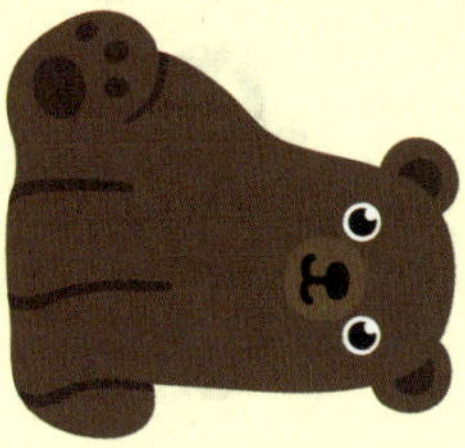
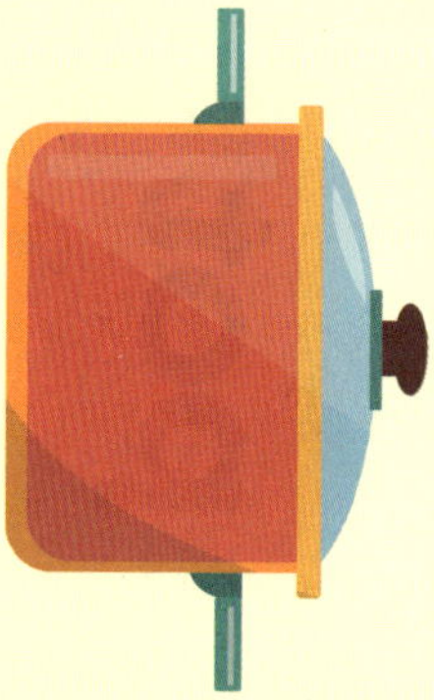
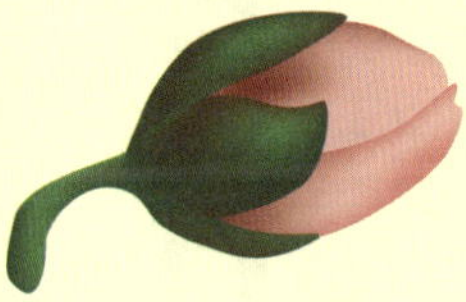
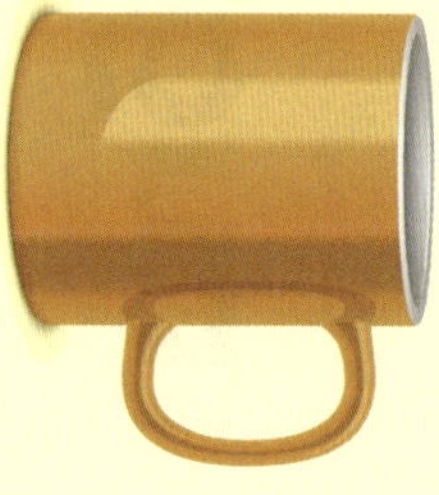
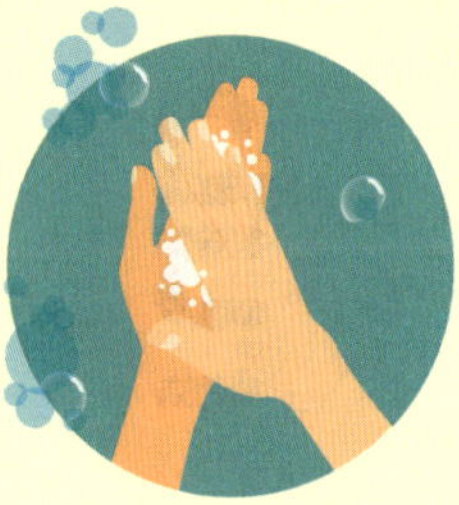
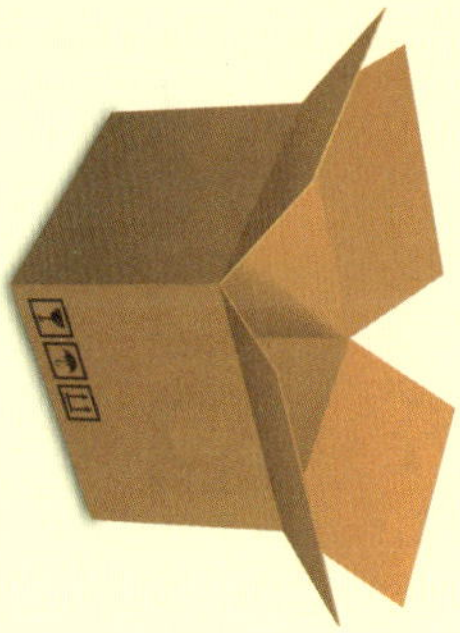
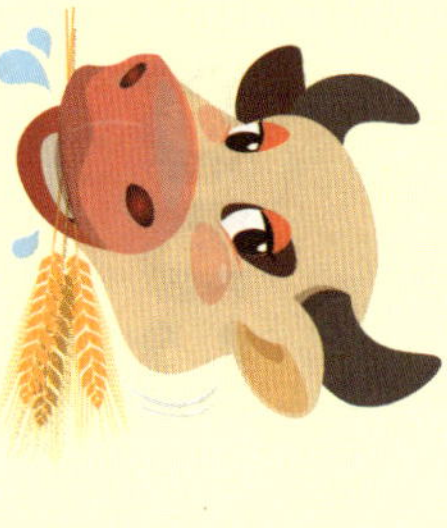
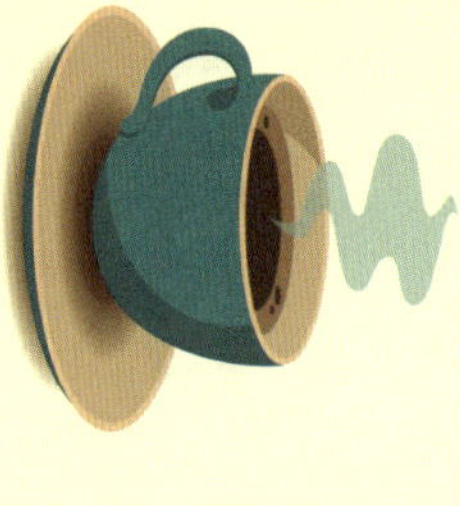
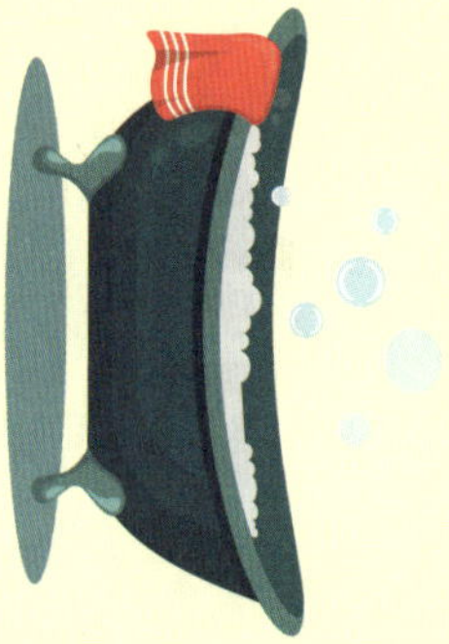
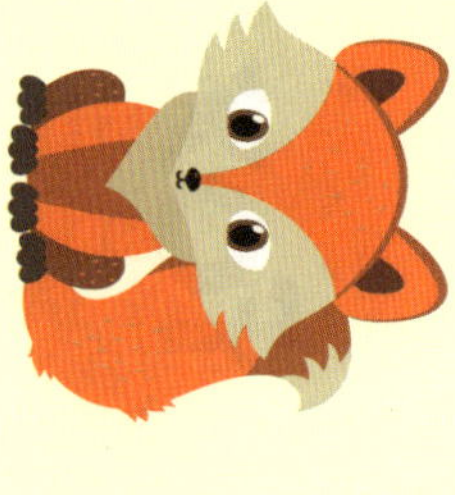

hot	ox	bug	pup
pot	cub	hug	up
box	rub	mug	bud
fox	tub	cup	cud

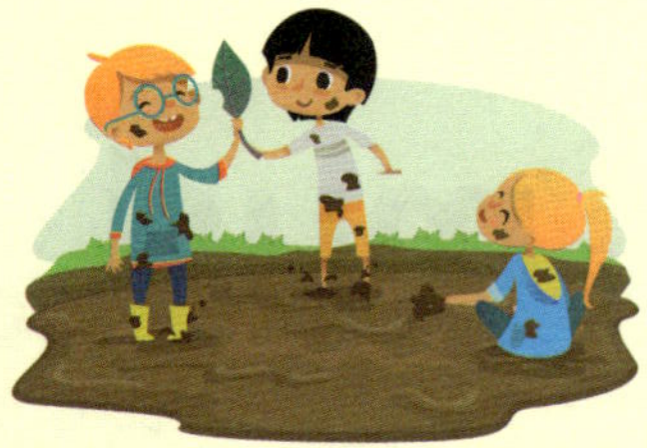
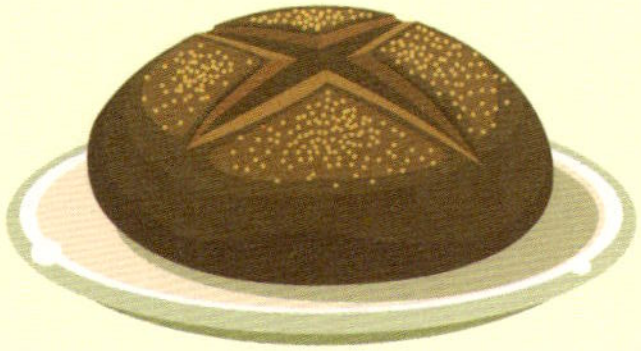
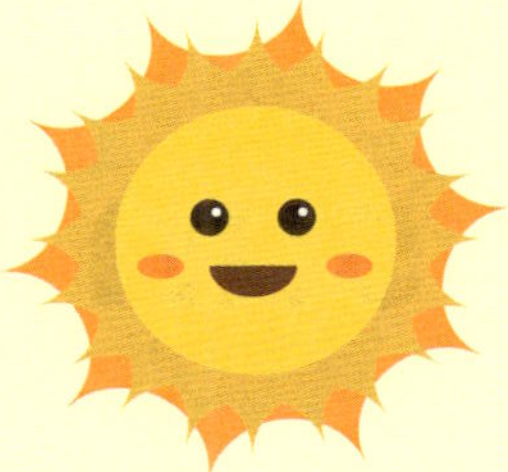
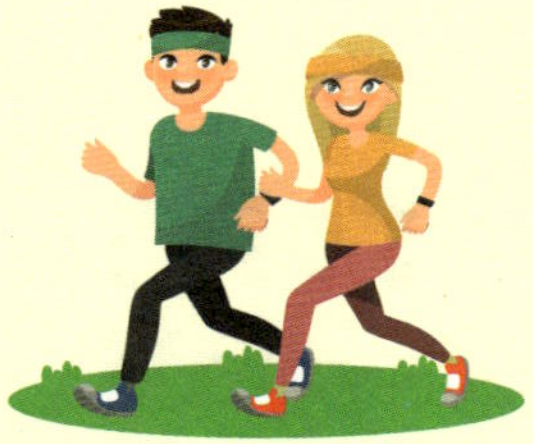
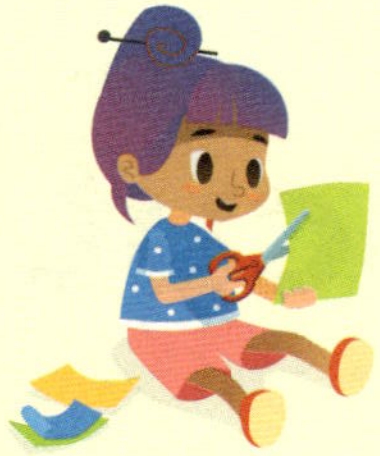
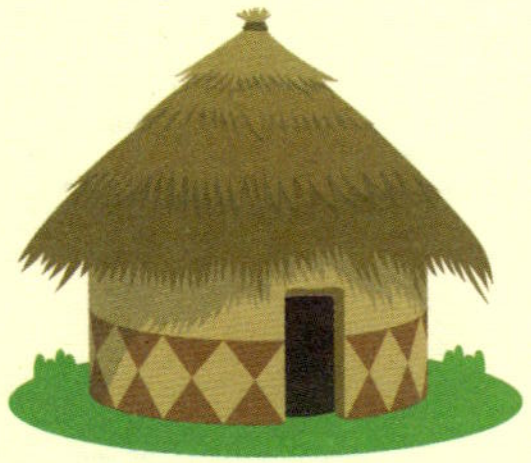
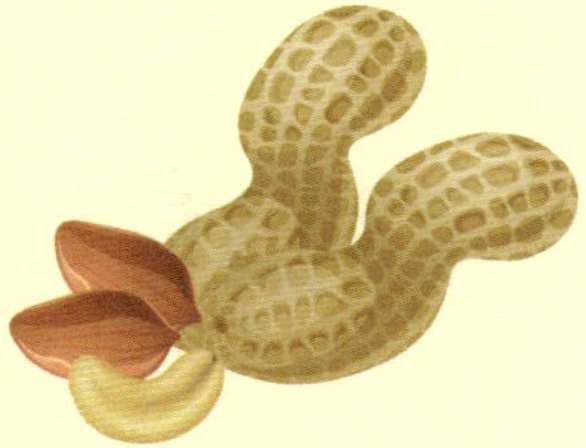
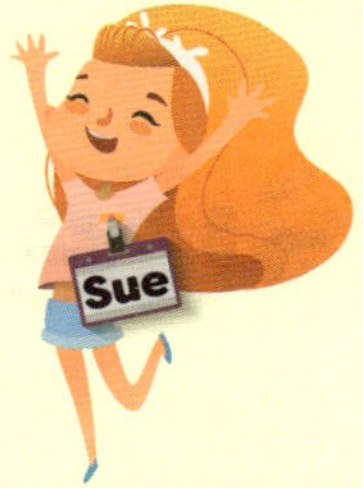
Sue
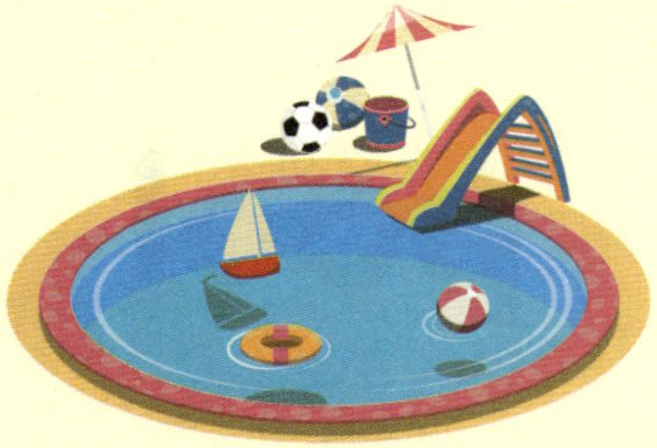
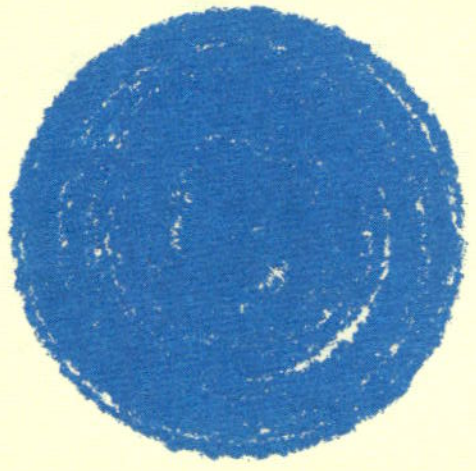
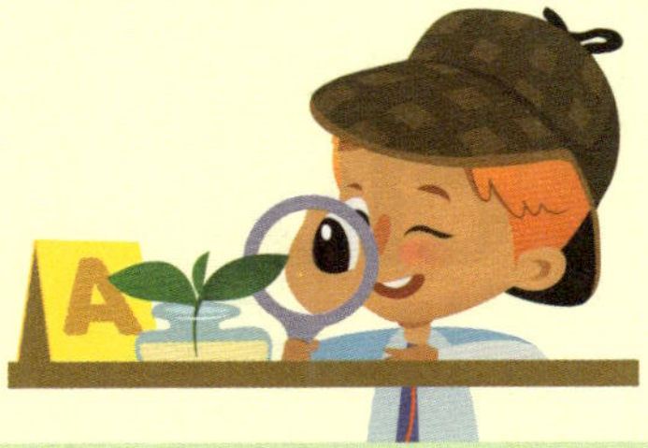
A
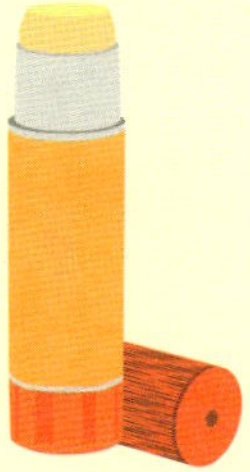

mud	bun	sun	run
cut	hut	nut	Sue
pool	blue	clue	glue

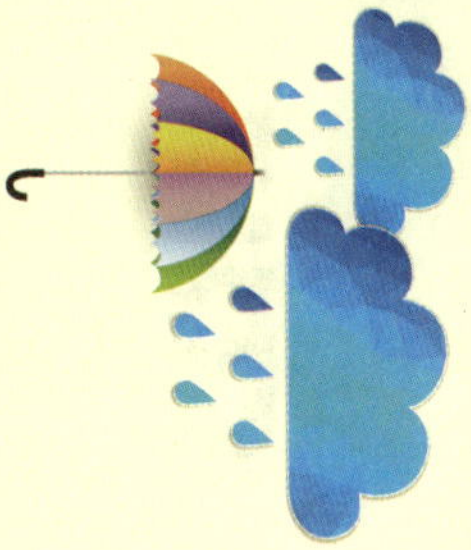
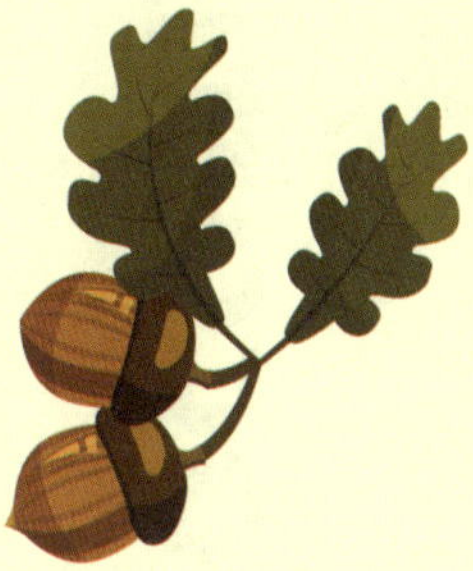
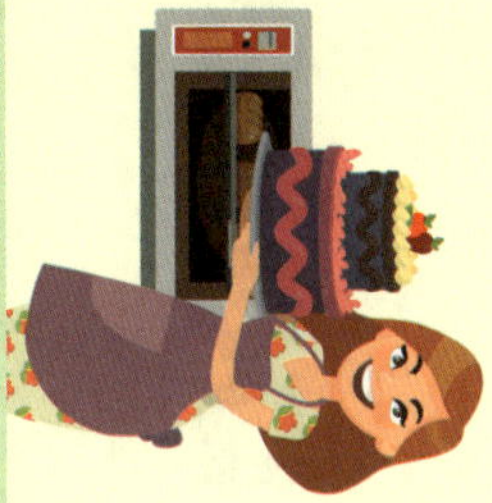
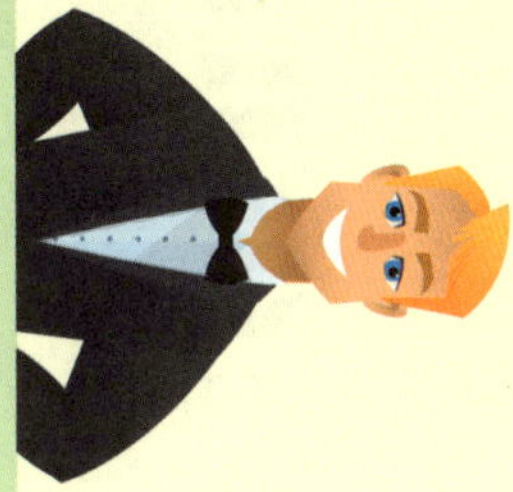
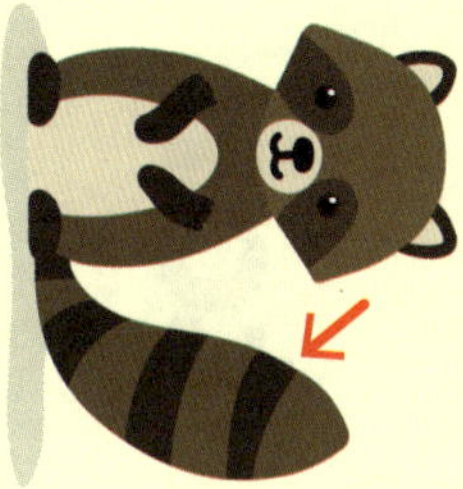
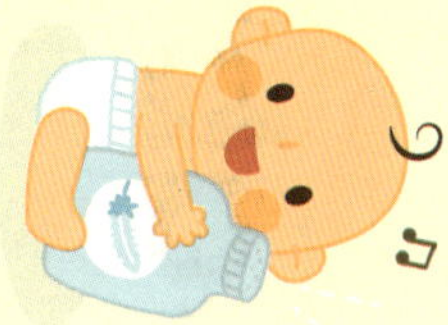
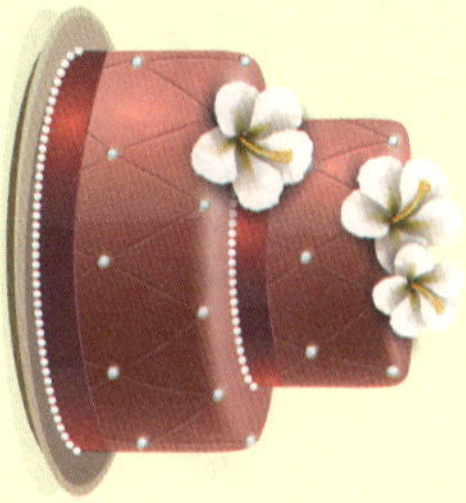
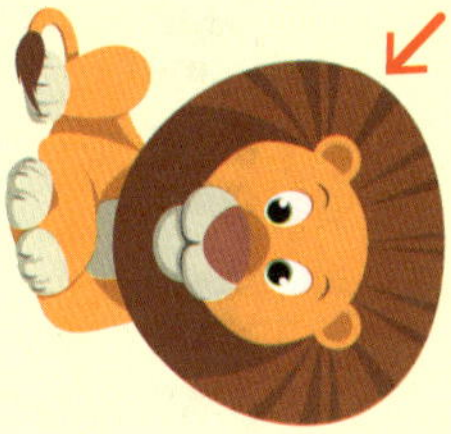
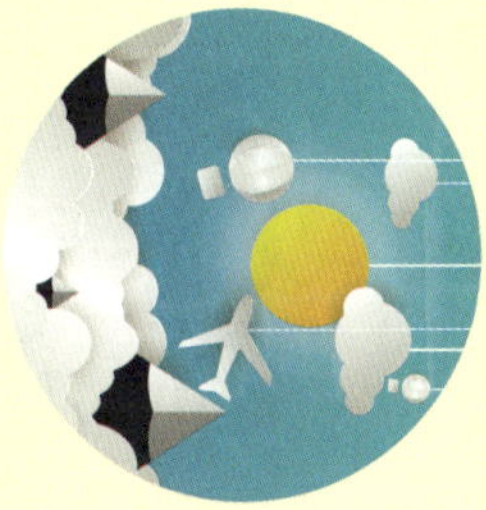

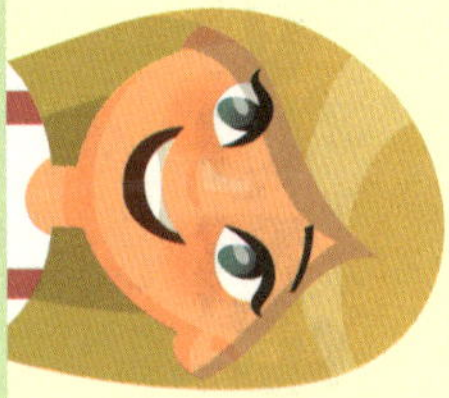
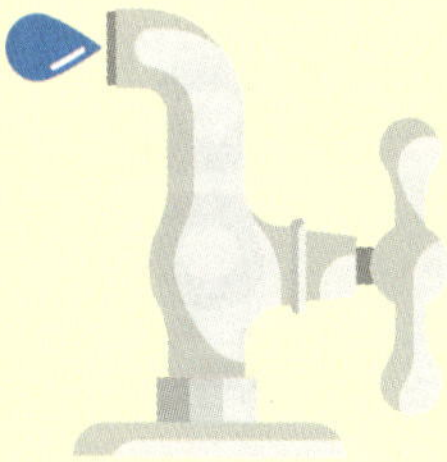
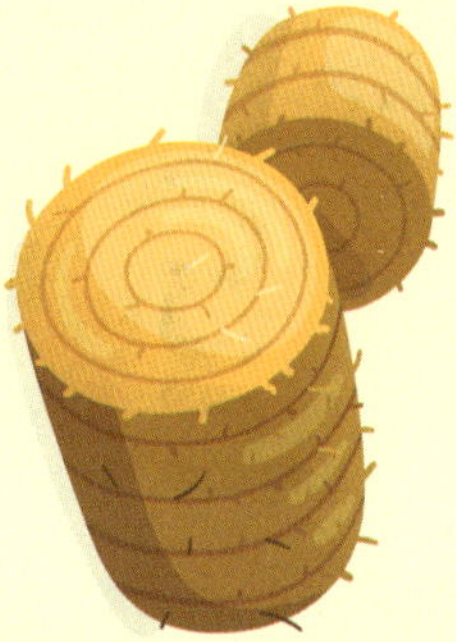
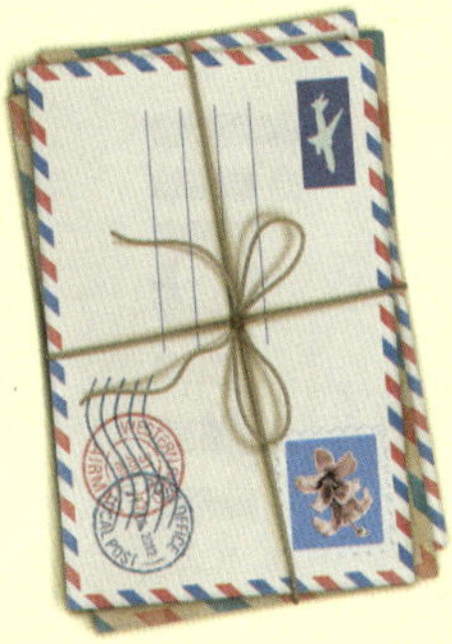
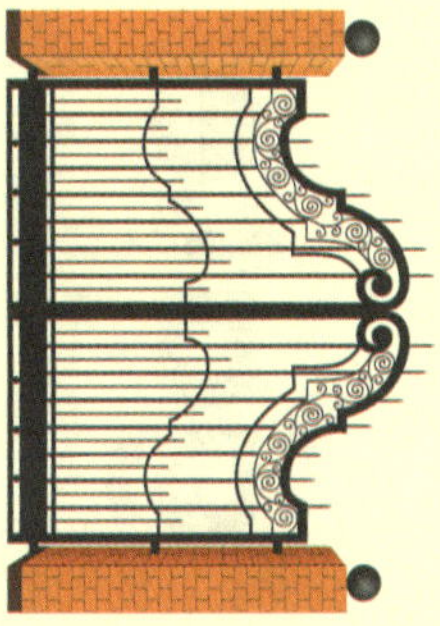
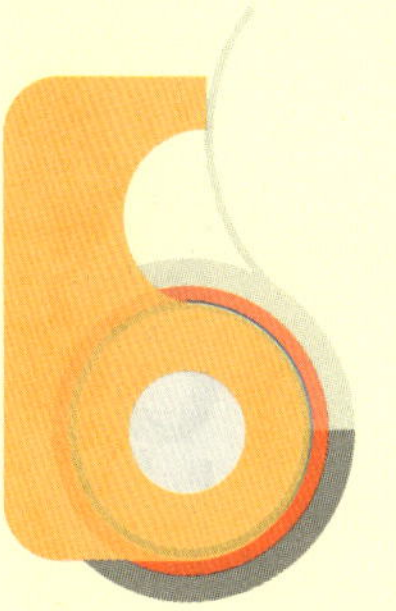

man	bake	acorn	rain
mane	cake	baby	tail
tap	face	paper	day
tape	gate	mail	hay

say	eve	city	pea
he	here	tiny	weak
me	Steve	eat	bee
we	body	leaf	need

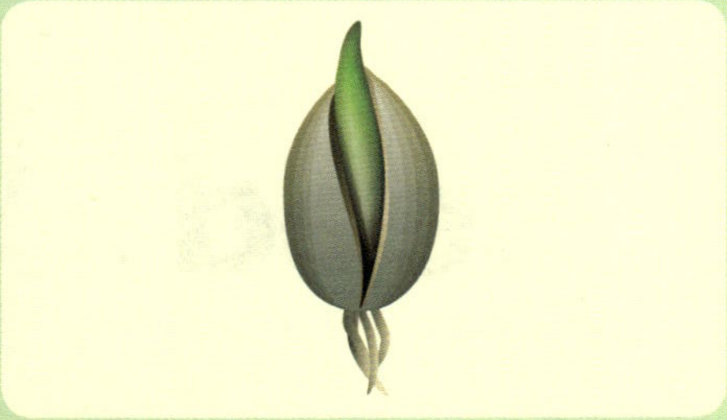
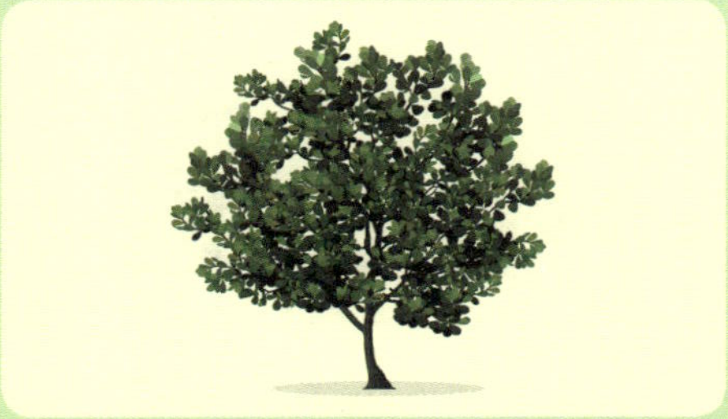
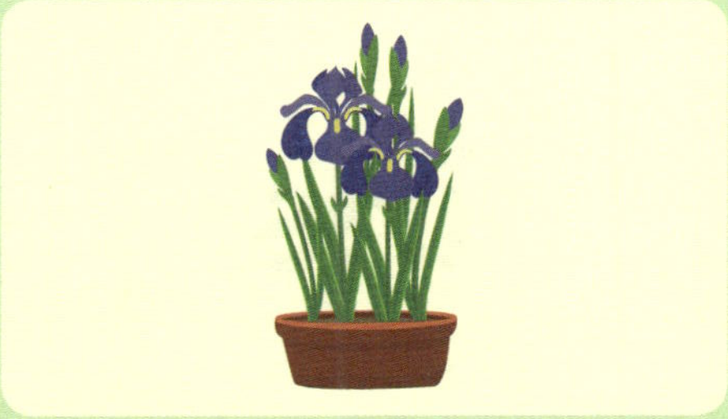
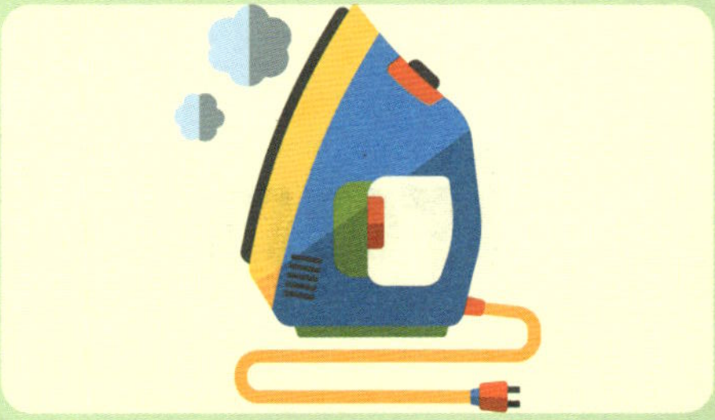
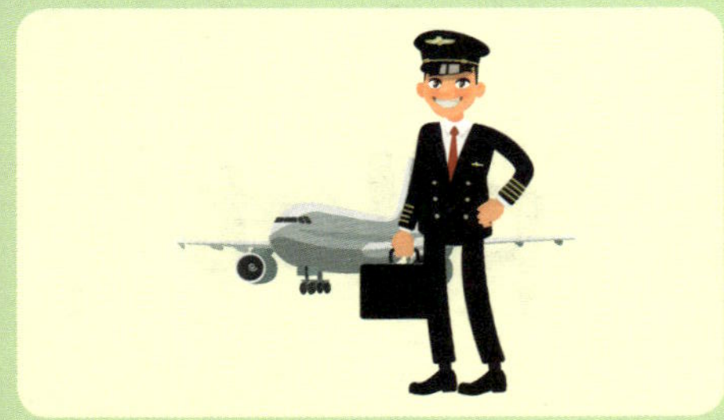
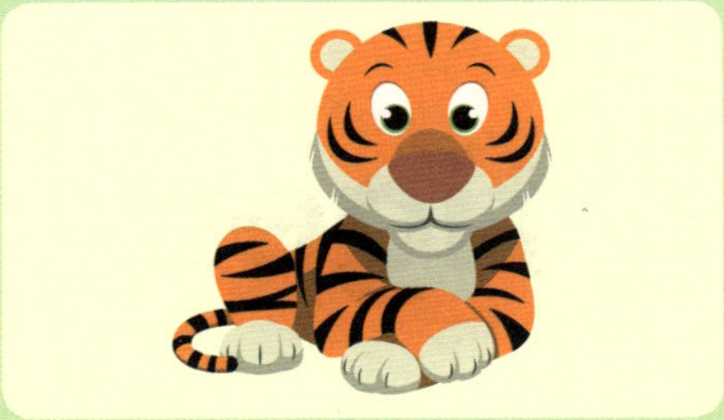
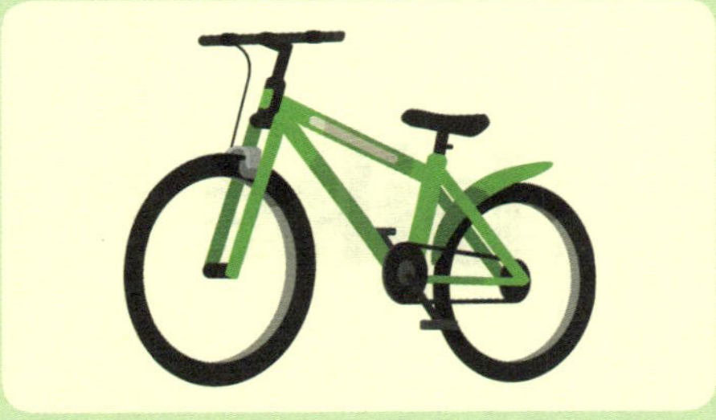
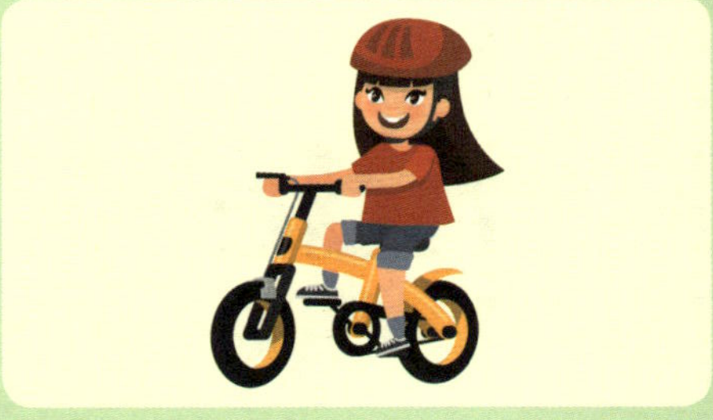
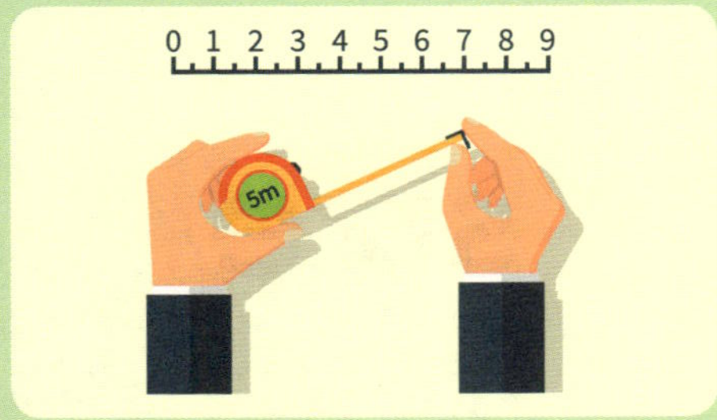
0 1 2 3 4 5 6 7 8 9
5m
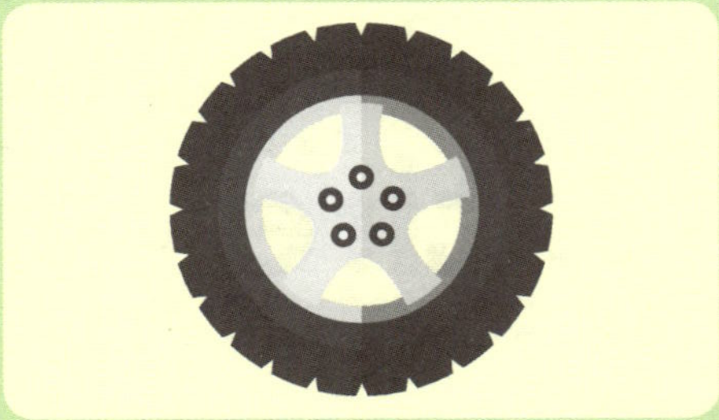
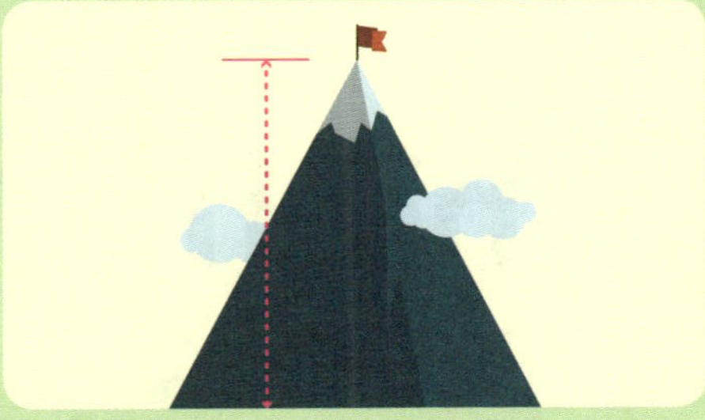
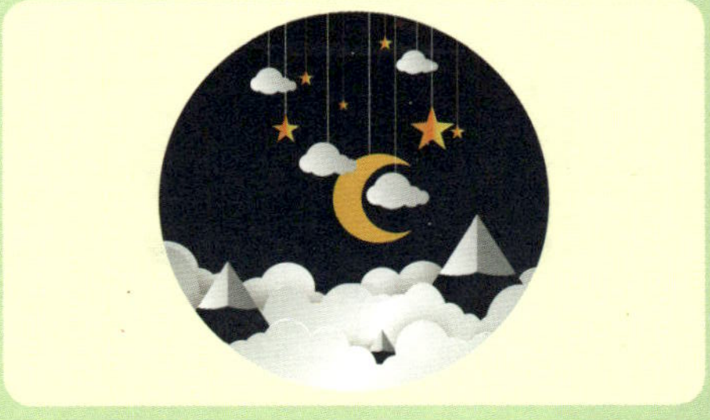
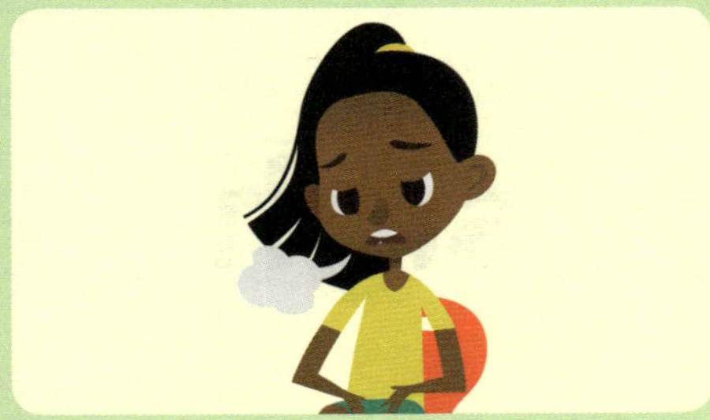
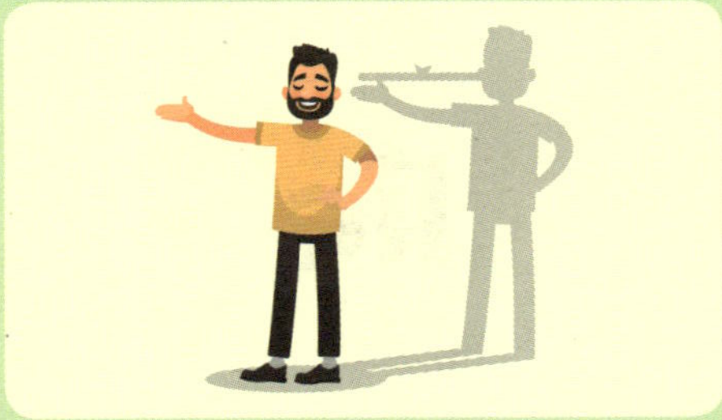
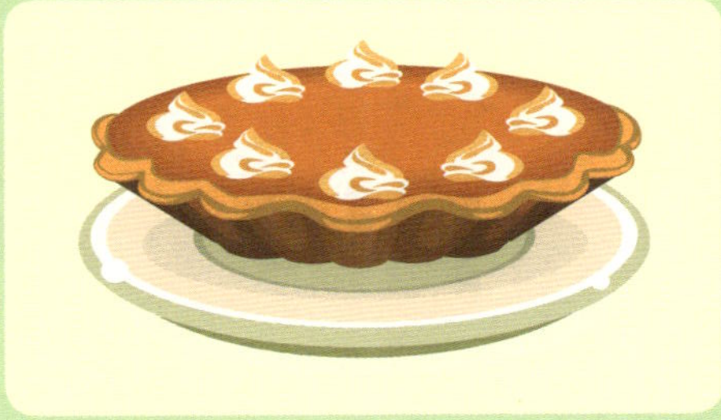
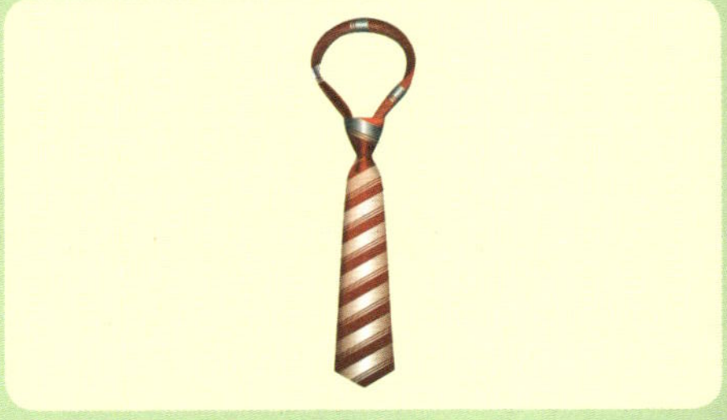

seed	pilot	size	sigh
tree	tiger	tire	lie
iris	bike	high	pie
iron	ride	night	tie

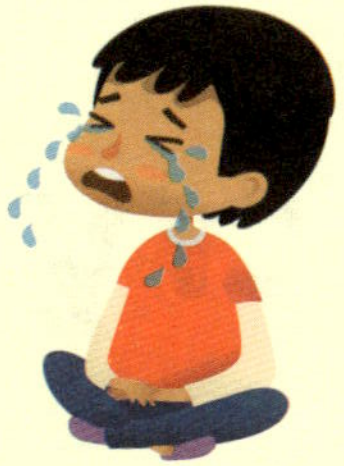
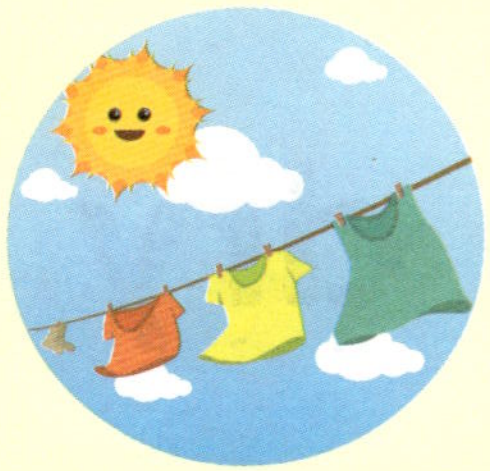
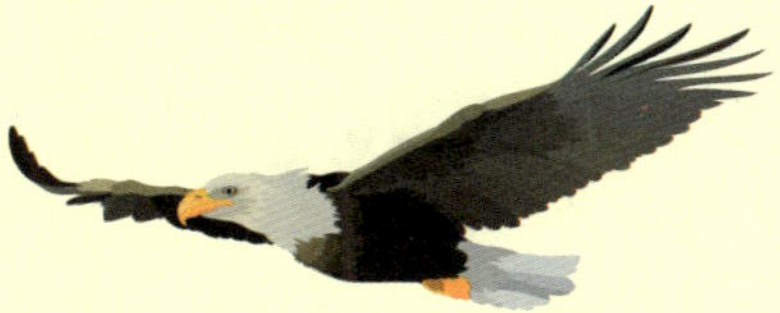
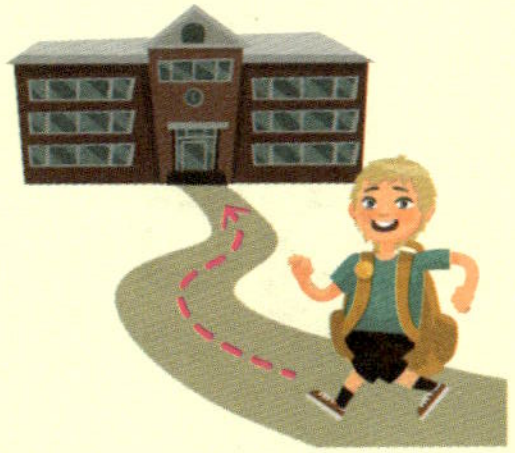
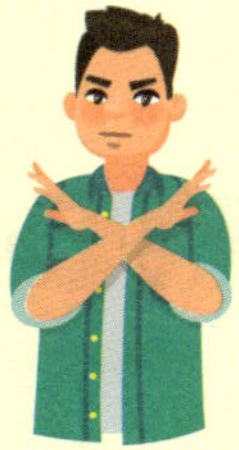
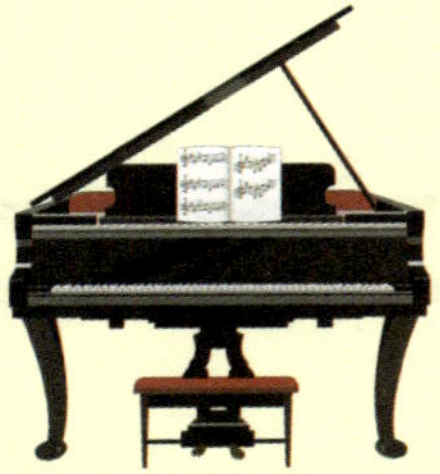
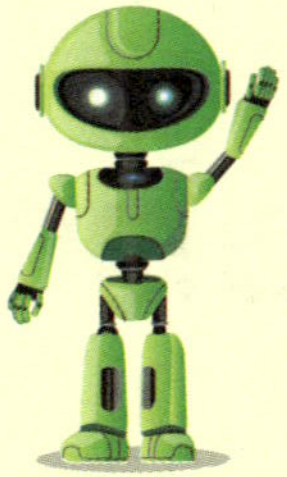

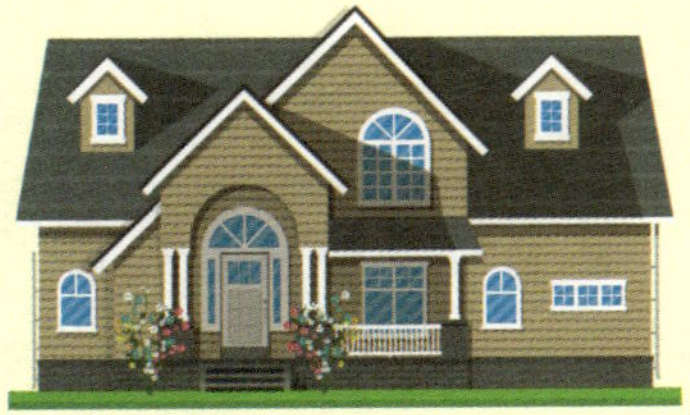
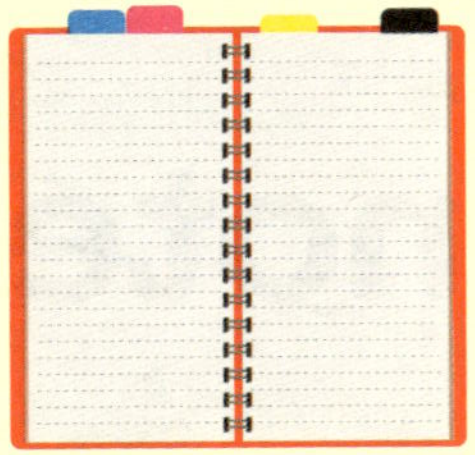
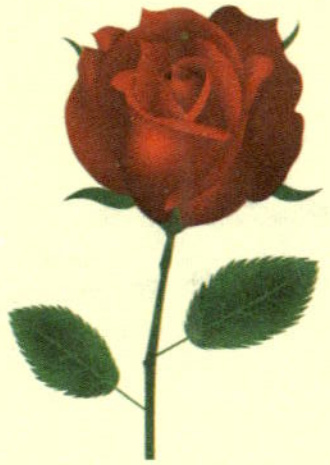
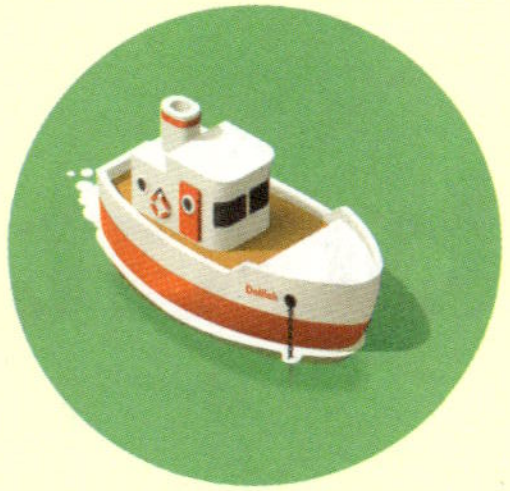
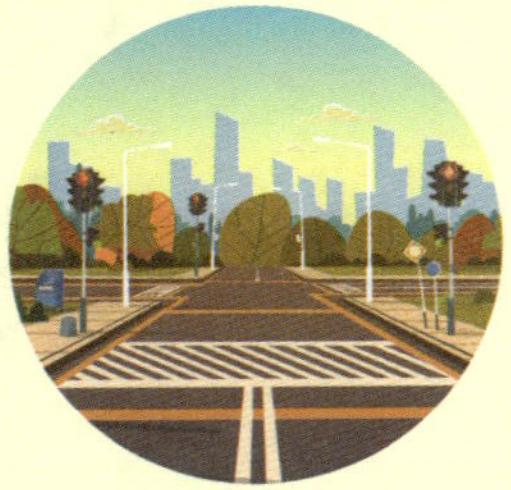

Natural Soap
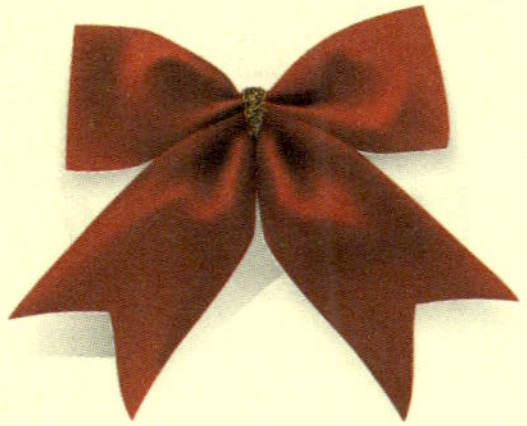
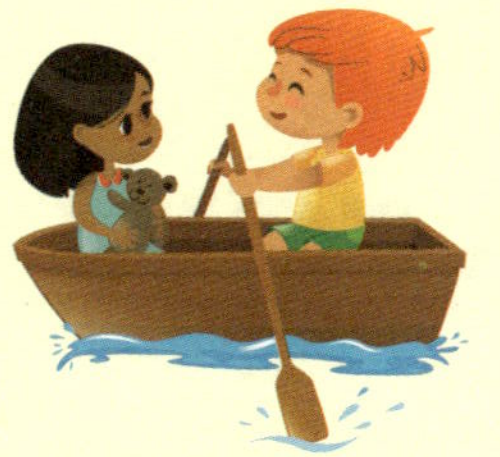

cry	no	home	road
dry	piano	note	soap
fly	robot	rose	bow
go	cone	boat	row

slow	cupid	huge	new
Joe	music	tube	cool
hoe	unicorn	chew	food
toe	cute	few	moon

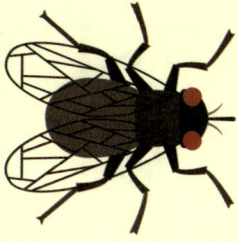

black	cliff	fly	plant
block	clock	globe	plate
blouse	flag	glass	plug
clap	flame	glow	sleep

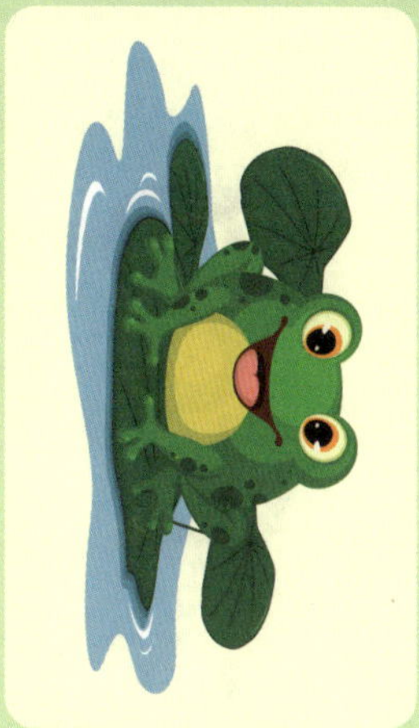
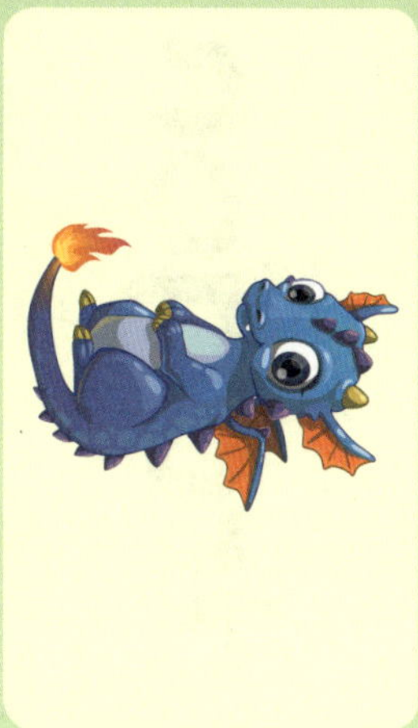
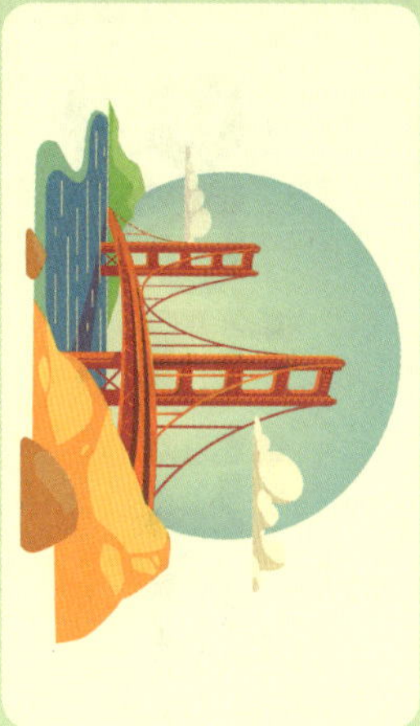
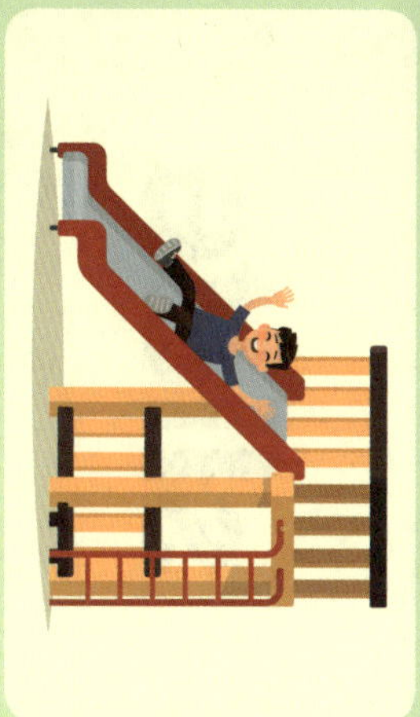
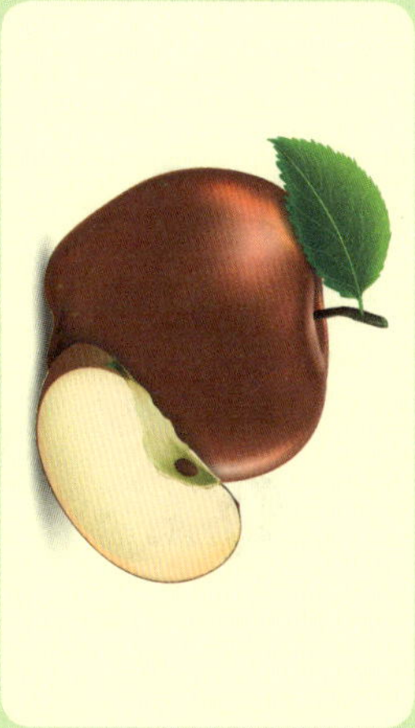
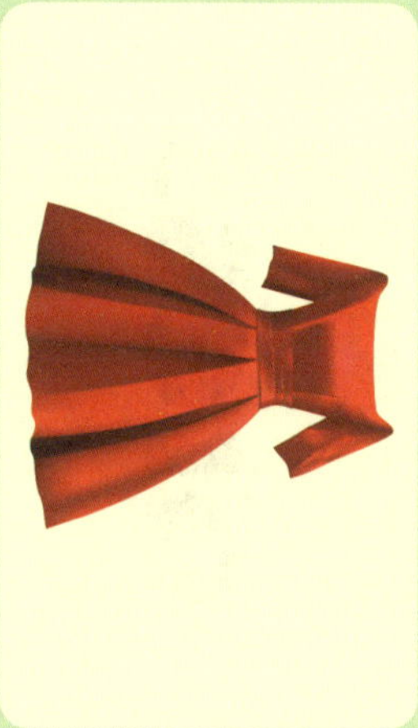
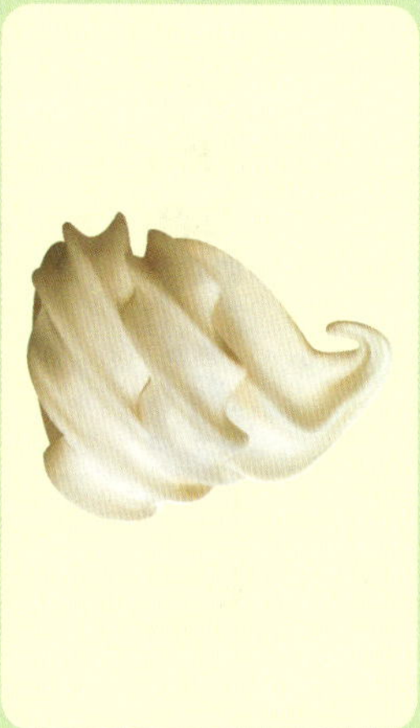
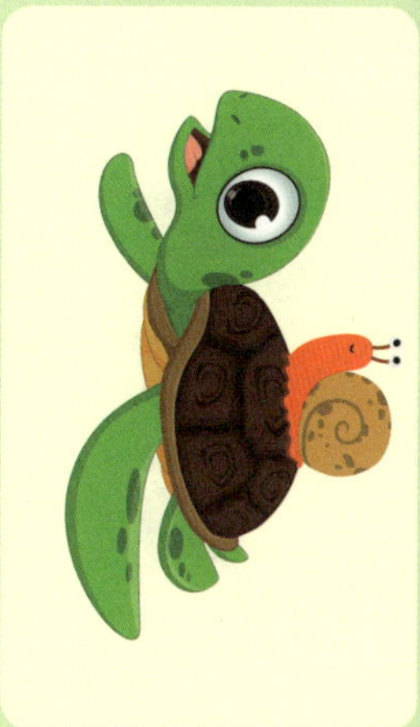
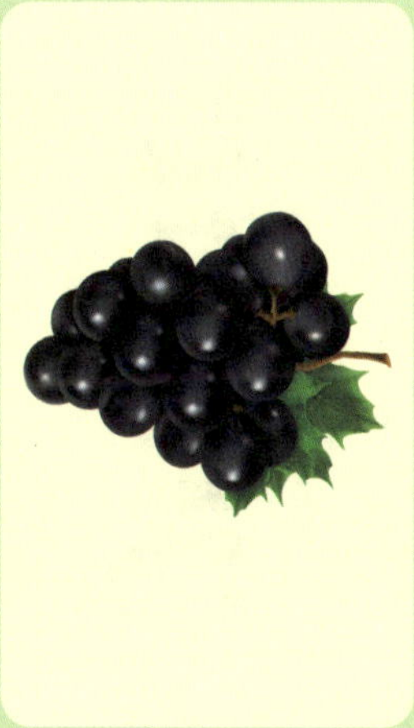
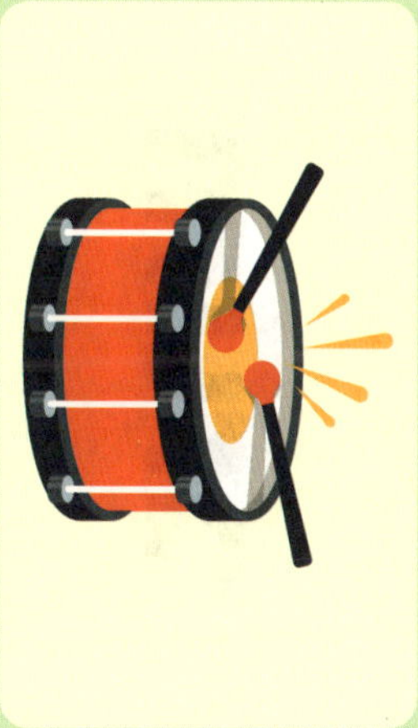
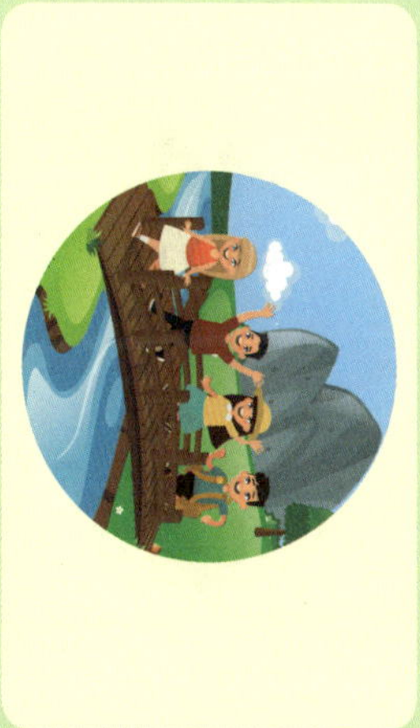
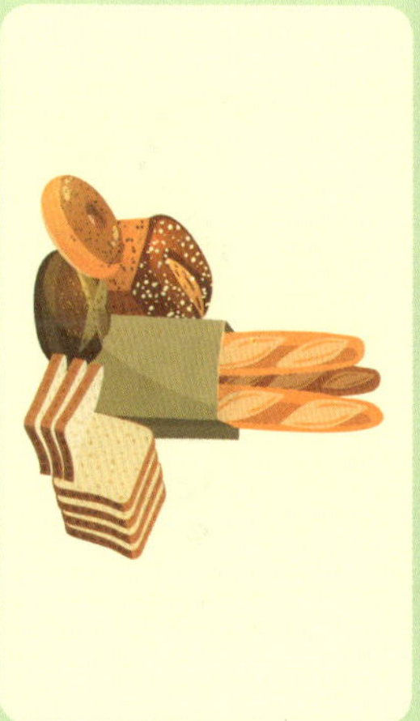
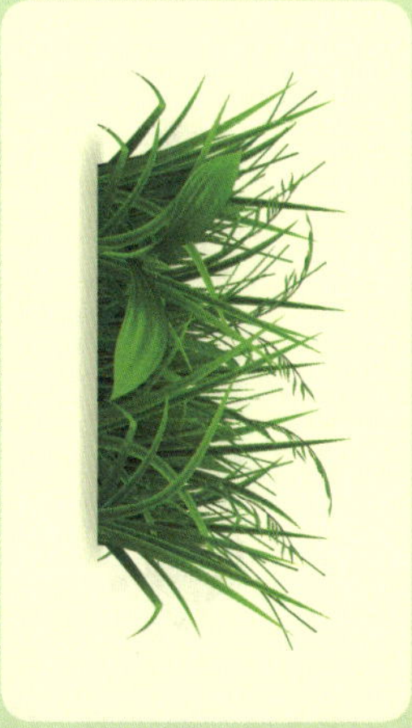
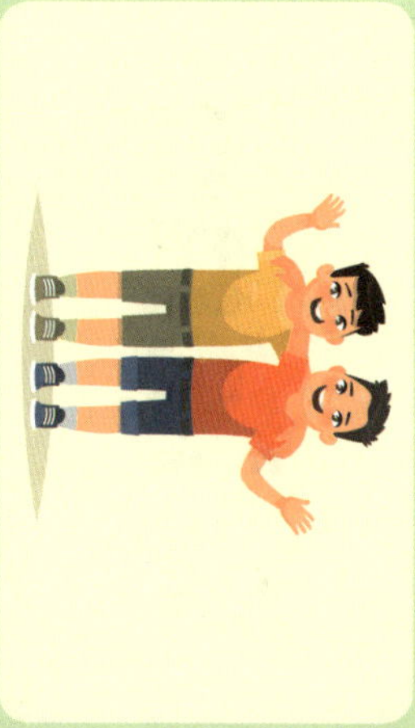
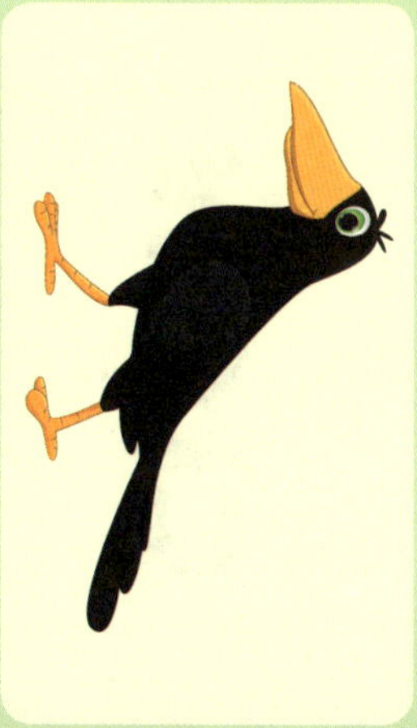
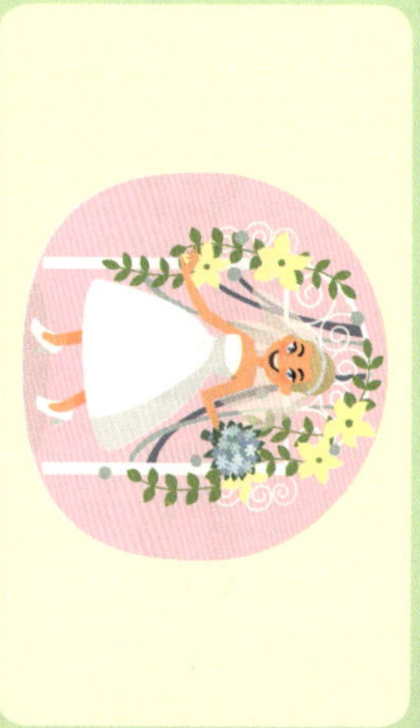

slide	bridge	dragon	frog
slow	cream	dress	fruit
bread	cross	drum	grape
bride	crow	friend	grass

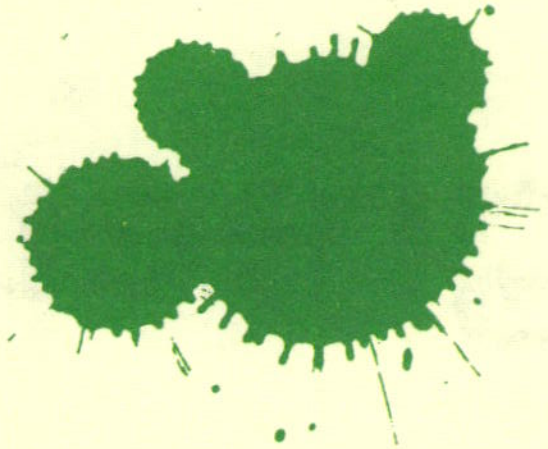
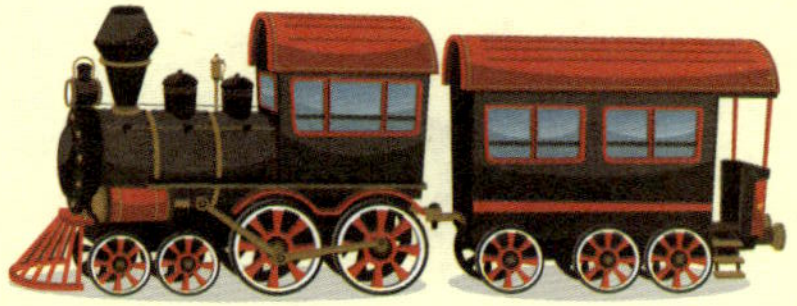
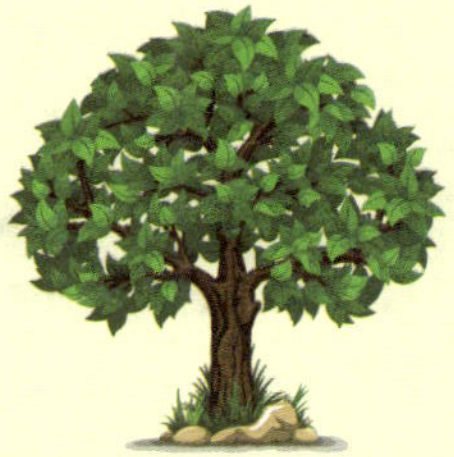
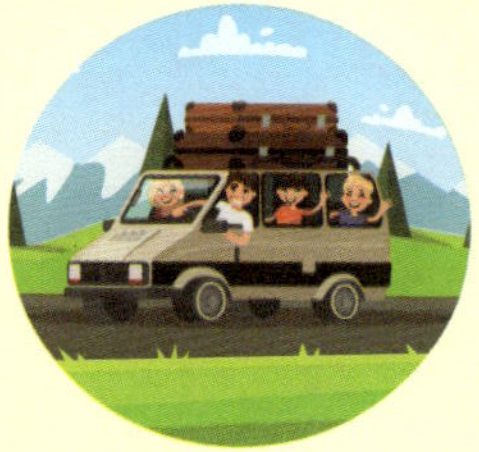
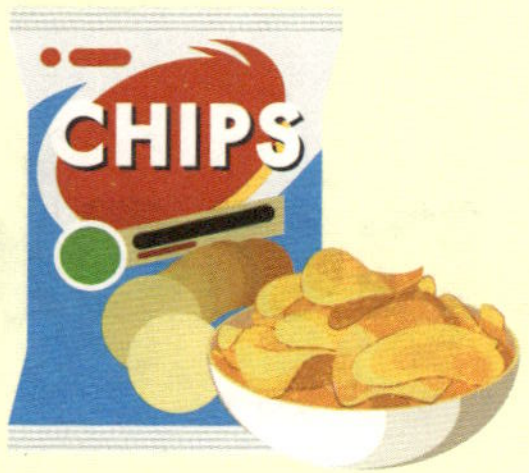
CHIPS
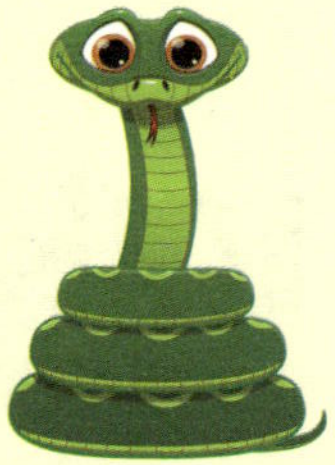
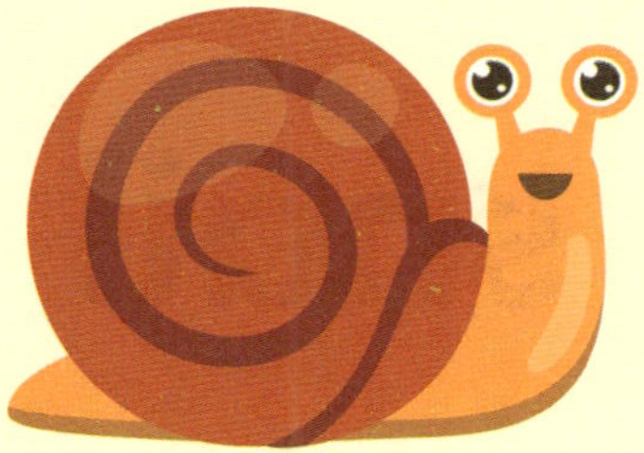
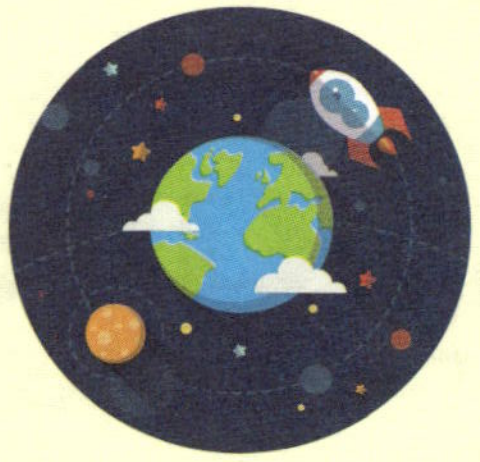
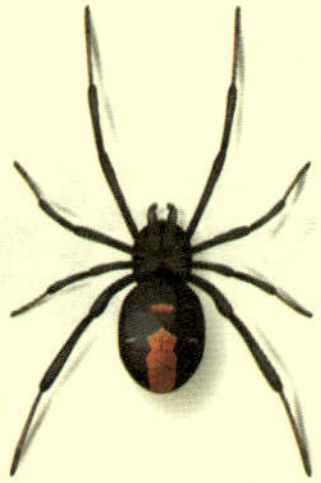
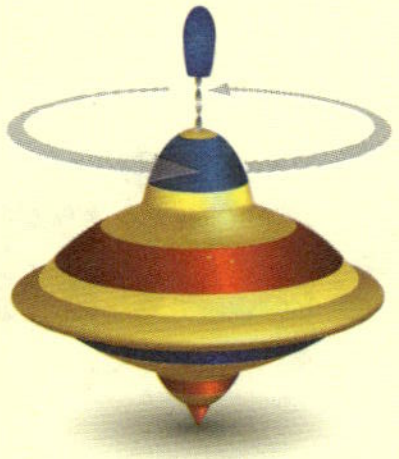
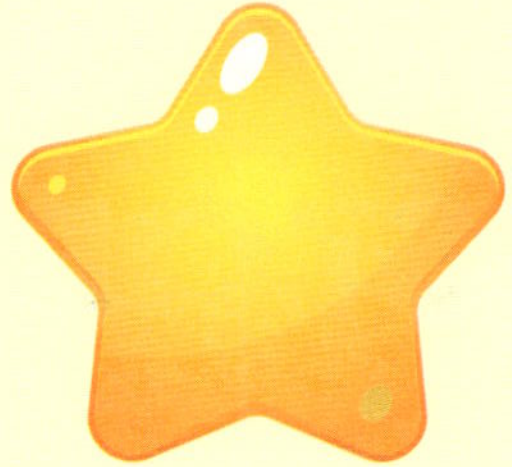
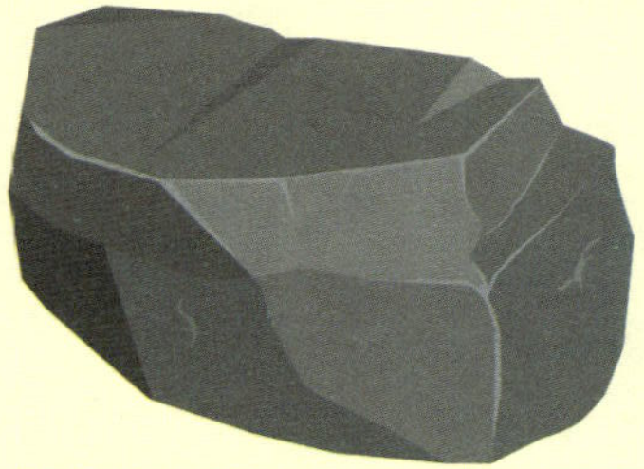

STOP
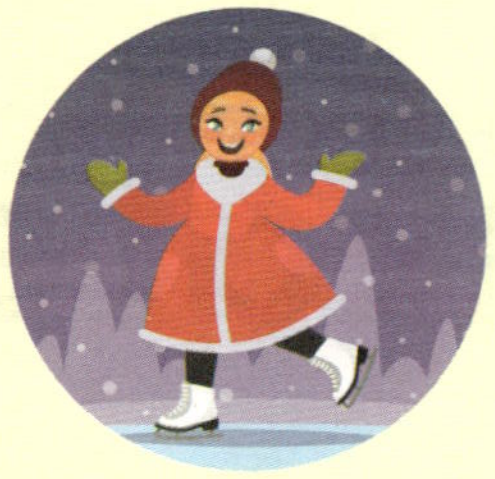

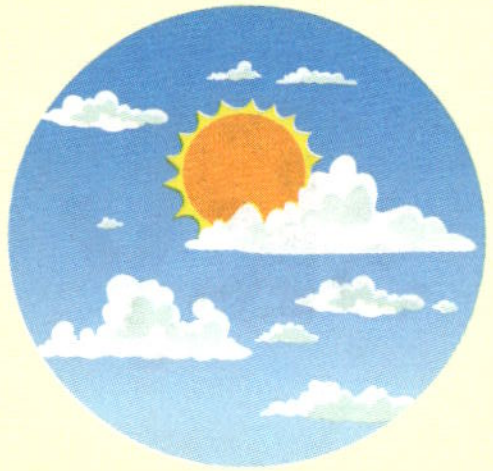

green	snack	spider	stop
train	snake	spin	skate
tree	snail	star	ski
trip	space	stone	sky

small	sweet	chin	sheep
smell	swim	chop	shirt
smile	cheese	shake	whale
swan	cherry	shape	what

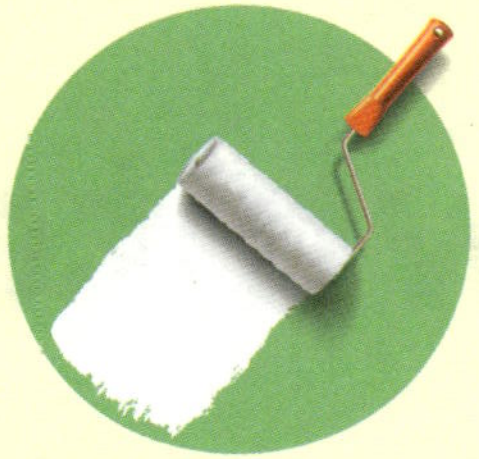
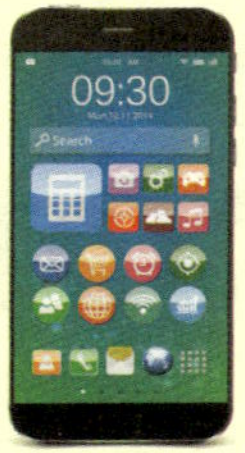
09:30
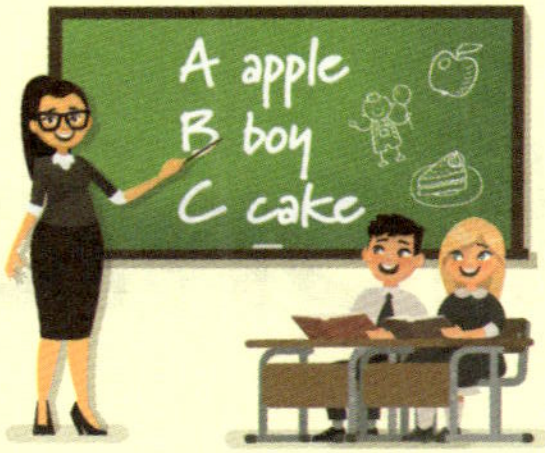
A apple
B boy
C cake
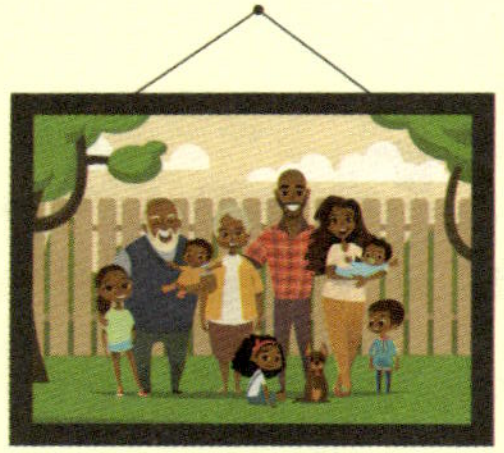

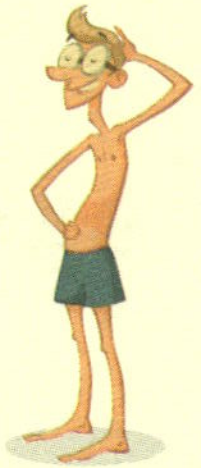

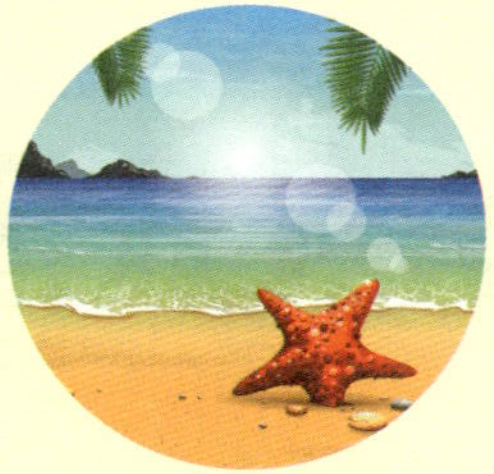
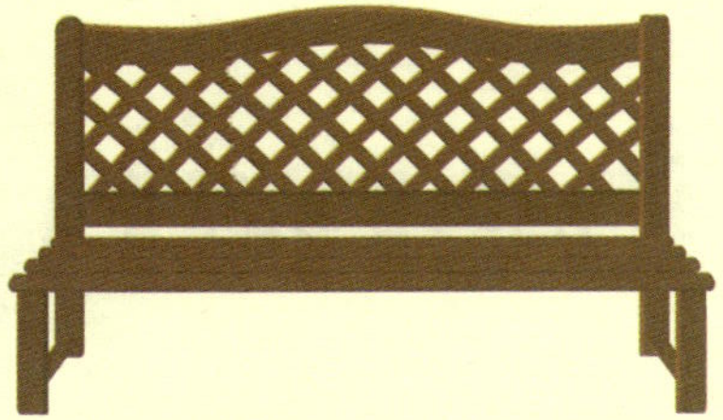
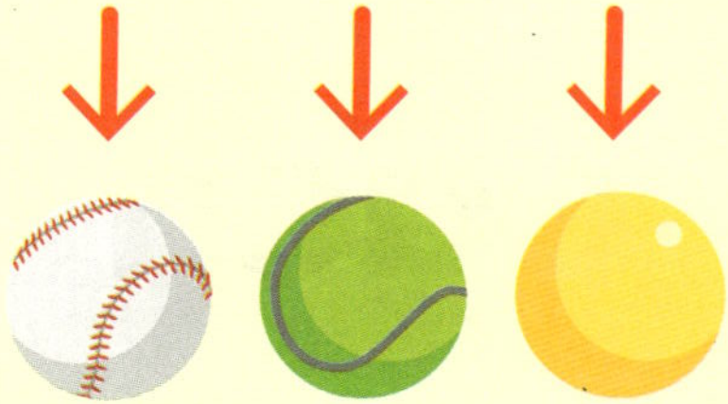
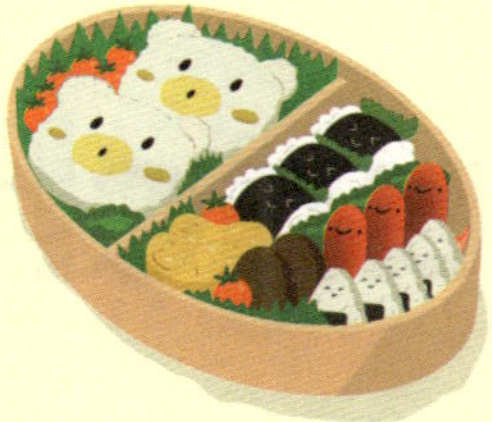
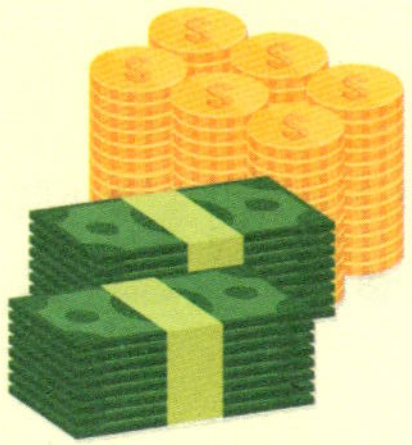

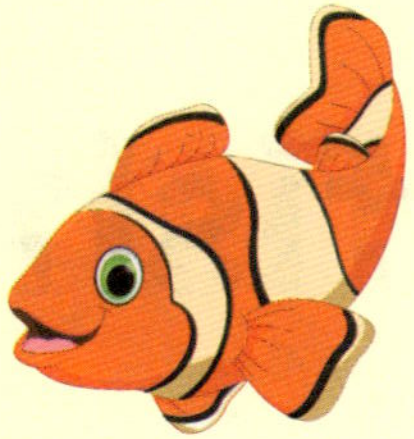
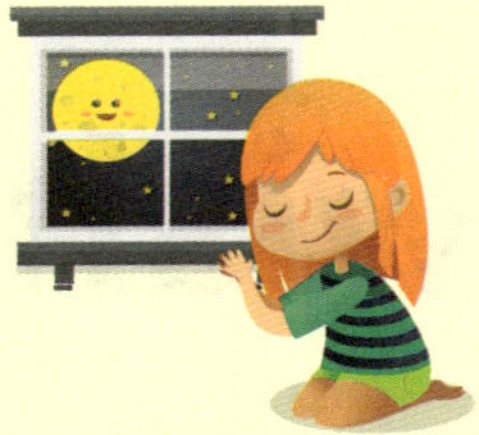
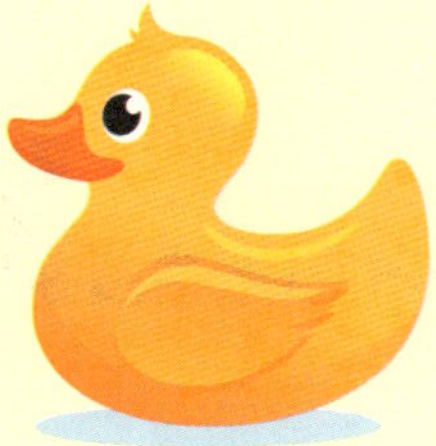

white	that	bench	dish
phone	thin	each	fish
phonics	think	lunch	wish
photo	beach	cash	duck

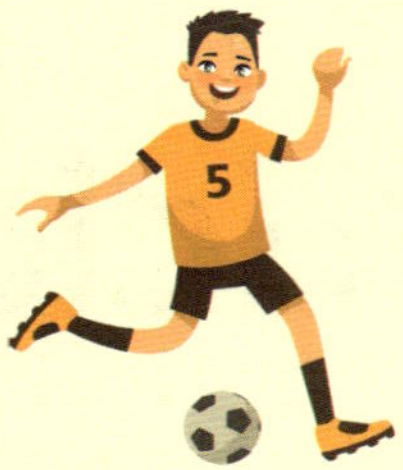

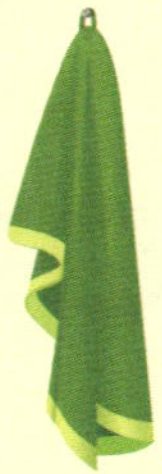

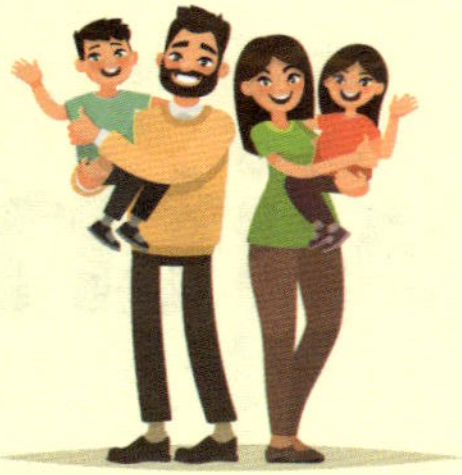

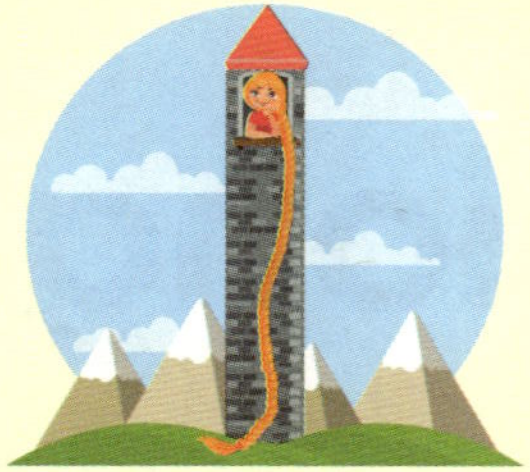

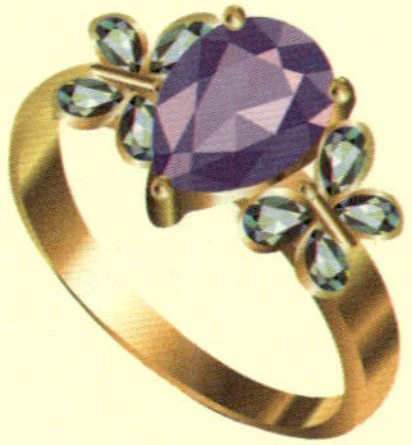

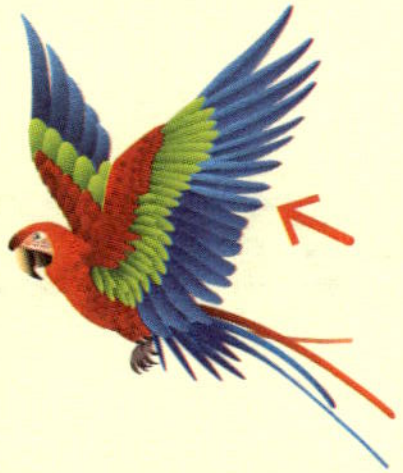

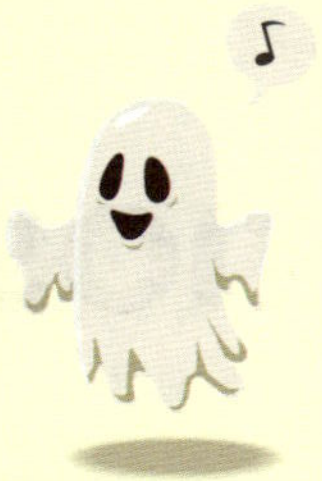

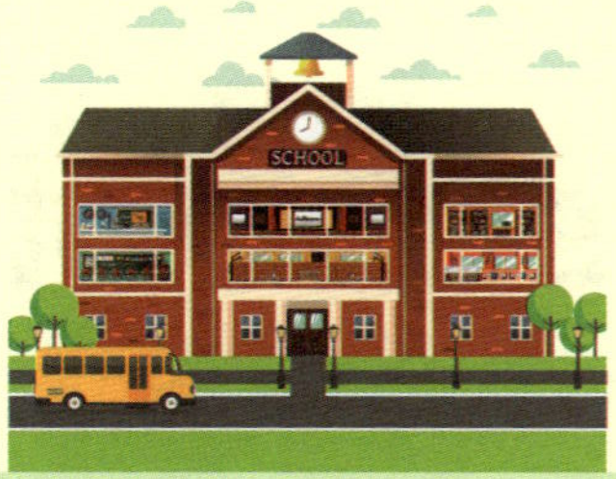
SCHOOL

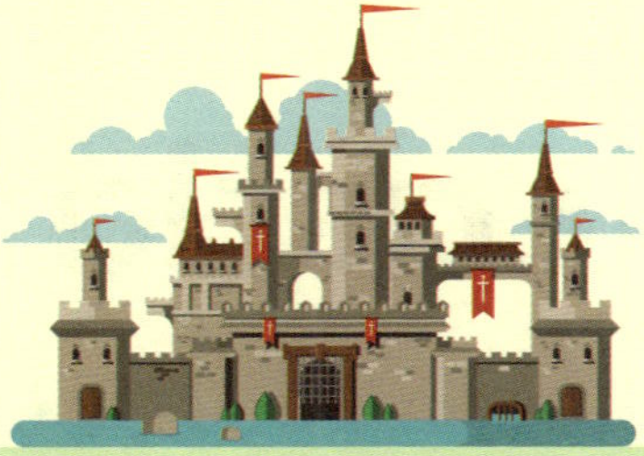

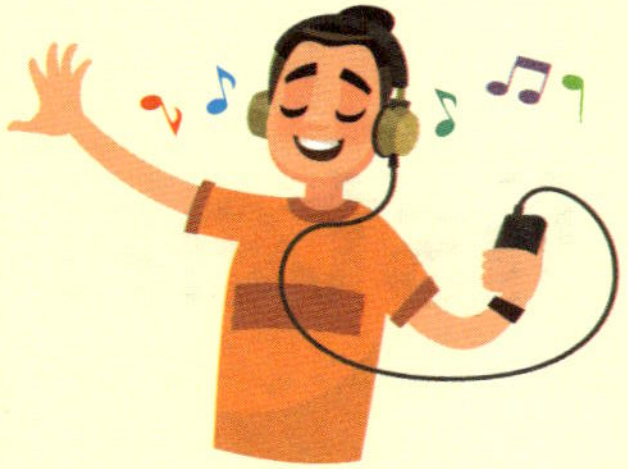

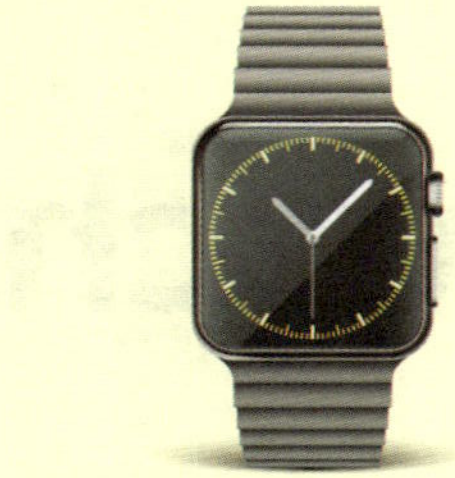

kick	with	ghost	watch
neck	long	school	
cloth	ring	castle	
smooth	wing	listen	

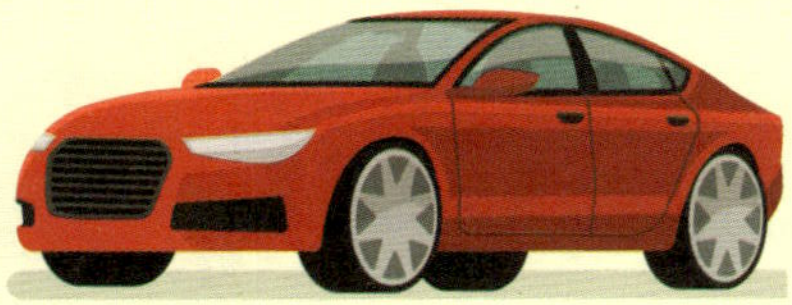

Invitation
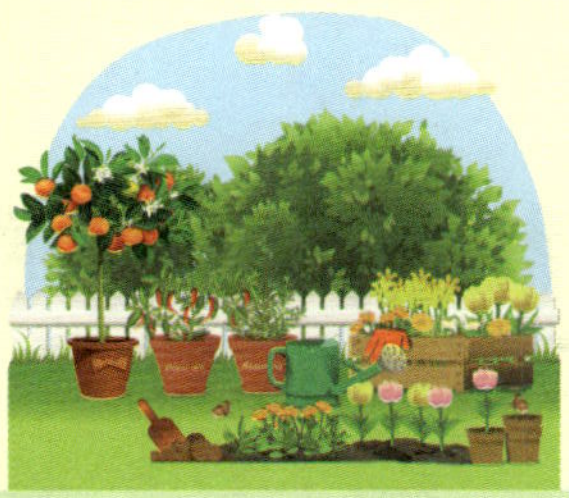
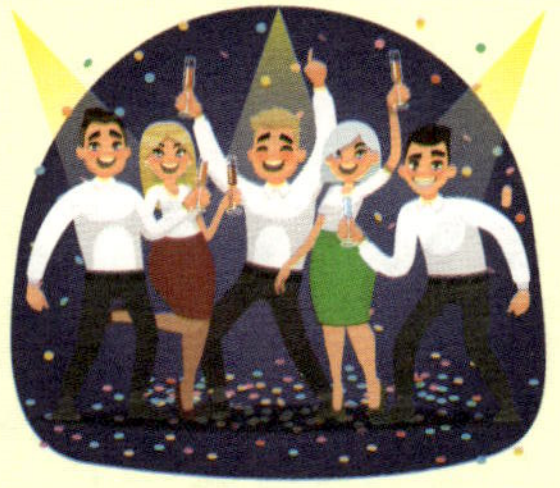
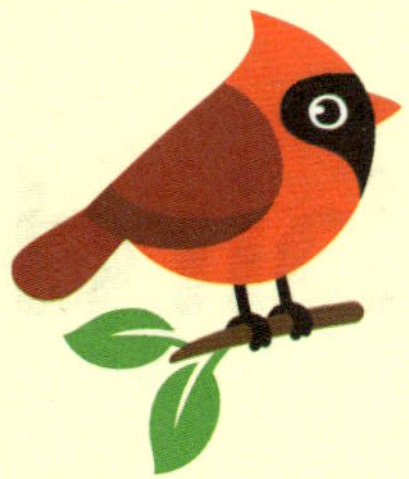
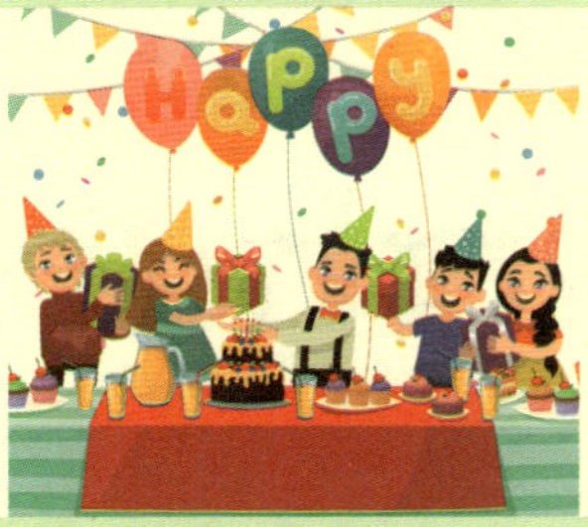
Happy
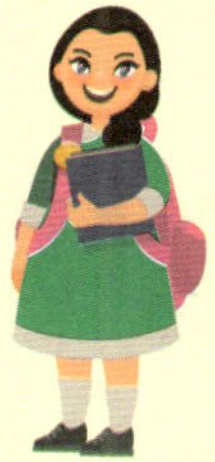
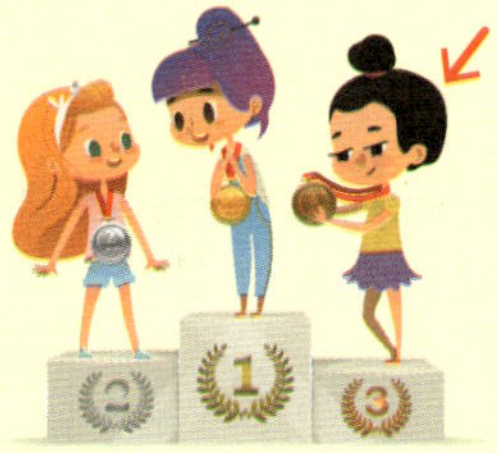
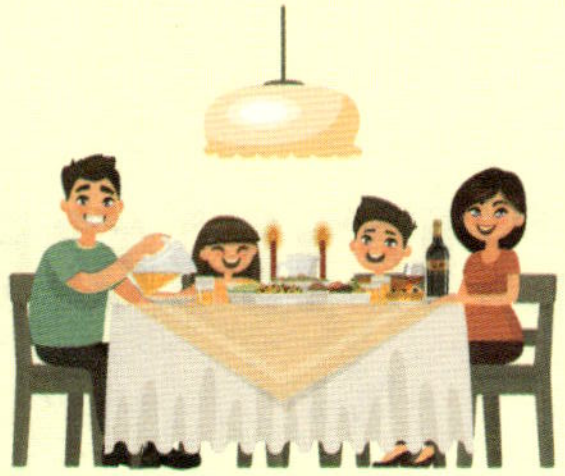
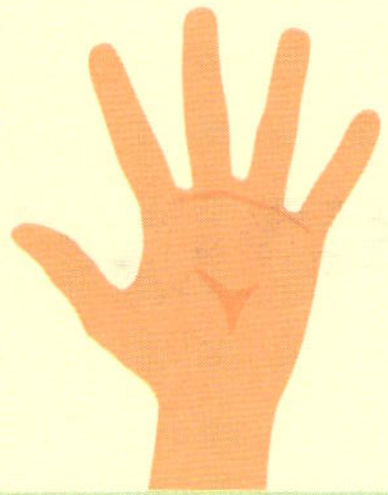
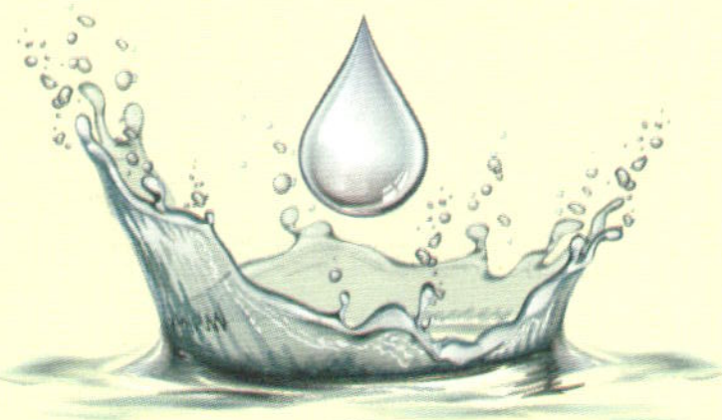
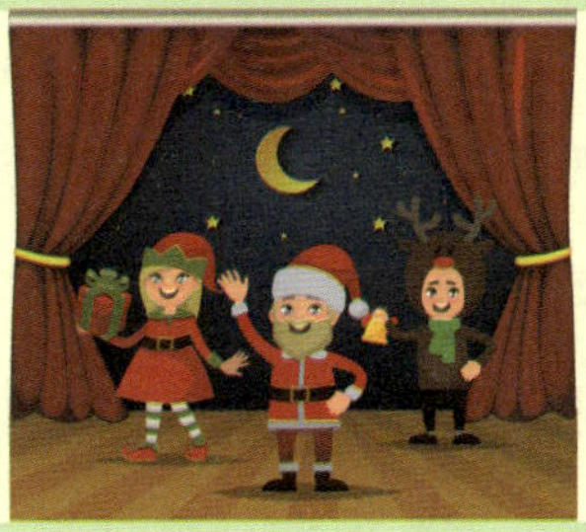
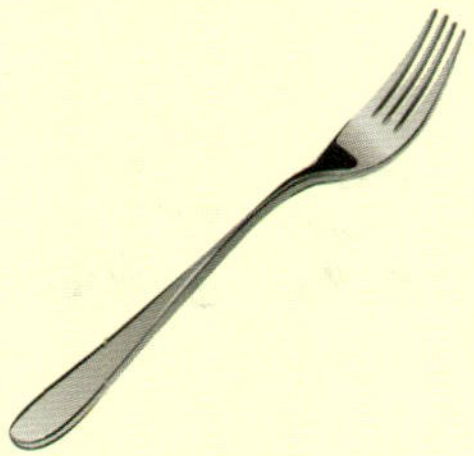
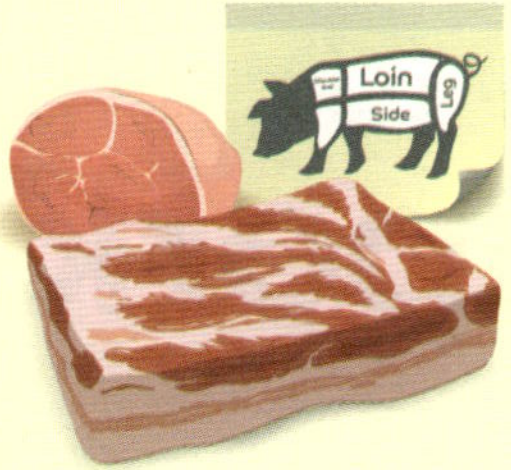
Loin
Side
Leg
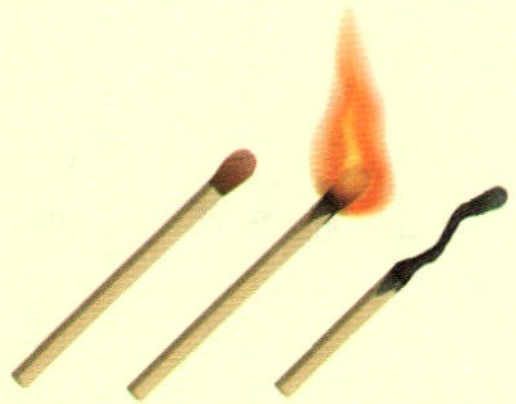
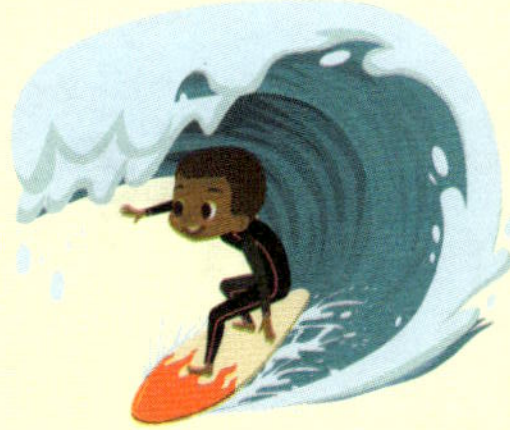

car	bird	dinner	fork
card	birthday	finger	pork
garden	girl	water	burn
party	third	actor	surf

turn	Paul	saw	point
author	awesome	coin	boy
autumn	awful	oink	joy
Laura	prawn	noise	soy

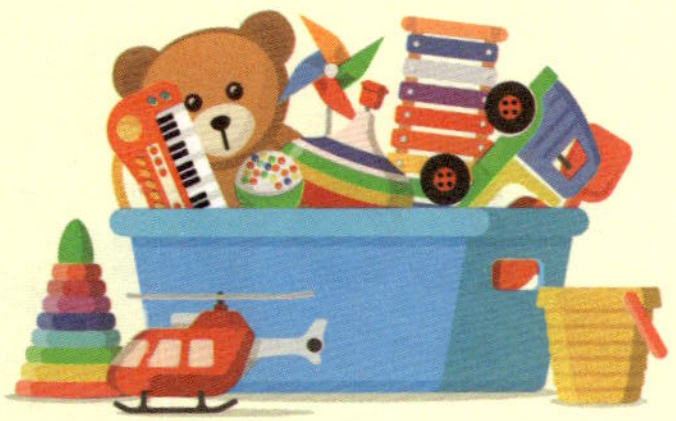
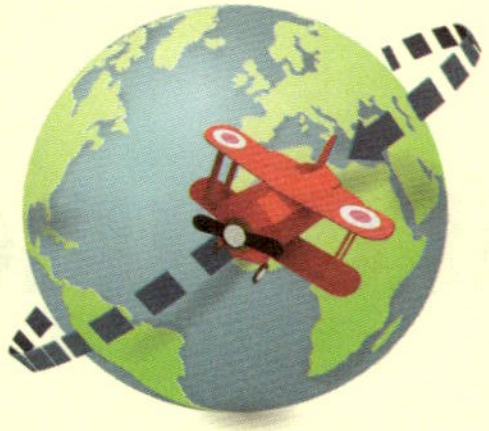

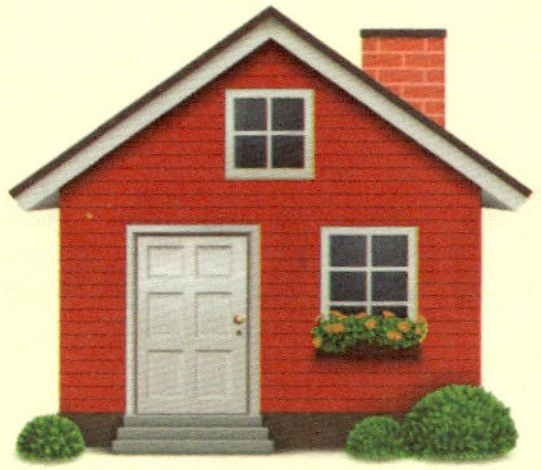
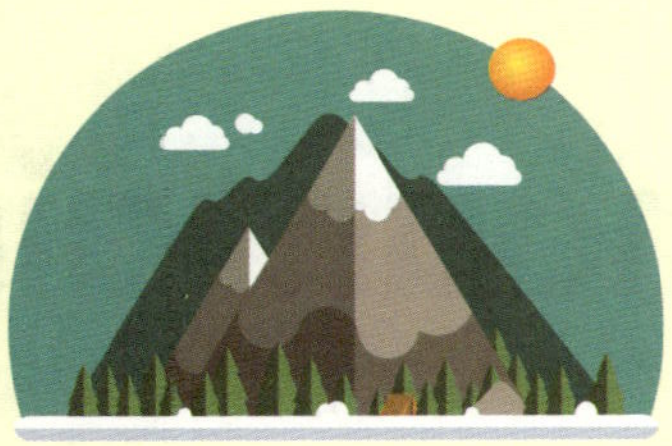
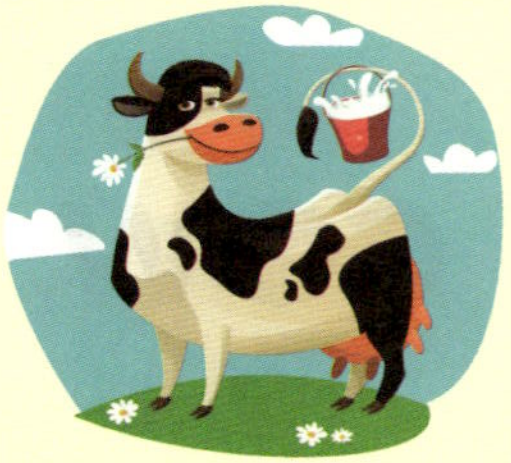
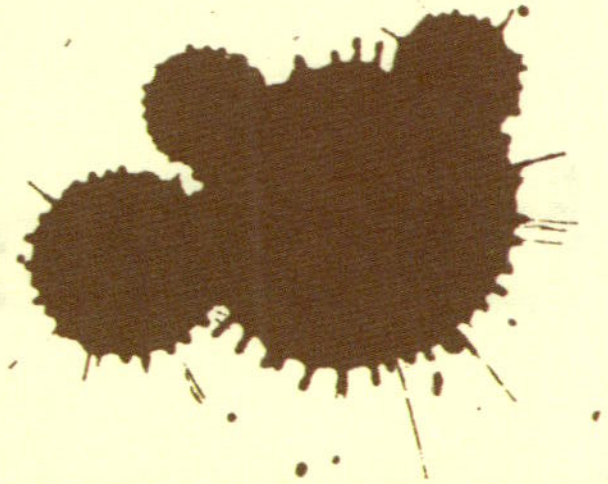
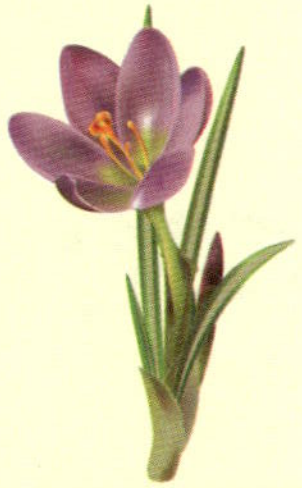
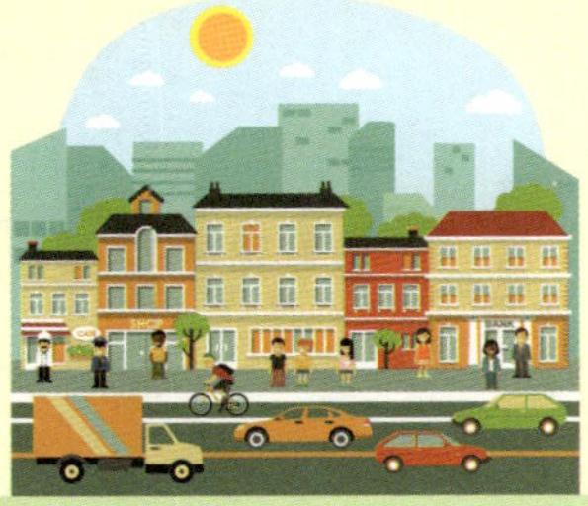
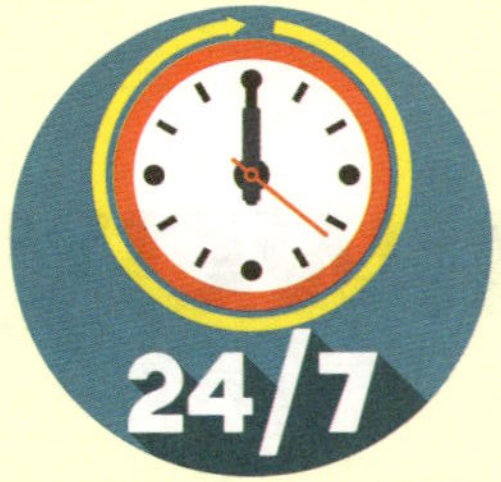
24/7
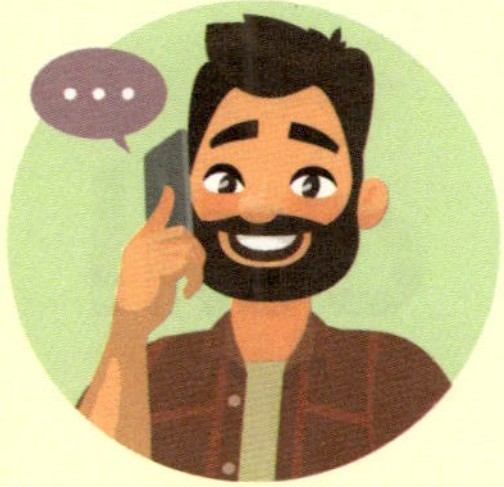
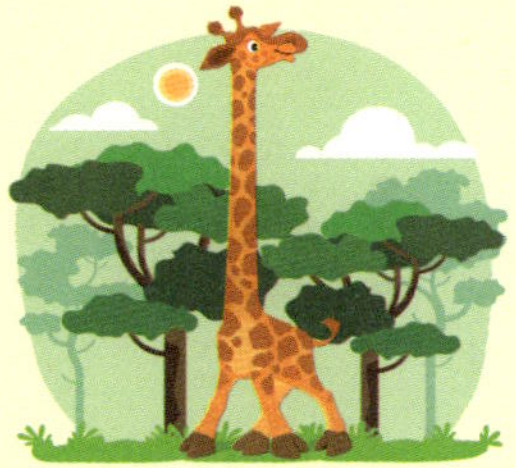
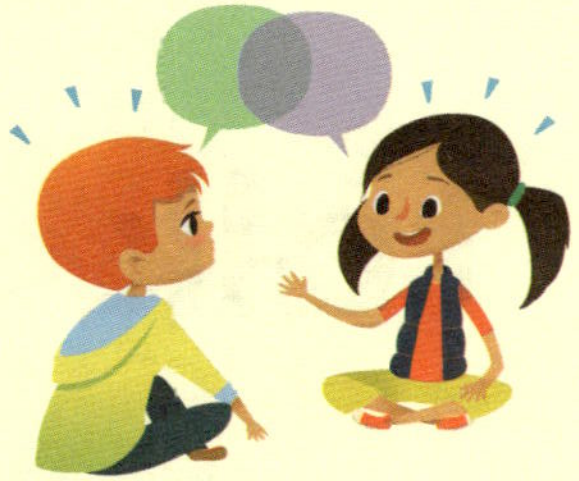
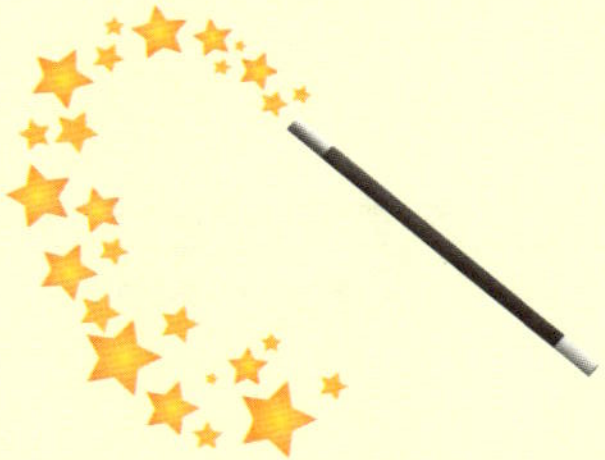
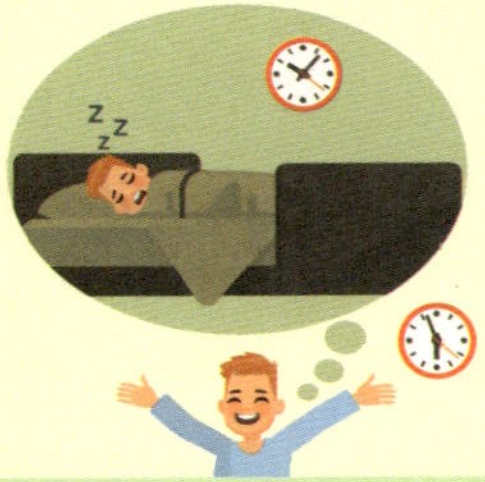
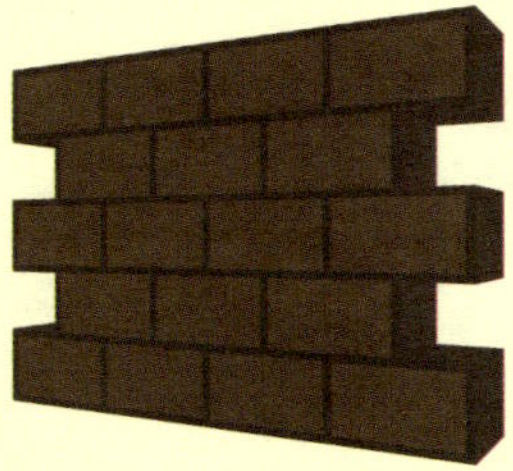

toy	mountain	town	talk
around	cow	always	wand
cloud	brown	call	was
house	flower	tall	wall

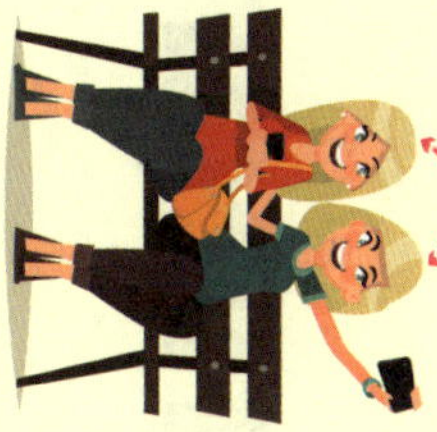
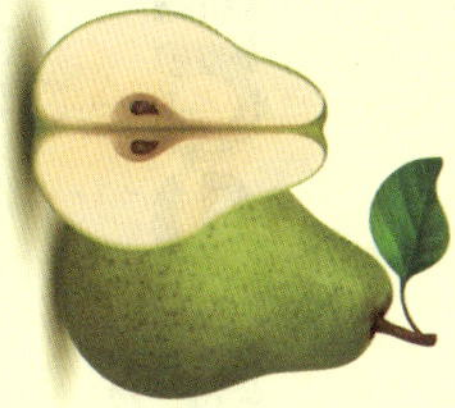
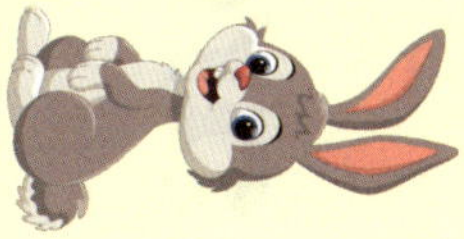
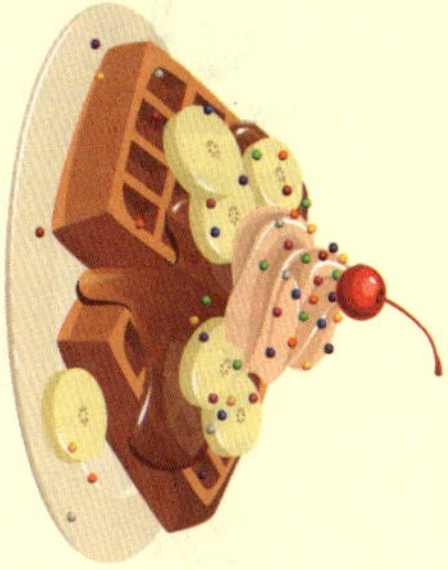
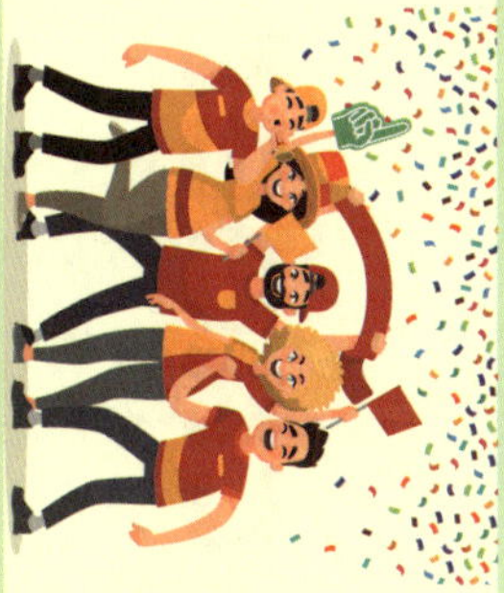

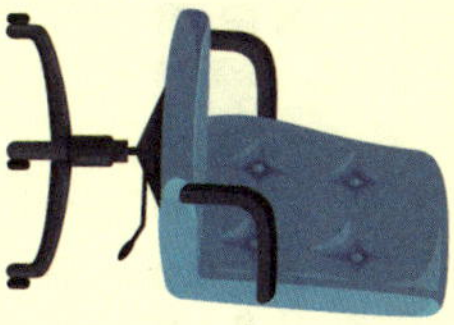
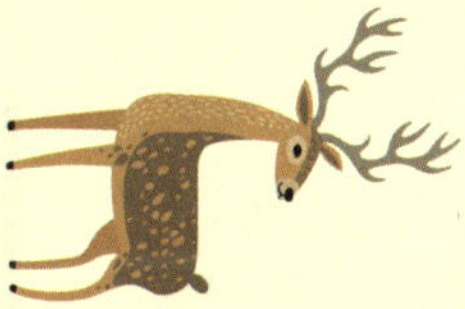
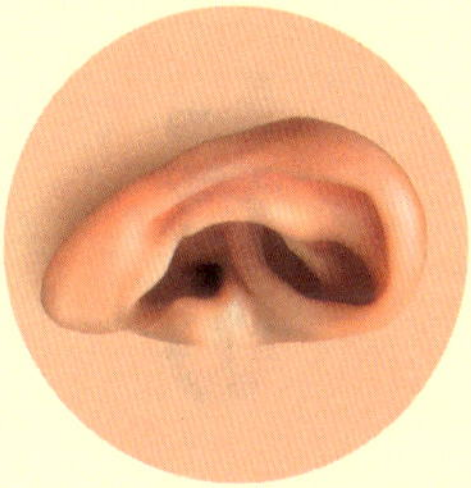

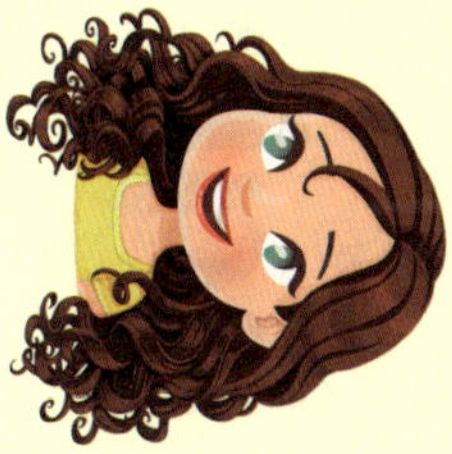
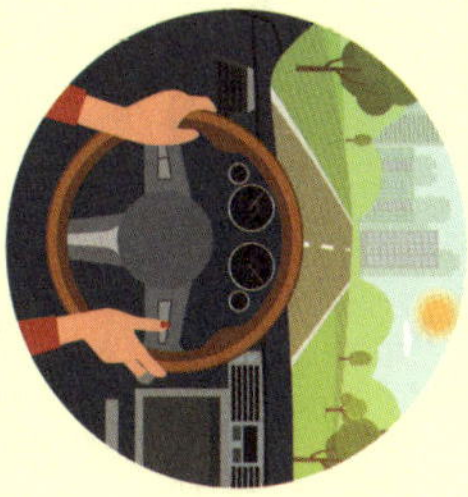
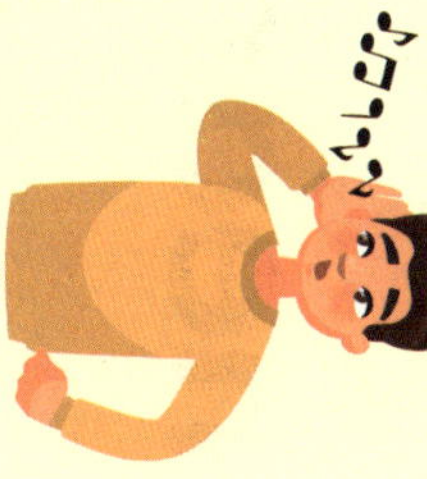
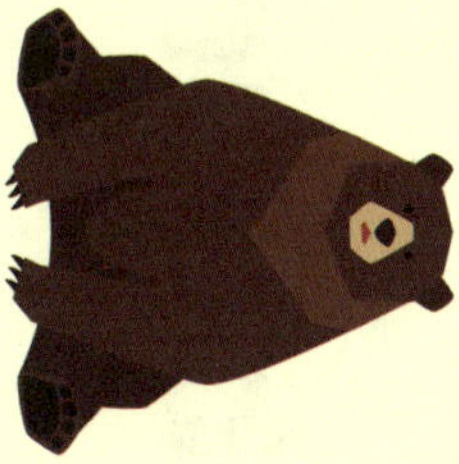
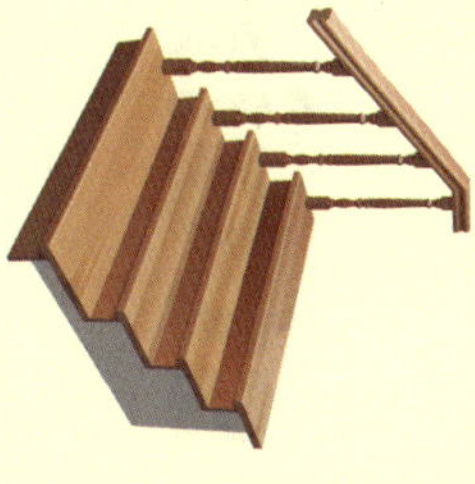

waffle	hare	pear	near
chair	square	wear	cheer
hair	stare	ear	deer
stair	bear	hear	steer

adhere	knife	write	design
here	knock	climb	eight
sphere	wrap	lamb	sigh
knee	wrist	thumb	hour

Amazing PHONICS

神奇的
自然拼读

阅读指导手册

ZHEJIANG UNIVERSITY PRESS
浙江大学出版社

《神奇的自然拼读》由韩国英语学习方法研究所（Key ELL and Learning Strategies Lab）编著，根据亚洲3岁以上孩子学习英语的特点和习惯，利用精美插图、有趣的互动方式来激发孩子的学习兴趣，增强学习效果。

《神奇的自然拼读》包含4册课本和4册配套练习册，覆盖《义务教育英语课程标准》所要求掌握的高频词、常见词与句型，实践证明可有效提高孩子的英语成绩。

《神奇的自然拼读》采用了丰富多样的学习方式，书中有涂色、贴纸、单词卡、连线等互动方式；并附赠发音讲解视频、全书配套音频、动画片等多媒体资源；而且我们还制作了"神奇的自然拼读"小程序，增加互动游戏，有效提升孩子学习兴趣。

Vol. 1：SHORT VOWEL SOUNDS

学习要点：短元音中常见的27个字母组合发音规则。掌握87个常见单词和15个高频词，达到拼读本册单词、阅读短文、组词造句的学习目标。

Vol.2：LONG VOWEL SOUNDS

学习要点：长元音中常见的24种字母组合发音规则。掌握85个常见单词和16个高频词，达到拼读本册单词、阅读短文、组词造句的学习目标。

Vol.3：CONSONANT BLENDS & DIGRAPHS

学习要点：复合辅音和辅音连读中28种字母组合发音规则。掌握88个常见单词和10个高频词，达到拼读本册单词、阅读短文、组词造句的学习目标。

Vol.4：ADVANCED VOWELS & SILENT LETTERS

学习要点：复杂元音（带R元音、双元音等）、不发音字母的拼读规则。掌握85个常见单词和10个高频词，达到拼读本册单词、阅读短文、组词造句的学习目标。

自然拼读课本

《神奇的自然拼读》课本每册有十个单元，每单元有九大板块，各板块学习要点如下：

Listen & Blend Up

了解常见字母组合的发音，进行跟读练习，达到认读、熟读和拼读的效果。

Focus On

认识字母组合构成的常见单词，进行字母发音及单词拼读的练习。

Match Up

将图片与对应的单词进行连线，巩固掌握单词与发音。

Color Up

根据图片，选择正确的单词进行涂色，巩固单词学习效果。

Sight Word Fun

认识高频词，找出高频词所在的图片并进行涂色。

Sight Word Check

跟读音频，圈出句中的高频词，进一步巩固对高频词的认识。

Reading Fun

跟着音频读句子，熟练掌握本单元的单词与拼读发音。虚线框内都可以贴上对应的图片贴纸（对应贴纸在图书的最后几页）。

Story Build Up

使用本单元的单词，尝试自主读出这些句子，巩固单词发音。虚线框内都可以贴上对应的单词贴纸（对应贴纸在图书的最后几页）。

针对本单元的学习内容，听音频并选择正确的答案，进行一次整体的复习和巩固练习。

REVIEW

✅ Check Up 01 ▶ TRACK 01-6

1. Listen and check the right picture.

2. Listen and check the right word.

sat	fan	dad

🅰 Check Up 02

1. Read the sentence and write the right number.

a. ☐ A man has a bad fan.

b. ☐ A cat sat on a mat.

c. ☐ A bad cat.

AMAZING PHONICS
神奇的
自然拼读
WORKBOOK
1
Vol.
SHORT VOWEL
SOUNDS

AMAZING PHONICS
神奇的
自然拼读
WORKBOOK
2
Vol.
LONG VOWEL
SOUNDS

AMAZING PHONICS
神奇的
自然拼读
WORKBOOK
3
Vol.
CONSONANT
BLENDS & DIGRAPHS

AMAZING PHONICS
神奇的
自然拼读
WORKBOOK
4
Vol.
ADVANCED
VOWELS
& SILENT LETTERS

　　每册课本都有配套的练习册，针对每个单元的学习内容，设置了Step 1–Step 4的练习，针对所学知识进行巩固练习。

Step 1　写单词：
根据图片提示，写出正确的单词。

Step 2　描红、写句子：
先描红，再独立书写一整句话。

Step 3　造句：
挑选本单元单词和高频词来造句，进行描红书写。

Step 4　自主造句：
利用本单元单词和高频词进行造句并书写。

音频、视频

本书附有完整的音频与视频资源，可通过三种方式获取：小程序播放、网页播放、点读笔点读。

一、小程序播放

微信扫码，进入"神奇的自然拼读"小程序：

点击进入相应的图书单元页面，即可观看其中的视频（Video），或收听相应的音频（MP3）。

快捷方式：在小程序首页点击下方的"兔子"进入扫码页面，扫描书中相应页面上方的二维码，即可直接进入该单元的小程序页面。

二、网页播放

打开手机上的"扫一扫"（微信或网络浏览器的"扫一扫"都可以），扫描书中相应页面上方的二维码，可直接进入音频、视频（MP3/Video）的播放页面。

Pre-learning	∨
Unit 01	∨
Unit 02	∨
Unit 03	∨
Unit 04	∨
Unit 05	∨
Unit 06	∨
Unit 07	∨
Unit 08	∨
Unit 09	∨
Unit 10	∨
Final Review	∨

Unit 01		
MP3	Track 01-1	
	Track 01-2	
	Track 01-3	
	Track 01-4	
	Track 01-5	
	Track 01-6	
Video	Pronunciation	
	Chant 1	
	Chant 2	
	Chant 3	

三、点读笔点读

每册课本中，凡带有 ▶ TRACK 标志的页面，都可以使用小达人点读笔进行点读。

获取点读包和安装方法，请阅读指导手册最后一页。

安装完成后，先点读扉页，听到书名后即可点读内文。

小程序

用微信扫码，进入"神奇的自然拼读"小程序。

每一单元都有：视频、音频、连线游戏（Match Up）、故事构建（Story Building）、单词测验（Word Quiz）等互动方式。

Video

Match Up

Story Building

Word Quiz

MP3

验证解锁

　　小程序中，每册Unit 02以后的页面需验证解锁。进入页面后会提示输入问题的答案，只需输入对应的单词即可解锁本册全部内容。

亲子英文系列图书全家福

适读年龄 **3岁+**

适读年龄 **6岁+**

适读年龄 **3岁+**

适读年龄 **6岁+**

适读年龄 **9岁+**

✦ 建议与反馈 ✦

　　扫码关注亲子学乐（kidsfund）公众号，关于本书的任何建议与反馈，都可以通过公众号留言的方式反馈给我们，我们重视您的每一份意见。

　　发送"神奇"，获取关于本书阅读与使用的详细介绍。

　　发送"自然拼读"，获取本书点读包的下载和安装说明。

AMAZING PHONICS
Vol.1 Short Vowel Sounds

CONTENTS

FUN

Reading Fun
Match Up
Blend Up
Color Up
Stickers
Chants

EASY

Comprehensible Input
Simple Lesson Plans
Repeated Activities
Simple Activities
Step by Step

INDEPENDENT

Self-Perfection
Self-Correction
Individual Work
Hands-On Work

Hello, I am Jay!

I want to be a magician when I grow up.

Can you help me make something amazing happen?

Vol. 1
Short Vowel Sounds

Amazing Phonics Vol.1
Short Vowel Sounds

Vol. 2
Long Vowel Sounds

Vol. 3
Consonant Blends & Digraphs

Vol. 4
Advanced Vowels & Silent Letters

Hello, I am Curi!

I am very curious. If you follow me, we will have so much fun!

Welcome to *Amazing Phonics*!

Amazing Phonics introduces a fun, easy, and effective way to start your phonics journey.

Phonics is a method for teaching reading and writing of the English language by developing children's phonemic awareness.
Amazing Phonics teaches the phonemes (sounds) associated with the graphemes (letters). The sounds are taught in isolation then blended together to form words. This way, the children can develop phonemic awareness along with the corresponding letter shapes.

Amazing Phonics also focuses on "the way of learning". Children perfect themselves by repeating their work. They work toward mastery of the task. This repetition leads not only to mastery of the task, but also to a heightened ability to concentrate and an increased sense of accomplishment. So, if children are given enough time to practise, they can perfect their skills while feeling that they are learning well.

We hope every child can experience the joy of learning with *Amazing Phonics*. Have fun learning, everyone!

Features of *Amazing Phonics*

A truly amazing experience!

Amazing Phonics Vol. 1

Short Vowel Sounds

a   **e**   **i**   **o**   **u**

Unit 1
ad, an, at

Unit 2
ag, am, ap

Unit 3
ed, eg

Unit 4
en, et

Unit 5
id, ig, in

Unit 6
ip, it, ix

Unit 7
og, op

Unit 8
od, ot, ox

Unit 9
ub, ug, up

Unit 10
ud, un, ut

1 | ★ Books ★

Student Book

Pronunciation & Chant
Videos

Step by Step
Day by Day

Sight Word Fun
One Step Closer to
Reading

Now I can read
phonics & sight words
in the story!

I get more confident!
Everything is so easy!
Now I am ready for MORE!

Yay!

Workbook (My Writing Note)

I can write the words
& sentences I learned!

I am so confident.
I can make my own sentences.
It is so much fun!

Features of *Amazing Phonics*

Videos

Fun phonics lectures with Mr. David, the magician!

I can understand the pronunciation better!

Guess the words!
Time to meet the words and become friends with them.

a + d = -ad

b ad
d ad
s ad

I love my phonics chants!
I want to sing them again and again.
It is easy and so much fun!

-ad	bad	dad	sad
-an	can	fan	man
-at	cat	mat	sat

Pronunciation & Chant Videos Are
Included with the Book
Full Lectures Are Available at

2 ★ Multimedia ★

Applet

vol. 1

Short Vowel Sounds

ă	Unit 01	ad,an,at
	Unit 02	ag,am,ap
ĕ	Unit 03	ed,eg
	Unit 04	en,et
ĭ	Unit 05	id,ig,in
	Unit 06	ip,it,ix
ŏ	Unit 07	og,op
	Unit 08	od,ot,ox
ŭ	Unit 09	ub,ug,up
	Unit 10	ud,un,ut

HOME CONTENTS TRACKER

Unit 01 ad,an,at

Video   Match Up

Story Building   Word Quiz

MP3

HOME CONTENTS TRACKER

AMAZING PHONICS

GO!

Unit 01 ad,an,at
Video
- Pronunciation
- Chant 1. -ad
- Chant 2. -an
- Chant 3. -at

Video

Unit 01 ad,an,at
Match Up
- bad
- cat
- can

Match Up

Unit 01 ad,an,at
Story Building

Reading Fun

A cat.
A cat sat.
A cat sat on a mat.
A man.
A man has a fan.
A man has a bad fan.

Story Building

Unit 01 ad,an,at
Word Quiz

a b c d e
f g h i j
k l m

Word Quiz

Amazing PHONICS

- Pre-ABC_Song
- Pre-Blend_Up
- Track 01-1
- Track 01-2
- Track 01-3
- Track 01-4
- Track 01-5
- Track 01-6

MP3

I want to do it again and again!
I am perfecting myself by repeating the work.
I feel so confident! Now I can read more!

ABC song

Aa	Bb	Cc	Dd	Ee
Ff	Gg	Hh	Ii	Jj
Kk	Ll	Mm	Nn	Oo
Pp	Qq	Rr	Ss	Tt
Uu	Vv	Ww	Xx	Yy
Zz				

Sing the alphabet!

Blend Up

Sound out each letter and blend them together.

1 c — a — t

c - a - t

cat

Point!

2 d — o — g

d - o - g

dog

Are you ready?
Let's have fun!

CHAPTER 1

a

Unit 1 ad, an, at
bad, dad, sad, can, fan, man, cat, mat, sat

Unit 2 ag, am, ap
bag, tag, wag, ham, jam, ram, cap, map, nap

Guess the words!

ad **an** **at**

Listen & Blend Up ▶ TRACK 01-1

a

🔊 Listen > 🎯 Point > 🗨 Repeat

① a d → a d

② a n → a n

③ a t → a t

dad

fan

mat

Focus On

▶ TRACK 01-2

🎧 Listen > 🍅 Chant > ✏️ Highlight

1 -ad

bad

dad

sad

2 -an

can

fan

man

3 -at

cat

mat

sat

CHECK UP

⊙ Look > 🔊 Listen > ✏ Match

1  ● ─ ─ ─ ─ ─ ─ ● **sat**

2 🟦 ● ● **bad**

3  ● ● **man**

4 🙁 ● ● **fan**

5  ● ● **mat**

Color Up

START FINISH

Look > Say > Color

1 ♠
GAME

~~can~~ fan

2 ♥
GAME

dad sad

3 ♦
GAME

mat cat

4 ♣
GAME

bad dad

SIGHT WORD

Sight Word Fun

◉ Look > 🔍 Find > 🎨 Color

Find and color the bananas that have "has" on them.

has

das

has

has

pas

was

has

has

has

Sight Word Check

TRACK 01-4

Listen > Repeat > Circle

1  (has) a .

Dad (has) a cat.

2 has a .

Dad has a mat.

3  A  has a .

A man has a cat.

4 A has a .

A man has a fan.

Reading Fun

TRACK 01-5

Listen > Repeat > Put on the Stickers

A cat.

A cat sat.

A cat sat on a mat.

A man.

A man has a fan.

A man has a bad fan.

Story Build Up

DAY

Look > **Put on the Stickers** > **Read**

1

A cat.

A cat sat.

A [cat] [sat] on a [mat].

2

A man.

A man has a fan.

A [man] has a [bad] [fan].

REVIEW

🎧 ✅ Check Up 01 ▶ TRACK 01-6

1. Listen and check the right picture.

2. Listen and check the right word.

sat	fan	dad

📖 🅰 Check Up 02

1. Read the sentence and write the right number.

a. ☐ A man has a bad fan.

b. ☐ A cat sat on a mat.

c. ☐ A bad cat.

2. Read the sentence and circle the right word.

1 A [man | fan] has a cat.

2 A cat sat on a [mat | hat] .

3 A man [has | was] a fan.

4 A man has a [bad | dad] fan.

ag **am** **ap**

Listen & Blend Up

TRACK 02-1

a

Listen > Point > Repeat

① **a** **g** → **a** **g**

② **a** **m** → **a** **m**

③ **a** **p** → **a** **p**

bag

jam

map

Focus On

▶ TRACK 02-2

🔊 Listen > 🎵 Chant > ✏️ Highlight

1 -ag

bag

tag

wag

2 -am

ham

jam

ram

3 -ap

cap

map

nap

CHECK UP

Match Up

TRACK 02-3

START GAME FINISH

Look > Listen > Match

1. — cap

2.

3.

4.

5.

- ham
- wag
- cap
- map
- bag

Color Up

START   FINISH

Look > Say > Color

1 GAME

tag / **wag**

2 GAME

nap   **cap**

3 GAME

ram   **ham**

4 GAME

jam   **map**

Sight Word Fun

START GAME FINISH

Look > Find > Color

Color the parts that have "see" red, and then color the rest.

cee

sea

sat

see

see

see

see

see

see

dad

sad

has

cat

Sight Word Check

TRACK 02-4

Listen > Repeat > Circle

1

I _____ a 🧢 .

I (see) a cap.

2

I _____ a 🐏 .

I see a ram.

3

I _____ a 🗺️ .

I see a map.

4

I _____ a 🎒 .

I see a bag.

STORY BUILD UP

Reading Fun

TRACK 02-5

Listen > Repeat > Put on the Stickers

A bag.

I see a bag.

I see a tag on a bag.

A map.

I see a map.

I see a ram on a map.

Story Build Up

👁 Look > ❤ Put on the Stickers > 📖 Read

1

A bag.

I see a bag.

I [see] a [tag] on a [bag].

2

A map.

I see a map.

I [see] a [ram] on a [map].

REVIEW

Check Up 01 TRACK 02-6

1. Listen and check the right picture.

2. Listen and check the right word.

map	tag	ram

Check Up 02

1. Read the sentence and write the right number.

1 2 3

a. ☐ A man can nap.

b. ☐ Dad has jam.

c. ☐ A ram has a cap.

Well done!

2. Read the sentence and circle the right word.

1   I see ram | ham .

2   I see jam in a bag | wag .

3   I see a nap | map .

4   I see a ram | jam on a map.

CHAPTER 2

e

Unit 3 ed, eg
bed, red, Ted, wed, beg, egg, leg, Meg

Unit 4 en, et
hen, men, pen, ten, jet, net, pet, wet

Guess the words!

UNIT 3

ed **eg**

▶ TRACK 03-1

🎧 Listen › ✋ Point › 💬 Repeat

① e d → e d

② e g → e g

bed   egg

Focus On

▶ TRACK 03-2

🔊 Listen > 🎵 Chant > ✏️ Highlight

1 ♪ **-ed** ♫

bed	**red**	**Ted**	**wed**

2 ♪ **eg** ♫

*egg [eg] 'gg' makes a 'g' sound

beg	**egg***	**leg**	**Meg**

CHECK UP

Match Up
▶ TRACK 03-3

START GAME FINISH

👁 Look > 🔊 Listen > ✏ Match

1. • Ted

2. • Meg

3.  • bed

4.  • egg

Color Up

START | FINISH

Look > Say > Color

1
beg | egg

2
Meg | leg

3
bed | red

4
wed | Ted

Sight Word Fun

START GAME FINISH

Look > Find > Color

★ Sight Words ★
this, is

Color the letters in the word "this" different colors.

this

Find and circle the word "is".

as

is

is   at   is

is   has   see

Sight Word Check

▶ TRACK 03-4

🎧 Listen ❯ 💬 Repeat ❯ 🔴 Circle

1

👉 (is) an 🍳 .

~~(This)~~ (is) an egg.

2

👉 is a 🛏️ .

This is a bed.

3

👉 is a 👶 .

This is a leg.

4

👉 is 👰 .

This is Meg.

Reading Fun

TRACK 03-5

Listen > Repeat > Put on the Stickers

A **bed**.

This is a **bed**.

This is a **red bed**.

This is Ted.

This is Meg.

Ted weds **Meg**.

Story Build Up

◉ Look > ❤ Put on the Stickers > 📖 Read

1

A bed.

This is a bed.

[This] [is] a [red] [bed].

2

This is Ted.

This is Meg.

[Ted] [wed]s [Meg].

REVIEW

🔊 ✅ Check Up 01 ▶ TRACK 03-6

1. Listen and check the right picture.

2. Listen and check the right word.

leg	bed	wed

📖 🅰 Check Up 02

1. Read the sentence and write the right number.

1	2	3

a. ☐ Ted weds Meg.

b. ☐ This is Ted.

c. ☐ This is a bed.

Well done!

2. Read the sentence and circle the right word.

1 This is an   bed | egg   .

2 This is a   led | red   bed.

3 Ted   weds | begs   Meg.

4 I see a   leg | Meg   .

en

et

Listen & Blend Up

▶ TRACK 04-1

e

Listen > Point > Repeat

① e n → en

② e t → et

hen

jet

Focus On ▶ TRACK 04-2

🔊 Listen ＞ 💿 Chant ＞ ✏️ Highlight

1 -en 🎵

hen   men   pen   ten

2 -et 🎵

jet   net   pet   wet

CHECK UP

👁 Look > 🎧 Listen > Match

1  •·············· • **ten**

2 ✈ • • **jet**

3 🖊 • • **pen**

4  • • **pet**

Color Up

START   FINISH

Look > Say > Color

1 ♠

wet   **pet**

2 ♥

men   **ten**

3 ♦

jet   **net**

4 ♣

pen   **hen**

Sight Word Fun

START   GAME   FINISH

Look > Find > Color

★ Sight Words ★
there, are

Color the correct word box in the sentence.

There [is] [are] a hen.

There [is] [are] a jet.

There [is] [are] men.

Sight Word Check

TRACK 04-4

Listen > Repeat > Circle

1 (There) is a  .

(There) is a jet.

2 There are .

There are men.

3 There is a .

There is a pet.

4 There are  .

There are ten pens.

STORY BUILD UP

Reading Fun

TRACK 04-5

Listen > Repeat > Put on the Stickers

A jet.

There is a jet.

There are men on a jet.

A hen.

There is a hen.

There is a hen in a net.

✨ Story Build Up ✨

⊙ Look ❯ ♥ Put on the Stickers ❯ 📖 Read

1

A jet.

There is a jet.

(There) (are) (men) on a (jet).

2

A hen.

There is a hen.

(There) is a (hen) in a (net).

🔊 ✅ Check Up 01 ▶ TRACK 04-6

1. Listen and check the right picture.

2. Listen and check the right word.

net	pet	wet

📖 🅐 Check Up 02

1. Read the sentence and write the right number.

1 2 3

a. ☐ There are men.

b. ☐ There are ten eggs.

c. ☐ There is a jet.

2. Read the sentence and circle the right word.

1. There is a | pet | net | .

2. There | is | are | a hen in a net.

3. There are | ten | hen | pens.

4. There | is | are | men on a jet.

CHAPTER 3

Unit 5 id, ig, in

hid, kid, lid, big, dig, pig, bin, fin, win

Unit 6 ip, it, ix

dip, hip, zip, hit, kit, sit, fix, mix, six

Guess the words!

UNIT 5 id ig in

Listen & Blend Up ▶ TRACK 05-1

Listen 〉 Point 〉 Repeat

① **i** **d** → **i** **d**

② **i** **g** → **i** **g**

③ **i** **n** → **i** **n**

kid

pig

bin

1
DAY

Focus On ▶ TRACK 05-2

🔊 Listen > 🎵 Chant > ✏️ Highlight

1 -id

hid

kid

lid

2 -ig

big

dig

pig

3 -in

bin

fin

win

CHECK UP

Match Up

TRACK 05-3

START GAME FINISH

Look > Listen > Match

1. • · · · · · · · · · · · · · · win

2. • hid

3. • · · · · · · · · · · · · · · bin

4. • pig

5. • big

Color Up

START FINISH

Look > Say > Color

1 ♠ GAME

lid   hid

2 ♥ GAME

dig   big

3 ♦ GAME

kid   pig

4 ♣ GAME

win   fin

Sight Word Fun

START GAME1 GAME2 FINISH

Look > Find > Color

Color "can" red and "find" yellow.

find

can

can

find

find

can

find

can

find

can

can find

Sight Word Check

TRACK 05-4

Listen > Repeat > Circle

1

(Find) a  .

Find a **pig.**

2

Find a .

Find a **bin.**

3

A can a  .

A kid can find a bin.

4

A can a  .

A kid can find a fin.

STORY BUILD UP

Reading Fun

TRACK 05-5

Listen > Repeat > Put on the Stickers

A kid.

A man hid a lid.

A kid can find it in a bin.

A pig.

A pig can dig.

A pig digs to find a lid.

Story Build Up

👁 Look > ❤ Put on the Stickers > 📖 Read

1

A kid.

A man hid a lid.

A kid   can find it in a bin .

2

A pig.

A pig can dig .

A pig digs to find a lid .

REVIEW

🔊 ✅ Check Up 01 ▶ TRACK 05-6

1. Listen and check the right picture.

2. Listen and check the right word.

lid	hid	kid

📖 🅰 Check Up 02

1. Read the sentence and write the right number.

a. ☐ A kid hid a lid.

b. ☐ A pig can find a lid.

c. ☐ A pig can dig.

Well done!

2. Read the sentence and circle the right word.

1 **Find** | **Bind** a pig.

2 A kid can find a **win** | **fin** .

3 A kid **hid** | **bid** a lid in a bin.

4 A pig **big** | **digs** to find a lid.

UNIT **6**

ip   it   ix

Listen & Blend Up

▶ TRACK 06-1

Listen > Point > Repeat

① i p → i p

② i t → i t

③ i x → i x

zip   hit   six

Focus On

▶ TRACK 06-2

🎧 Listen > 🎵 Chant > ✏️ Highlight

1 -ip

dip

hip

zip

2 -it

hit

kit

sit

3 -ix

fix

mix

six

Match Up ▶ TRACK 06-3

👁 Look > 👂 Listen > ✏ Match

1.   •   • kit

2.   •   • dip

3.   •   • sit

4.   •   • zip

5.   •   • mix

Color Up

START   FINISH

Look > Say > Color

1 ♠ GAME

mix   fix

2 ♥ GAME

sit   hit

3 ♦ GAME

six   fix

4 ♣ GAME

hip   dip

Sight Word Fun

START   GAME   FINISH

Look > Find > Color

Color the parts that have "the" red and then color the rest.

this

is

the

see

the

dad

the

the

the

the

has

the

sad

see

there

Sight Word Check

TRACK 06-4

Listen > Repeat > Circle

1 (The)  !
....
(The) cat!

2 I the .
....
I see the bed.

3 The !
....
The cap!

4 I the  .
....
I see the kit.

STORY BUILD UP

Reading Fun

Listen > Repeat > Put on the Stickers

It is a **zip**.

Dad has **the** **kit**.

Dad can **fix** **the** **zip**.

I see **six** men.

The **six** men **sit**.

The **six** men **sit** on **the** mat.

Story Build Up

◉ Look > ❤ Put on the Stickers > 📖 Read

1

It is a zip.

Dad has the kit.

Dad can fix the zip .

2

I see six men.

The six men sit.

The six men sit on the mat .

REVIEW

Check Up 01 ▶ TRACK 06-6

1. Listen and check the right picture.

2. Listen and check the right word.

six	hip	kit

Check Up 02

1. Read the sentence and write the right number.

1
2
3

a. ☐ Dad can fix the zip.

b. ☐ A kid can sit.

c. ☐ A kid can mix the dip.

Well done!

5 DAY

2. Read the sentence and circle the right word.

1   The   hit   kit   !

2   Dad can   six   fix   it.

3   I can see   there   the   bed.

4   A kid   sits   six   on the mat.

CHAPTER 4

Unit 7 og, op
dog, fog, jog, log, hop, mop, pop, top

Unit 8 od, ot, ox
cod, nod, pod, dot, hot, pot, box, fox, ox

Guess the words!

UNIT 7

og **op**

Listen & Blend Up

▶ TRACK 07-1

Listen > Point > Repeat

① o g → **og**

② o p → **op**

dog

mop

DAY 1

Focus On ▶ TRACK 07-2

Listen > Chant > Highlight

1 -og

dog **fog** **jog** **log**

2 -op

hop **mop** **pop** **top**

CHECK UP

Match Up

▶ TRACK 07-3

START GAME FINISH

Look > Listen > Match

1 dog

2 pop

3 mop

4 log

Color Up

START FINISH

Look > Say > Color

1 ♠

GAME

~~jog~~ log

2 ♥

GAME

pop hop

3 ♦

GAME

dog fog

4 ♣

GAME

top mop

SIGHT WORD

Sight Word Fun

START GAME FINISH

Look > Find > Color

Find and color the lily pads that have "he" on them.

he

he

he

pe

he

ha

he

he

Sight Word Check

TRACK 07-4

Listen > Repeat > Circle

1

(He) can .

(He) can jog.

2

He can .

He can hop.

3

He has a .

He has a cat.

4

He is on a .

He is on a log.

STORY BUILD UP

Reading Fun

TRACK 07-5

Listen > Repeat > Put on the Stickers

There is a dog.
He is on a log.
He can hop.

In a fog,
He can see a top.
He can see a mop.

Story Build Up

◉ Look > ♥ Put on the Stickers > 📖 Read

1

There is a dog .
He is on a log .
He can hop .

2

In a fog ,
He can see a top .
He can see a mop .

Check Up 01 ▶ TRACK 07-6

1. Listen and check the right picture.

2. Listen and check the right word.

mop	jog	top

Check Up 02

1. Read the sentence and write the right number.

a. ☐ He can hop.

b. ☐ There is a dog on a log.

c. ☐ There is a top.

2. Read the sentence and circle the right word.

1. He   She   has a cat.

2. I can see a   mop   hop .

3. He can   top   hop .

4. He can   log   jog .

od **ot** **ox**

Listen & Blend Up

▶ TRACK 08-1

🎧 Listen > 👆 Point > 💬 Repeat

① o d → o d

② o t → o t

③ o x → o x

cod   hot   fox

DAY 1

Focus On ▶ TRACK 08-2

🎧 Listen > 🍅 Chant > ✏️ Highlight

1 -od

cod

nod

pod

2 -ot

dot

hot

pot

3 ox

box

fox

ox

CHECK UP

Match Up ▶ TRACK 08-3

START GAME FINISH

◉ Look › 🔊 Listen › 🟠 Match

1 ●   • **pot**

2 🐟   • **box**

3 📦   • **dot**

4 🐂   • **ox**

5 🍲   • **cod**

Color Up

START FINISH

Look > Say > Color

1 GAME

fox | ox

2 GAME

cod | pod

3 GAME

dot | hot

4 GAME

nod | box

SIGHT WORD

Sight Word Fun

START GAME1 GAME2 FINISH

Look > Find > Color

Color "it" red and color 'is' yellow.

is

it

it

is

it

is

it

it

is

is

it

is

it is

Sight Word Check

TRACK 08-4

Listen > Repeat > Circle

1

(It) (is) .

(It) (is) hot.

2

The 🍲 is .

The pot is hot.

3

It is a 🦊 .

It is a fox.

4

It is a 🐟 .

It is a cod.

STORY BUILD UP

Reading Fun

TRACK 08-5

Listen > Repeat > Put on the Stickers

It is hot.
The pot is hot.

It is a dot.
There are dots on the box.

It is a fox.
The fox is in the box.

✨ Story Build Up ✨

◉ Look > ♥ Put on the Stickers > 📖 Read

1

It is hot.
The pot is hot.

2

It is a dot.
There are dots on the box.

3

It is a fox.
The fox is in the box.

REVIEW

Check Up 01 ▶ TRACK 08-6

1. Listen and check the right picture.

2. Listen and check the right word.

fox	hot	nod

Check Up 02

1. Read the sentence and write the right number.

1

2

3

a. ☐ There is a fox in the box.

b. ☐ He can nod.

c. ☐ It is a pod.

2. Read the sentence and circle the right word.

1. It **is** | has hot.

2. A pod has **pots** | dots .

3. It is a nod | **cod** .

4. The **fox** | ox is in the box.

u

Unit 9 ub, ug, up
cub, rub, tub, bug, hug, mug, cup, pup, up

Unit 10 ud, un, ut
bud, cud, mud, bun, sun, run, cut, hut, nut

Guess the words!

UNIT 9

ub **ug** **up**

Listen & Blend Up

▶ TRACK 09-1

u

Listen > Point > Repeat

① u b → u b

② u g → u g

③ u p → u p

cub

mug

pup

Focus On ▶ TRACK 09-2

🔊 Listen > 🎵 Chant > ✏️ Highlight

1 -ub

cub

rub

tub

2 -ug

bug

hug

mug

3 up

cup

pup

up

CHECK UP

Match Up ▶ TRACK 09-3

START GAME FINISH

👁 Look > 👂 Listen > 🏅 Match

1  • · · · · · · · · · · · · · · · · · ·• **cup**

2  •   • **pup**

3 • • **mug**

4  •   • **cub**

5 •   • **tub**

Color Up

START FINISH

Look > Say > Color

1 ♠ GAME

up **pup**

2 ♥ GAME

mug **hug**

3 ♦ GAME

tub **bug**

4 ♣ GAME

rub **cub**

Sight Word Fun

START GAME FINISH

Look > Find > Color

Color the letters in the word "she" different colors.

she

Find and circle the word "she".

he

she

(she)

she

he

he

see

she

Sight Word Check

TRACK 09-4

Listen > Repeat > Circle

1

(She) has a .

(She) has a cup.

2

She  a .

She rubs a mug.

3
She has a .

She has a bug.

4

She  a .

She hugs a pup.

STORY BUILD UP

Reading Fun

TRACK 09-5

Listen > Repeat > Put on the Stickers

She has a pup.
She hugs a pup.
She hugs a wet pup.

She has a mug.
She rubs a mug.
She rubs a hot mug.

Story Build Up

◉ Look > ♥ Put on the Stickers > 📖 Read

1

She has a pup.
She hugs a pup.
She hugs a wet pup.

2

She has a mug.
She rubs a mug.
She rubs a hot mug.

REVIEW

Check Up 01 ▶ TRACK 09-6

1. Listen and check the right picture.

2. Listen and check the right word.

| cup | hug | pup |

Check Up 02

1. Read the sentence and write the right number.

a. ☐ She has a mug.

b. ☐ She hugs a wet pup.

c. ☐ She rubs a hot mug.

2. Read the sentence and circle the right word.

1 He | She has a cup.

2 She hugs a wet pup | cup .

3 She has a hub | mug .

4 She cubs | rubs a hot mug.

ud **un** **ut**

Listen & Blend Up ▶ TRACK 10-1

u

🦻 Listen > 👆 Point > 👄 Repeat

❶ u d → u d

❷ u n → u n

❸ u t → u t

mud   sun   cut

DAY 1
5 2
4 3

Focus On

▶ TRACK 10-2

🎧 Listen ﹥ 🎵 Chant ﹥ ✏️ Highlight

1 -ud

bud

cud

mud

2 -un

bun

run

sun

3 -ut

cut

hut

nut

CHECK UP

Match Up

▶ TRACK 10-3

START GAME FINISH

◉ Look ❯ Listen ❯ Match

1 • mud

2 • cut

3 • bud

4 • sun

5 • nut

Color Up

START FINISH

Look > Say > Color

1 ♠
GAME

hut / nut

♠ 1

2 ♥
GAME

cut cud

♥ 2

3 ♦
GAME

bud bun

♦ 3

4 ♣
GAME

run sun

♣ 4

Unit 10 ud, un, ut **115**

Sight Word Fun

Look > Find > Color

★ Sight Words ★
look, at

Fill in the missing letters.

l_ook l_ook

lo_k loo_

Fill in the missing letters.

Look at this!

at a_ _t

Sight Word Check

Listen > Repeat > Circle

1

the ☀.

(Look) (at) the sun.

2

the 🛖.

Look at the hut.

3

the 🧒.

Look at the mud.

4

the 🌷.

Look at the bud.

STORY BUILD UP

Reading Fun

TRACK 10-5

Listen > Repeat > Put on the Stickers

Look at the mud.

She can run.

She can run in the mud.

Look at the sun.

There is a hut.

There is a hut in the sun.

Story Build Up

◉ Look > ♥ Put on the Stickers > 📖 Read

1

Look at the mud.

She can run.

She can run in the mud.

2

Look at the sun.

There is a hut.

There is a hut in the sun.

REVIEW

Check Up 01 ▶ TRACK 10-6

1. Listen and check the right picture.

2. Listen and check the right word.

run	hut	cut

Check Up 02

1. Read the sentence and write the right number.

1

2

3

a. ☐ Look at the sun.

b. ☐ He can run in the sun.

c. ☐ Look at the mud.

2. Read the sentence and circle the right word.

1 Look | Book at the bud.

2 I can nut | cut .

3 There is a cud | hut .

4 She can sun | run .

FINAL REVIEW 01

TRACK 11-1

1. Listen and circle the right picture.

a

b

c

2. Listen and circle the right word.

a **red** **nod**

b **pot** **pet**

c **fix** **fin**

d **six** **sun**

Well done!

3. Look and complete the word.

a
d _ g

b
t _ b

c
z _ p

d
s _ d

4. Read the sentence and circle the right word.

a
A man has a | bed | bad | fan.

b
There is a dog on a | jog | log | .

c
I can find | ten | hit | eggs.

d
It is a | wet | Meg | pup.

FINAL REVIEW 02

TRACK 11-2

1. Listen and circle the right picture.

a		

b		

c		

2. Listen and circle the right word.

a	b
cap **cud**	**kid** **kit**

c	d
wed **win**	**hut** **hen**

Well done!

3. Look and complete the word.

a f _ x

b b _ _ n

c n _ p

d h _ p

4. Read the sentence and circle the right word.

a I see a cat on a | mud | mat | .

b | He | She | has a box.

c This is a | top | tag | .

d She | hugs | rubs | a pet.

MEMO

Unxit 01 pp20-21

cat

mat

man

bad

fan

sat

Unit 02 pp30-31

see

tag

bag

see

ram

map

Unit 03 pp42-43

Ted   Meg

This   is   red   bed

Ted   wed   Meg

Unit 04   pp52-53

There

are

men

jet

There

hen

net

Unit 05   pp64-65

hid

kid

can

bin

dig

pig

find

lid

Unit 06   pp74-75

fix   zip   six   sit   mat

Unit 07 pp86-87

dog

log

He

hop

fog

top

He

mop

Unit 08 pp96-97

It

hot

pot

is

dot

dots

fox

box

Unit 09 pp108-109

She pup hugs wet

She mug She rubs

Unit 10 pp118-119

Look at run mud

Look at hut sun

AMAZING PHONICS

神奇的
自然拼读

发音·单词·句子·故事

韩国钥匙英语学习方法研究所 / 著

Vol. **2**

LONG VOWEL
SOUNDS

ZHEJIANG UNIVERSITY PRESS
浙江大学出版社

**Nice to meet you.
What is your name?**

My name is...

- -

AMAZING PHONICS
Vol.2 Long Vowel Sounds

CONTENTS

FUN

Reading Fun
Match Up
Blend Up
Color Up
Stickers
Chants

EASY

Comprehensible Input
Simple Lesson Plans
Repeated Activities
Simple Activities
Step by Step

INDEPENDENT

Self-Perfection
Self-Correction
Individual Work
Hands-On Work

Hello,
I am Jay!

I want to be a magician when I grow up.

Can you help me make something amazing happen?

Vol.2 Long Vowel Sounds

Vol.1 Short Vowel Sounds

Vol.3 Consonant Blends & Digraphs

Vol.4 Advanced Vowels & Silent Letters

Hello, I am Curi!

I am very curious.
If you follow me,
we will have
so much fun!

Welcome to *Amazing Phonics*!

Amazing Phonics introduces a fun, easy, and effective way
to start your phonics journey.

Phonics is a method for teaching reading and writing of the English language by developing children's phonemic awareness.
Amazing Phonics teaches the phonemes (sounds) associated with the graphemes (letters). The sounds are taught in isolation then blended together to form words. This way, the children can develop phonemic awareness along with the corresponding letter shapes.

Amazing Phonics also focuses on "the way of learning". Children perfect themselves by repeating their work. They work toward mastery of the task. This repetition leads not only to mastery of the task, but also to a heightened ability to concentrate and an increased sense of accomplishment. So, if children are given enough time to practise, they can perfect their skills while feeling that they are learning well.

We hope every child can experience the joy of learning with *Amazing Phonics*. Have fun learning, everyone!

Features of *Amazing Phonics*

A truely amazing experience!

Amazing Phonics Vol. 2

Long Vowel Sounds

a · **e** · **i** · **o** · **u**

a	e	i	o	u
Unit 1 magic 'e', a_e	**Unit 3** e, e_e, y	**Unit 5** i, i_e	**Unit 7** o, o_e	**Unit 9** u, u_e, ew
Unit 2 a, ai, ay	**Unit 4** ea, ee	**Unit 6** igh, ie, y	**Unit 8** oa, ow, oe	**Unit 10** oo, ue

1 ★ Books ★

Student Book

Pronunciation & Chant Videos

Step by Step Day by Day

Sight Word Fun One Step Closer to Reading

Now I can read phonics & sight words in the story!

I get more confident! Everything is so easy! Now I am ready for MORE!

Yay!

Workbook (My Writing Note)

I can write the words & sentences I learned!

I am so confident. I can make my own sentences. It is so much fun!

Features of *Amazing Phonics*

Videos

Fun phonics lectures with Mr. David, the magician!

I can understand the pronunciation better!

Guess the words!
Time to meet the words and become friends with them.

I love my phonics chants!
I want to sing them again and again.
It is easy and so much fun!

Pronunciation & Chant Videos Are
Included with the Book
Full Lectures Are Available at

2 ★ Multimedia ★

Applet

Video

Match Up

Story Building

Word Quiz

MP3

> I want to do it again and again!
> I am perfecting myself by repeating the work.
> I feel so confident! Now I can read more!

ABC song

Aa	Bb	Cc	Dd	Ee
Ff	Gg	Hh	Ii	Jj
Kk	Ll	Mm	Nn	Oo
Pp	Qq	Rr	Ss	Tt
Uu	Vv	Ww	Xx	Yy
Zz				

Sing the alphabet!

Meet the Magic 'e'

1

tap ······ e ·····> tape

2

cub ······ e ·····> cube

Are you ready?
Let's have fun!

CHAPTER 1

a

Unit 1 magic 'e', a_e
man, mane, tap, tape, bake, cake, face, gate

Unit 2 a, ai, ay
acorn, baby, paper, mail, rain, tail, day, hay, say

Guess the words!

Magic e a_e

Listen & Blend Up ▶ TRACK 01-1

a

Listen > **Point** > **Repeat**

① man + e → mane

② tap + e → tape

man

tape

Focus On

TRACK 01-2

Listen > Chant > Highlight

1 Magic e

man mane tap tape

2 a_e

bake cake face gate

CHECK UP

Match Up

TRACK 01-3

START   GAME   FINISH

Look > Listen > Match

1

2

3

4

a

a_e

5

6

7

8

Color Up

START GAME FINISH

Look > Say > Color

1 man
mane

2 man
mane

3 tape
tap

4 tape
tap

5 cake
bake

6 gate
bake

7 face
gate

8 face
cake

Sight Word Fun

START GAME1 GAME2 FINISH

⊙ Look > 🔍 Find > Color

★ Sight Words ★
big, little

Color the words.

big
little

Circle the word little, triangle the word big in the box.

big   little   big

little

little   big   little

big   big

little   big

little   big

Sight Word Check

TRACK 01-4

Listen > Repeat > Circle

1

It is a 🐘 🎂 .

It is a (big) cake.

2

It is a 🐘 🎂 .

It is a little cake.

3

There is a 🐘 🚪 .

There is a big gate.

4

There is a 🐘 🎞️ .

There is a little tape.

Reading Fun

TRACK 01-5

Listen > Repeat > Put on the Stickers

I see a little man.

He can bake a cake.

He can bake a big cake.

Look at the tap!

The tap is little.

Look at the gate!

The gate is big.

Story Build Up

Look > Put on the Stickers > Read

1

I see a little man.

He can bake a cake .

He can bake a big cake.

2

Look at the tap .

The tap is little .

Look at the gate .

The gate is big .

REVIEW

🔊 ✅ Check Up 01 ▶ TRACK 01-6

1. Listen and check the right picture.

2. Listen and check the right word.

tape	face	tap

📖 🅰 Check Up 02

1. Complete the word puzzle.

1

		1	
		c	
	2	a	
		k	
3		e	

2

		1	
		m	
	2	a	
		n	
3		e	

2. Check the box with the right sentence for the picture.

1

☐ I see a mane.

☐ I see a name.

2

☐ I can bake a lake.

☐ I can bake a cake.

3

☐ I see a little gate.

☐ I see a big gate.

4

☐ There is a tap.

☐ There is a tape.

a ai ay

Listen & Blend Up

▶ TRACK 02-1

Listen > Point > Repeat

1. **a**

2. **ai**

3. **ay**

baby

rain

day

Focus On ▶ TRACK 02-2

Listen > Chant > Highlight

1 **a** ♪

acorn

baby

paper

2 **ai** ♪

mail

rain

tail

3 **ay** ♪

day

hay

say

CHECK UP

Match Up

▶ TRACK 02-3

START GAME FINISH

◉ Look › Listen › Match

1 2 3 4

a **ai** **ay**

5 6 7 8

Color Up

START GAME FINISH

Look > Say > Color

1 Hi | say / day

2 | acorn / paper

3 | mail / tail

4 | tail / rain

5 | acorn / paper

6 | say / hay

7 | rain / mail

8 | hay / day

SIGHT WORD

Sight Word Fun

START GAME FINISH

◉ Look > 🔍 Find > 🎨 Color

★ Sight Word ★
my

Find and color any mail that has "my" on it.

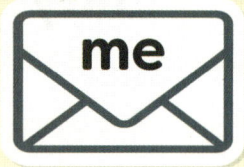

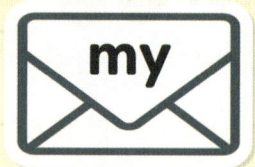

my

me

my

my

my

ny

me

my

my

Sight Word Check

Listen > Repeat > Circle

1

Oh, (my)  !

Oh, (my) baby!

2

It is my  .

It is my tail.

3

This is my   .

This is my paper.

4

Look at my .

Look at my acorn.

STORY BUILD UP

TRACK 02-5

Listen > Repeat > Put on the Stickers

It is a nice day.
There is a dog.
My baby can see the dog.
He can say "A tail!"

It is a nice day.
There is a man.
My baby can see a paper.
He can say "Mail!"

A tail!

Mail!

Story Build Up

Look > Put on the Stickers > Read

1

It is a nice day .
There is a dog.

My baby can see the dog.

He can say "A tail !"

2

It is a nice day.

There is a man.

My baby can see a paper .

He can say " Mail !"

REVIEW

🔊 ✅ Check Up 01 ▶ TRACK 02-6

1. Listen and check the right picture.

2. Listen and check the right word.

baby	rain	say

📖 🅰 Check Up 02

1. Complete the word puzzle.

1

1. b
2. a
   b
3. y

2

1. r
2. a
   i
   n

2. Check the box with the right sentence for the picture.

1
☐ My baby can see a rail.

☐ My baby can see a tail.

2
☐ This is my hay.

☐ This is my bay.

3
☐ Look at the mail.

☐ Look at the rain.

4
☐ This is my paper.

☐ This is my acorn.

CHAPTER 2

Unit 3 e, e_e, y
he, me, we, eve, here, Steve, body, city, tiny

Unit 4 ea, ee
eat, leaf, pea, weak, bee, need, seed, tree

1
2
3
4
5
6
7
8
9
10
11
12
13
14
15
16
17

Guess the words!

UNIT 3

e e_e y

Listen & Blend Up ▶ TRACK 03-1

e

Listen > Point > Repeat

① e

② e_e

③ y

e

he   **here**   **city**

Focus On

TRACK 03-2

Listen > Chant > Highlight

1 e

he

me

we

2 e_e

eve

here

Steve

3 y

body

city

tiny

Match Up ▶ TRACK 03-3

START GAME FINISH

◉ Look > 👂 Listen > Match

1

2

3

4

e_e

y

e

5

6

7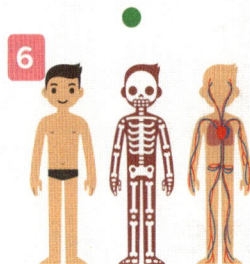

8

Color Up

START GAME FINISH

Look > Say > Color

1
me we

2
he we

3
he me

4
city Steve

5
eve paper

6
city tiny

7
eve here

8
tiny Steve

SIGHT WORD

Sight Word Fun

Look > Find > Color

★ Sight Word ★
come

Color the word **"come".**

come

Find the word **"come"** *and circle it.*

c	m	o	e
c	o	m	e
m	o	m	o
c	o	c	e

Sight Word Check

▶ TRACK 03-4

Listen > Repeat > Circle

1

(Come) 🗺️ .

(Come) here.

2

Come to 🧑, my pet.

Come to me, my pet.

3

👬 come to the 🏙️.

We come to the city.

4

Come with 🧑 .

Come with me.

STORY BUILD UP

Reading Fun

TRACK 03-5

Listen > Repeat > Put on the Stickers

"Come here, Steve.

It is a big city.

We are here.

We look tiny here.

There is a city map.

Let me get it."

Come here!

Steve

Story Build Up

Look > Put on the Stickers > Read

1

Come here, Steve.
It is a big city.
We are here.

2

We look tiny here.
There is a city map.
Let me get it.

Check Up 01 ▶ TRACK 03-6

1. Listen and check the right picture.

2. Listen and check the right word.

| tiny | here | body |

Check Up 02

1. Complete the word puzzle.

1

	2		3	
h	e	r	e	

2

			2
b	o	d	y

2. Check the box with the right sentence for the picture.

1.
- ☐ He is here.
- ☐ We are here.

2. Steve
- ☐ Come here, Steve.
- ☐ Come here, Eve.

3.
- ☐ We look big here.
- ☐ We look tiny here.

4.
- ☐ There is a city map.
- ☐ There is a tiny map.

ea

ee

Listen & Blend Up

▶ TRACK 04-1

Listen > Point > Repeat

❶ ea

❷ ee

e

pea

bee

Focus On ▶ TRACK 04-2

🎧 Listen › 🎵 Chant › 🖍 Highlight

1 ea

eat   **leaf**   **pea**   **weak**

2 ee

bee   **need**   **seed**   **tree**

CHECK UP

Match Up

TRACK 04-3

START GAME FINISH

Look > Listen > Match

1

2

3

4

ea **ee**

5

6

7

8

Color Up

START GAME FINISH

Look > Say > Color

1
tree
seed

2
leaf
pea

3
eat
need

4
pea
weak

5
leaf
weak

6
bee
eat

7
tree
seed

8
bee
need

Sight Word Fun

◉ Look > 🔍 Find > 🎨 Color

★ Sight Words ★
one, two, three

Color one bee.

Color two peas.

Color three trees.

Sight Word Check

TRACK 04-4

Listen > Repeat > Circle

1

I   see   ⓵ 🌿 .

I   see   (one)   leaf.

2

I   🧒   ⓷ 🫛 .

I   eat   three   peas.

3

I   need   ⓶ 🌱 .

I   need   two   seeds.

4

There   are   ⓷ 🐝 .

There   are   three   bees.

Reading Fun

▶ TRACK 04-5

👂 Listen ＞ 💬 Repeat ＞ ❤️ Put on the Stickers

One pea. Two peas.
Three peas. I am weak.
I need to eat peas.

One bee. Two bees.
Three bees.
There are three bees in
the tree.

Story Build Up

◉ Look > ❤ Put on the Stickers > 📖 Read

1

One pea. Two peas.
Three peas. I am weak.
I need to eat peas.

2

One bee. Two bees.
Three bee s.
There are three bees in the tree.

REVIEW

🔊 ✅ Check Up 01 ▶ TRACK 04-6

1. Listen and check the right picture.

2. Listen and check the right word.

eat	leaf	tree

📖 🅰 Check Up 02

1. Complete the word puzzle.

1

s
e
e
d

❶
❷
❸

2

t
r
e
e
e

❶
❷
❸

2. Check the box with the right sentence for the picture.

1
- [ ] I eat peas.
- [ ] I eat trees.

2
- [ ] I need a seed.
- [ ] I need a leaf.

3
- [ ] There are two bees.
- [ ] There are three bees.

4
- [ ] I am a leaf.
- [ ] I am weak.

CHAPTER 3

Unit 5 i, i_e
iris, iron, pilot, tiger, bike, ride, size, tire

Unit 6 igh, ie, y
high, night, sigh, lie, pie, tie, cry, dry, fly

Guess the words!

UNIT 5 i i_e

Listen & Blend Up

TRACK 05-1

Listen > Point > Repeat

① i

② i_e

i

tiger

bike

1 DAY 5 4 3 2

Focus On ▶ TRACK 05-2

🔊 Listen > 🎵 Chant > 🖊 Highlight

1 i 🎵

iris	**iron**	**pilot**	**tiger**

2 i_e 🎵

bike	**ride**	**size**	**tire**

CHECK UP

Match Up

TRACK 05-3

START GAME FINISH

Look > Listen > Match

1

2

3

4

i_e

i

5

6

7

8

Color Up

START GAME FINISH

Look > Say > Color

1

iron

iris

2

tire

bike

3

pilot

tiger

4

tiger

ride

5

size

bike

6

0 1 2 3 4 5 6 7 8 9

size

iron

7

pilot

tire

8

ride

iris

Sight Word Fun

START GAME FINISH

Look > Find > Color

★ Sight Word ★
like

Color the balloons that have "like".

ride

like

like

my

the

bike

like

play

like

like

like

Sight Word Check

TRACK 05-4

Listen > Repeat > Circle

1

I like (this) .

I like (this) iris.

2

I like to a .

I like to ride a bike.

3

I like .

I like tigers.

4

I like .

I like big sizes.

STORY BUILD UP

Reading Fun

TRACK 05-5

Listen > Repeat > Put on the Stickers

I have a bike.
Look at the size!
I like my big bike.

It has two tires.
I can ride my bike.
I like my bike.

Story Build Up

● Look > ♥ Put on the Stickers > 📖 Read

1

I have a **bike**.
Look at the **size**!
I **like** my big bike.

2

It has two **tires**.
I can **ride** my bike.
I like my **bike**.

REVIEW

TRACK 05-6

Check Up 01

1. Listen and check the right picture.

2. Listen and check the right word.

| tiger | ride | size |

Check Up 02

1. Complete the word puzzle.

1

1 t i r e

3 _ _ _ e

2

2 i r i s

Well done!

2. Check the box with the right sentence for the picture.

1
- ☐ I ride my bike.
- ☐ I ride my iron.

2
- ☐ I want to be a tiger.
- ☐ I want to be a pilot.

3
- ☐ It is a big size tire.
- ☐ It is a big ride tire.

4
- ☐ I like this iris.
- ☐ I like this size.

igh **ie** **y**

Listen & Blend Up
▶ TRACK 06-1

> 👂 Listen > 👆 Point > 💬 Repeat

❶ **igh**

❷ **ie**

❸ **y**

i

high

pie

cry

1
DAY

Focus On ▶ TRACK 06-2

🎧 Listen > 🎵 Chant > ✏️ Highlight

1 igh ♪

high

night

sigh

2 ie ♪

lie

pie

tie

3 y ♪

cry

dry

fly

Match Up

▶ TRACK 06-3

START GAME FINISH

◉ Look > 🔊 Listen > 🔴 Match

1

2

3

4

ie

y

igh

5

6

7

8

Color Up

START   GAME   FINISH

Look > Say > Color

1

fly

night

2

cry

bike

3

sigh

night

4

high

fly

5

dry

high

6

lie

dry

7

pilot

tie

8

pie

lie

SIGHT WORD

Sight Word Fun

Look > Find > Color

★ Sight Words ★
want, to

Color the jelly beans that have "want".

want	what	want
went	was	
want	want	west

Connect each "want" to "to".

want — to   want   to   want   to

want   to   want   to   want   to

Sight Word Check

▶ TRACK 06-4

🦻 Listen > 💬 Repeat > ⭕ Circle

1 I (want) (to)  .

I (want) (to) fly high.

2 I want to .

I want to eat pie.

3 I want to .

I want to cry.

4 I want to  it.

I want to dry it.

STORY BUILD UP

Reading Fun

TRACK 06-5

Listen > Repeat > Put on the Stickers

I am a pilot.
I **want to** **fly high**.
I can **fly high** at **night**.

Oh! The rain!
I am wet! I **sigh**.
I **want to** **cry**.

✨ Story Build Up ✨

◉ Look > ❤ Put on the Stickers > 📖 Read

1

I am a pilot.

I want to fly high .

I can fly high at night .

2

Oh! The rain!

I am wet! I sigh .

I want to cry .

REVIEW

🔊 ✅ Check Up 01 ▶ TRACK 06-6

1. Listen and check the right picture.

2. Listen and check the right word.

high	dry	tie

📖 ✏️ Check Up 02

1. Complete the word puzzle.

1

① ② ③

f	l	y
		e

2

② ① ③

	n	i	g	h	t

Well done!

2. Check the box with the right sentence for the picture.

1

☐ I want to fly high.

☐ I want to sigh.

2

☐ I want to eat pie.

☐ I want to eat a tie.

3

☐ I want to lie.

☐ I want to cry.

4

☐ I want a tie.

☐ I want to dry it.

CHAPTER 4

Unit 7 o, o_e
go, no, piano, robot, cone, home, note, rose

Unit 8 oa, ow, oe
boat, road, soap, bow, row, slow, Joe, hoe, toe

Guess the words!

o   o_e

Listen & Blend Up
▶ TRACK 07-1

o

Listen > Point > Repeat

① o

② o_e

go   rose

Focus On ▶ TRACK 07-2

🔊 Listen > 🎵 Chant > ✏️ Highlight

1 o

go   **no**   **piano**   **robot**

2 o_e

cone   **home**   **note**   **rose**

Match Up

TRACK 07-3

START   GAME   FINISH

Look > Listen > Match

1

2

3

4

o_e

o

5

6

7

8

Color Up

START GAME FINISH

👁 Look > 💬 Say > 🎨 Color

1

cone

rose

2

home

rose

3

piano

go

4

note

no

5

note

home

6

piano

cone

7

note

robot

8

go

no

Sight Word Fun

START GAME FINISH

Look > Find > Color

★ Sight Words ★
do, you

Draw a line to match the right picture.

1

Do you have a robot?

No, I don't.

2

Do you like me?

Yes, I do.

3

Do you want a rose?

Yes, I do.

Sight Word Check

▶ TRACK 07-4

Listen > Repeat > Circle

1

(Do) (you) have a 🤖 ?

(Do) (you) have a robot?

2

Yes, I do.

Yes, I do.

3

Do you play the 🎹 ?

Do you play the piano?

4

No, I don't.

No, I don't.

Reading Fun

TRACK 07-5

Listen > Repeat > Put on the Stickers

Do you have a **note**?
Yes, I **do**.

Do you have a **robot**?
Yes, I have it at **home**.

Do you want to **go home**?
No, I **don't**.*

*don't = do not

Story Build Up

◉ Look > ♥ Put on the Stickers > 📖 Read

1

Do you have a note ?
Yes, I do .

2

Do you have a robot ?
Yes, I have it at home .

3

Do you want to go home?
No , I don't.

REVIEW

🔊 ✅ Check Up 01 ▶ TRACK 07-6

1. Listen and check the right picture.

2. Listen and check the right word.

home	note	no

📖 ✏️ Check Up 02

1. Complete the word puzzle.

1

① ②

③

	2		3	
1 r	o	b	o	t

2

① ② ③

	1 r
2	o
	s
3	e

2. Check the box with the right sentence for the picture.

1

☐ I love my cone.

☐ I love my piano.

2

☐ Do you have a rose?

☐ Do you have a note?

3

☐ I have a robot at rose.

☐ I have a robot at home.

4

☐ I no home.

☐ I go home.

UNIT 8

oa **ow** **oe**

🎧 Listen > 👆 Point > 🗣️ Repeat

❶ **oa**

❷ **ow**

❸ **oe**

o

soap

bow

toe

1 DAY

Focus On ▶ TRACK 08-2

🔊 Listen > 🎵 Chant > 🖍 Highlight

1 oa 🎵	2 ow 🎵	3 oe 🎵
boat	bow	Joe
road	row	hoe
soap	slow	toe

CHECK UP

Match Up

TRACK 08-3

START GAME FINISH

Look > Listen > Match

1

2 Natural Soap

3

4

oa | oe | ow

5

6

7

8

Let's practice more!

App + cat Flash Cards

DAY 2

Color Up

START GAME FINISH

Look > Say > Color

1 Natural Soap — **boat** / **soap**

2  — **Joe** / **bow**

3 toe / Joe

4 — **road** / **row**

5 bow / toe

6  — **slow** / **row**

7 road / boat

8  — **soap** / **slow**

SIGHT WORD

Sight Word Fun

👁 Look > 🔍 Find > 🎨 Color

★ Sight Word ★
play

Color the word "play".

play

Color the box with the right word for the sentence.

I play | in | with | a box.

I play | in | with | a dog.

Sight Word Check

TRACK 08-4

Listen > Repeat > Circle

1

We (play) in a ⛵ .

We (play) in a boat.

2

I play with Joe .

I play with Joe.

3

I play with my 🦶 .

I play with my toes.

4

I play with my 🧼 .

I play with my soap.

Reading Fun

TRACK 08-5

Listen > Repeat > Put on the Stickers

Little Joe likes to play.
He wants to play in a tub.
He likes to play with a boat.

He can row the boat.
Joe plays with soap.
He likes to play in a tub.

Story Build Up

● Look > ❤ Put on the Stickers > 📖 Read

1

Little [Joe] likes to [play].

He wants to play in a tub.

He likes to play with a [boat].

2

He can [row] the boat.

Joe plays with [soap].

He likes to [play] in a tub.

REVIEW

🔊 ✅ Check Up 01 ▶ TRACK 08-6

1. Listen and check the right picture.

2. Listen and check the right word.

| slow | road | bow |

📖 🅰 Check Up 02

1. Complete the word puzzle.

1

1. b
2. o a
3. t

2

1. s o
   o
   a
   p

2
3

2. Check the box with the right sentence for the picture.

1
- [ ] I play with my boat.
- [ ] I play with my soap.

2
- [ ] Look at hoe!
- [ ] Look at Joe!

3
- [ ] Wow! A boat!
- [ ] Wow! A road!

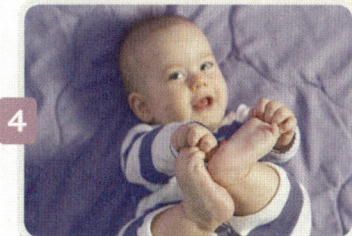

4
- [ ] I play with my toes.
- [ ] I play with my Joes.

u

Unit 9 u, u_e, ew
cupid, music, unicorn, cute, huge, tube, chew, few, new

Unit 10 oo, ue
cool, food, moon, pool, blue, clue, glue, Sue

Guess the words!

UNIT 9   u   u_e   ew

Listen & Blend Up ▶ TRACK 09-1

Listen > Point > Repeat

1 u

2 u_e

3 ew*

*'ew' makes a 'yoo' or 'oo' sound

unicorn

tube

chew

Focus On

TRACK 09-2

Listen > Chant > Highlight

1 u

cupid

music

unicorn

2 u_e

cute

huge

tube

3 ew

chew

few

new

CHECK UP

Match Up

TRACK 09-3

START GAME FINISH

Look > Listen > Match

1

2

3

4

| u_e | ew | u |

5

6

7

8

BRAND

Color Up

START GAME FINISH

👁 Look > 💬 Say > Color

1 cute / tube

2 new / few

3 cupid / huge

4 cupid / cute

5 cute / tube

6 unicorn / few

7 music / unicorn

8 huge / new

SIGHT WORD

Sight Word Fun

START · GAME1 · GAME2 · FINISH

Look > **Find** > **Color**

★ Sight Words ★
on, under

Color the balls on the table if they have "on" in them. Then color the blocks under the table if they have "under" in them.

on | on | on
on | in | on | under

under | under | under
on | under | on

Sight Word Check

► TRACK 09-4

🎧 Listen > 💬 Repeat > ⭕ Circle

1

I am (on) a 🦄 .

I am (on) a unicorn.

2

It is under the 🎁 🚲.

It is under the new bike.

3

There is a 🪥 on the table.

There is a tube on the table.

4

I see a 👼 under the 🌳.

I see a cupid under the tree.

Reading Fun

TRACK 09-5

Listen > Repeat > Put on the Stickers

I am **under** a **huge** tree.

I see a **cupid**.

The **cupid** is **cute**.

He is **on** a **unicorn**.

He can play **music**.

I like the **cupid** **on** a **unicorn**.

Story Build Up

👁 Look > ❤ Put on the Stickers > 📖 Read

1

I am (under) a (huge) tree.
I see a (cupid).
The cupid is (cute).

2

He is (on) a unicron.
He can play (music).
I like the cupid on a (unicorn).

REVIEW

Check Up 01 ▶ TRACK 09-6

1. Listen and check the right picture.

2. Listen and check the right word.

| new | cupid | few |

Check Up 02

1. Complete the word puzzle.

Puzzle 1

1 ① c h e w
2
3 ... e

Puzzle 2

2   3
1 c u t e

2. Check the box with the right sentence for the picture.

1

☐ It is on the piano.

☐ It is under the piano.

2

☐ It is under the boat.

☐ It is on the boat.

3

☐ Look at the cute cupid!

☐ Look at the huge cupid!

4

☐ I can chew it.

☐ I can few it.

oo

ue

Listen & Blend Up

▶ TRACK 10-1

u

Listen > Point > Repeat

① oo

② ue

u

moon

blue

1 DAY

Focus On

▶ TRACK 10-2

Listen > Chant > Highlight

1 oo

cook   food   moon   pool

2 ue

blue   clue   glue   Sue

CHECK UP

Match Up

TRACK 10-3

START GAME FINISH

Look > Listen > Match

1

2

3

4

ue

oo

5

6

7

8

Color Up

START GAME FINISH

Look > Say > Color

1
moon
pool

2
glue
blue

3
Sue
clue

4
food
cool

5
blue
clue

6
moon
pool

7
food
cool

8
glue
Sue

SIGHT WORD

Sight Word Fun

START   GAME   FINISH

👁 Look > 🔍 Find > 🍩 Color

★ Sight Word ★
yellow

Color the puzzle to match the color word.

blue

red

blue

red

yellow

yellow

yellow

yellow

yellow

yellow

red

yellow

blue

yellow

blue

red

Sight Word Check

TRACK 10-4

Listen > Repeat > Circle

1

The 😊 is ⬤ .

The moon is (yellow).

2

Sue likes ⬤ 🌹 .

Sue likes yellow roses.

3

A 🍌 is a ⬤ 🍲 .

A banana is a yellow food.

4

I like 🔴 🔵 and ⬤ .

I like red, blue and yellow.

STORY BUILD UP

Reading Fun

Listen > Repeat > Put on the Stickers

Sue can see food.

The food is yellow.

She can see a pool.

The pool is blue.

She can see a moon.

The moon is yellow.

Story Build Up

DAY 4

◉ Look ＞ ❤ Put on the Stickers ＞ 📖 Read

1

Sue can see food .
The food is yellow .

2

She can see a pool .
The pool is blue .

3

She can see a moon .
The moon is yellow .

REVIEW

🔊 ✅ **Check Up 01** ▶ TRACK 10-6

1. Listen and check the right picture.

2. Listen and check the right word.

pool	food	blue

📖 🅰 **Check Up 02**

1. Complete the word puzzle.

1

❶ ❷ ❸

1		2		3
c	o	o	l	

2

❶ ❷ ❸

1		2		3
b	l	u	e	

2. Check the box with the right sentence for the picture.

1

☐ I have a blue tube.

☐ I have a blue glue.

2

☐ I see a yellow moon.

☐ I see a yellow pool.

3

☐ I am cool in the glue.

☐ I am cool in the pool.

4

Sue

☐ Sue eats food.

☐ Sue eats glue.

FINAL REVIEW 01

TRACK 11-1

1. Listen and circle the right picture.

a

b

c

2. Listen and circle the right word.

a rain · hay	**b** pea · bee
c tire · iron	**d** here · tiny

Well done!

3. Unscramble the word.

a i e p

pie

b e o s r

c n m o o

d c k e a

4. Read the sentence and circle the right word.

a There is a leaf seed under the tree.

b I want to go home cone .

c Come here to see a cupid glue .

d The unicorn has a big little tail.

FINAL REVIEW 02

1. Listen and circle the right picture.

a

b

c

2. Listen and circle the right word.

a cone | no

b tire | eat

c music | new

d he | city

For answers, go to p.47 in the workbook!

Well done!

3. Unscramble the word.

a z e i s

b y a d

c e m h o

d e e d s

4. Read the sentence and circle the right word.

a Do you like a [big | little] robot?

b I like [yellow | blue] tigers.

c I play with [me | my] big robot.

d Sue can [bake | face] a cake.

Unit 01 pp20-21

little

cake

bake

big

tap

little

gate

big

Unit 02 pp30-31

day

baby

tail

My

paper

say

Mail

Unit 03 pp42-43

Come Steve here

tiny city me

Unit 04 pp52-53

One

Two

Three

weak

One

bee

three

Unit 05 pp64-65

bike

size

like

tires

ride

bike

Unit 06 pp74-75

to high fly night sigh

want   cry

Unit 07   pp86-87

note

do

robot

home

you

No

Unit 08   pp96-97

Joe

play

boat

row

soap

play

Natural Soap

Unit 09 pp108-109

under   huge   cupid   cute

on   music   unicorn

Unit 10 pp118-119

food   yellow   pool   blue

moon   yellow

AMAZING PHONICS

神奇的自然拼读

发音·单词·句子·故事

韩国钥匙英语学习方法研究所 / 著

Vol. **3**

CONSONANT BLENDS & DIGRAPHS

ZHEJIANG UNIVERSITY PRESS
浙江大学出版社

**Nice to meet you.
What is your name?**

My name is...

_____

AMAZING PHONICS
Vol.3 Consonant Blends & Digraphs

CONTENTS

FUN

Reading Fun
Match Up
Blend Up
Color Up
Stickers
Chants

EASY

Comprehensible Input
Simple Lesson Plans
Repeated Activities
Simple Activities
Step by Step

INDEPENDENT

Self-Perfection
Self-Correction
Individual Work
Hands-On Work

Hello,
I am Jay!

I want to be a magician
when I grow up.

Can you help me
make something
amazing happen?

Hello, I am Curi!

I am very curious.
If you follow me,
we will have
so much fun!

Amazing Phonics Vol.3
Consonant
Blends
& Digraphs

Vol.1 Short Vowel Sounds

Vol.2 Long Vowel Sounds

Vol.3 Consonant Blends & Digraphs

Vol.4 Advanced Vowels & Silent Letters

Welcome to *Amazing Phonics*!

Amazing Phonics introduces a fun, easy, and effective way
to start your phonics journey.

Phonics is a method for teaching reading and writing of the English language by developing children's phonemic awareness.
Amazing Phonics Vol.3 teaches consonant blends & digraphs. Consonant blends are consonant pairs in which each consonant makes its own sound. Consonant digraphs are clusters of consonants pronounced as a single sound.

Amazing Phonics also focuses on "the way of learning". Children perfect themselves by repeating their work. They work toward mastery of the task. This repetition leads not only to mastery of the task, but also to a heightened ability to concentrate and an increased sense of accomplishment. So, if children are given enough time to practise, they can perfect their skills while feeling that they are learning well.

We hope every child can experience the joy of learning with *Amazing Phonics*. Have fun learning, everyone!

Features of *Amazing Phonics*

A truely amazing experience!

Amazing Phonics Vol. 3
Consonant Blends & Digraphs

L	R	S	Beginning	Ending
Blends	**Blends**	**Blends**	**Digraphs**	**Digraphs**
•	•	•	•	•
Unit 1 bl, cl, fl	**Unit 3** br, cr, dr	**Unit 5** sn, sp, st	**Unit 7** ch-, sh-	**Unit 9** -ch, -sh
Unit 2 gl, pl, sl	**Unit 4** fr, gr, tr	**Unit 6** sk, sm, sw	**Unit 8** wh-, ph-, th-	**Unit 10** -ck, -th, -ng

1 ★ Books ★

Student Book

Pronunciation & Chant Videos

Step by Step Day by Day

Sight Word Fun One Step Closer to Reading

Now I can read phonics & sight words in the story!

I get more confident! Everything is so easy! Now I am ready for MORE!

Yay!

Workbook (My Writing Note)

I can write the words & sentences I learned!

I am so confident.
I can make my own sentences.
It is so much fun!

Features of *Amazing Phonics*

Videos

Fun phonics lectures with Mr. David, the magician!

I can understand the pronunciation better!

L-Blends
bl, cl, fl

Guess the words!
Time to meet the words and become friends with them.

black   clock   flag

UNIT 1
Chant 1

b + l = bl

black
block
blouse

I love my phonics chants!
I want to sing them again and again.
It is easy and so much fun!

black   block   blouse

bl-   black   block   blouse
cl-   clap   cliff   clock
fl-   flag   flame   fly

Pronunciation & Chant Videos Are
Included with the Book
Full Lectures Are Available at

2 ★ Multimedia ★

Applet

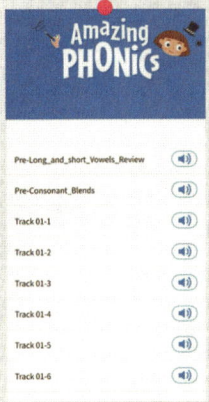

Video	Match Up	Story Building	Word Quiz	MP3

Video   **Match Up**   **Story Building**   **Word Quiz**   **MP3**

I want to do it again and again!
I am perfecting myself by repeating the work.
I feel so confident! Now I can read more!

1 Pre-Learning
Long & Short Vowels Review

MP3

★ Circle the right word for the picture. ★

1

name man mane

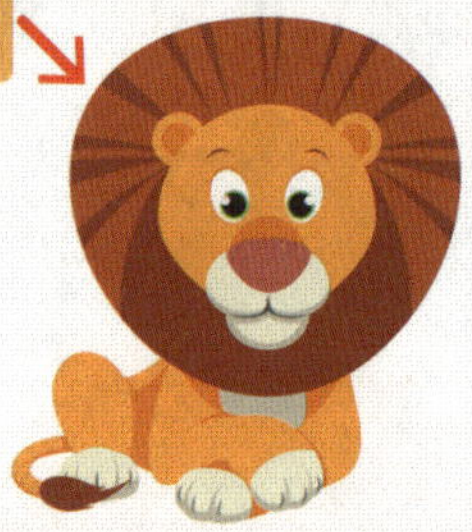

2

kite hit kit

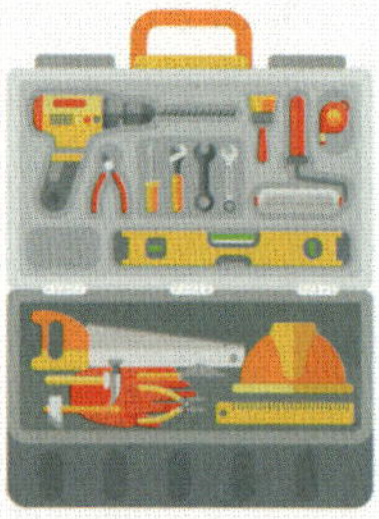

3

rub tube tub

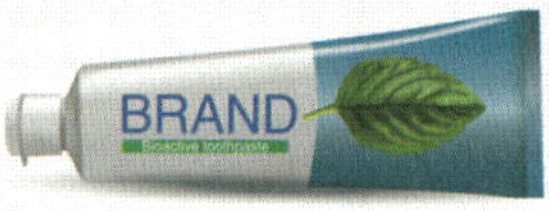

4

jet he net

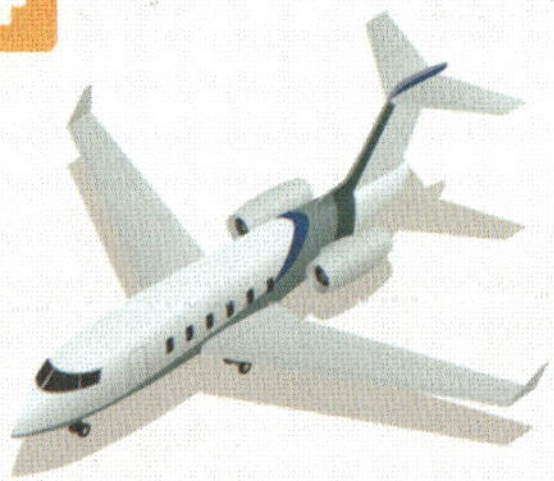

★ Listen and repeat. ★

1

I see a **bl**ack **fl**y in the **tr**ee.

2

There is a **gr**een **fr**og in the **gr**ass.

Are you ready?
Let's have fun!

CHAPTER 1

Consonant Blends

L Blends

Unit 1 bl, cl, fl
black, block, blouse, clap, cliff, clock, flag, flame, fly

Unit 2 gl, pl, sl
globe, glass, glow, plant, plate, plug, sleep, slide, slow

Guess the words!

bl **cl** **fl**

Listen & Blend Up

▶ TRACK 01-1

L— Blends

Listen > Point > Repeat

① **bl** ack → **bl** ack

② **cl** ock → **cl** ock

③ **fl** ag → **fl** ag

black   **cl**ock   **fl**ag

1 DAY
5 2
4 3

Focus On

▶ TRACK 01-2

Listen > Chant > Highlight

1 bl

black

block

blouse

2 cl

clap

cliff

clock

3 fl

flag

flame

fly

CHECK UP

Match Up

▶ TRACK 01-3

START GAME FINISH

◉ Look > 👂 Listen > 🎯 Match

1

2

3

4

cl

bl

fl

5

6

7

8

Color Up

START FINISH

Look > Say > Color

1 GAME

fly / flag

2 GAME

flame clap

3 GAME

clock cliff

4 GAME

block black

SIGHT WORD

Sight Word Fun

START GAME FINISH

👁 Look > 🔍 Find > 🎨 Color

★ Sight Word ★
next

Find and color the blocks that have the word **"next"** on them.

next

my

next

next

on

next

Sight Word Check

TRACK 01-4

Listen > Repeat > Circle

1. I see a (fly) next to a (block).

I see a fly next to a block.

2. I am next to a (flag).

I am next to a flag.

3. There is a (clock) next to you.

There is a clock next to you.

4. I find my (blouse) next to my bed.

I find my blouse next to my bed.

STORY BUILD UP

Reading Fun

TRACK 01-5

Listen > Repeat > Put on the Stickers

I am a fly.

I am a black fly.

I sit next to a little block.

I can see a flag.

It is next to a big clock.

I can fly high to the clock.

Story Build Up

◎ Look > ♥ Put on the Stickers > 📖 Read

1

I am a fly.

I am a black fly.

I sit next to a little block.

2

I can see a flag.

It is next to a big clock.

I can fly high to the clock.

REVIEW

🥨 ✅ Check Up 01 ▶ TRACK 01-6

1. Listen and check the right picture.

2. Listen and check the right word.

block	clock	clap

📖 🍪 Check Up 02

1. Look and circle the right blend for the picture.

1 cl fl

2 fl bl

3 cl bl

2. Circle the right word to complete the sentence.

1

I am a .... fly.

a. block   b. black   c. blouse

2

It is .... to a big clock.

a. want   b. are   c. next

3

I like my new ....

a. blouse   b. cliff   c. flame

4

I want to play with my ....

a. cliff   b. blocks   c. flame

gl

pl

sl

Listen & Blend Up

TRACK 02-1

L- Blends

> Listen > Point > Repeat

① **gl** obe → **gl** obe

② **pl** ate → **pl** ate

③ **sl** eep → **sl** eep

 globe

 plate

 sleep

Focus On

TRACK 02-2

Listen > Chant > Highlight

1 gl

globe

glass

glow

2 pl

plant

plate

plug

3 sl

sleep

slide

slow

Match Up

▶ TRACK 02-3

START GAME FINISH

◉ Look ＞ 🔊 Listen ＞ Match

1

2

3

4

5

6

7

8

sl

pl

gl

Color Up

START   FINISH

👁 Look > 💬 Say > 🎨 Color

1 ♠

plate   plant

2 ♥

glass   glow

3 ♦

slow   slide

4 ♣

globe   plug

SIGHT WORD

Sight Word Fun

START GAME FINISH

Look > Find > Color

★ Sight Word ★
when

Color the glasses that have the same words on them.

when
when

when
glow

when
when

when
when

slow
when

when
when

when
when

Sight Word Check

TRACK 02-4

Listen > Repeat > Circle

1

(When) do you go to 🛏.

(When) do you go to sleep?

2

I like it when it 💡.

I like it when it glows.

3

When it is red, you need to 🐢 down.

When it is red, you need to slow down.

4

🔌 it in when you need to.

Plug it in when you need to.

STORY BUILD UP

Reading Fun

TRACK 02-5

Listen > Repeat > Put on the Stickers

I have a glass globe.
I have it on a big plate.
It glows at night.

When I go to sleep,
I plug in the globe.
I love it when it glows.

Story Build Up

👁 Look > ❤ Put on the Stickers > 📖 Read

1

I have a [glass] globe.
I have it on a big [plate].
It [glows] at night.

2

When I go to [sleep],
I [plug] in the globe.
I love it [when] it glows.

REVIEW

🦻 ✅ Check Up 01 ▶ TRACK 02-6

1. Listen and check the right picture.

2. Listen and check the right word.

slide	plate	plant

📖 🍪 Check Up 02

1. Look and circle the right blend for the picture.

1

sl　gl

2

gl　pl

3

sl　pl

2. Circle the right word to complete the sentence.

1

I have a .... globe.

a. plate   b. glass   c. plant

2

I plug in the globe .... I go to bed.

a. next   b. when   c. sleep

3

At night, I go to ....

a. sleep   b. slide   c. globe

4

I see a .... next to a plant.

a. slide   b. glow   c. slow

CHAPTER 2

Consonant Blends

R

Blends

Unit 3 br, cr, dr
bread, bride, bridge, cream, cross, crow, dragon, dress, drum

Unit 4 fr, gr, tr
friend, frog, fruit, grape, grass, green, train, tree, trip

1	2	3	4
5	6	7	8
9	10	11	12
13	14	15	16
17	18	**Guess the words!**	

br **cr** **dr**

Listen & Blend Up ▶ TRACK 03-1

R ▬ Blends

Listen > Point > Repeat

① **br** **ead** → **br** **ead**

② **cr** **eam** → **cr** **eam**

③ **dr** **agon** → **dr** **agon**

bread

cream

dragon

Focus On

▶ TRACK 03-2

🔊 Listen > 🎵 Chant > ✏️ Highlight

1 br

bread

bride

bridge

2 cr

cream

cross

crow

3 dr

dragon

dress

drum

Match Up

▶ TRACK 03-3

START GAME FINISH

👁 Look > 👂 Listen > Match

1

cr

br

dr

2

3

4

5

6

7

8

Color Up

START   FINISH

Look > Say > Color

1 ♠

cream cross

2 ♥

bride bread

3 ♦

dress drum

4 ♣

dragon bridge

SIGHT WORD

Sight Word Fun

START GAME FINISH

👁 Look > 🔍 Find > 🎨 Color

★ Sight Word ★
put

Color the word "put".

put

Color the shapes that match the word "put".

put

Sight Word Check

▶ TRACK 03-4

🦻 Listen ＞ 💬 Repeat ＞ 🔴 Circle

1

I (put) on my 👗 .

I (put) on my dress.

2

I put 🍦 on 🥖 .

I put cream on bread.

3

I put my 🏷️ on it.

I put my name on it.

4

I put 📼 on it.

I put tape on it.

STORY BUILD UP

Reading Fun

TRACK 03-5

Listen > Repeat > Put on the Stickers

I am a bride.
I put on a dress.
I cross the bridge
in my dress.

When I come home,
I eat bread.
I put cream on my bread.
I like cream bread.

Story Build Up

👁 Look > ❤ Put on the Stickers > 📖 Read

1

I am a ⸢ bride ⸥.

I put on a ⸢ dress ⸥.

I ⸢ cross ⸥ the bridge in my dress.

2

When I come home,

I eat ⸢ bread ⸥.

I ⸢ put ⸥ cream on my bread.

I like ⸢ cream ⸥ bread.

🔊 ✅ Check Up 01 ▶ TRACK 03-6

1. Listen and check the right picture.

2. Listen and check the right word.

dress	bridge	bride

📖 ✏️ Check Up 02

1. Look and circle the right blend for the picture.

1 cr br

2 dr br

3 cr dr

2. Circle the right word to complete the sentence.

1

I put on a ....

   a. dragon   b. drum   c. dress

2

I .... the bridge.

   a. cross   b. cream   c. crow

3

I like to eat cream ....

   a. bride   b. bread   c. bridge

4

I can play the ....

   a. drums   b. cross   c. bread

fr **gr** **tr**

Listen & Blend Up

▶ TRACK 04-1

R - Blends

Listen > Point > Repeat

① **fr** **og** → **fr** **og**

② **gr** **een** → **gr** **een**

③ **tr** **ain** → **tr** **ain**

frog

green

train

Focus On ▶ TRACK 04-2

🔊 Listen > 🎵 Chant > ✏️ Highlight

1 fr 🎵

friend

frog

fruit

2 gr 🎵

grape

grass

green

3 tr 🎵

train

tree

trip

Match Up

▶ TRACK 04-3

START GAME FINISH

👁 Look > 👂 Listen > 🖊 Match

1

5

tr

2

6

gr

3

7

fr

4

8

Color Up

START FINISH

Look > Say > Color

1 ♠

grass grape

2 ♥

tree green

3 ♦

fruit friend

4 ♣

train trip

SIGHT WORD

Sight Word Fun

START   GAME   FINISH

Look > Find > Color

★ Sight Word ★
get

Color the grapes that have the word "get" on them.

get   get   go
put   go   get   get   go
get   get   get   put   get
go   put   get   get
get

Sight Word Check

TRACK 04-4

Listen > Repeat > Circle

1

I (get) some 🍇 .

I (get) some grapes.

2

I get on a 🚂

I get on a train.

3

I get to eat 🍊 .

I get to eat fruits.

4

I get on a 🚲 .

I get on a bike.

STORY BUILD UP

Reading Fun

TRACK 04-5

Listen > Repeat > Put on the Stickers

I go on a trip.

I get on a train.

I get to see a frog.

I see green grass.

I see a grape vine.

Look at my little friend.

Phonics St.

Story Build Up

👁 Look > 💛 Put on the Stickers > 📖 Read

1

I go on a trip.

I get on a train.

I get to see a frog.

2

I see green grass.

I see a grape vine.

Look at my little friend.

🔊 ✅ Check Up 01 ▶ TRACK 04-6

1. Listen and check the right picture.

2. Listen and check the right word.

| fruit | tree | friend |

📖 🖊 Check Up 02

1. Look and circle the right blend for the picture.

1

fr | tr

2

fr | gr

3

tr | gr

2. Circle the right word to complete the sentence.

1 I get on a ....

a. grape   b. train   c. friend

2 I see a .... vine.

a. friend   b. grape   c. grass

3 There is a big .... tree.

a. green   b. grass   c. train

4 I go to get some ....

a. friend   b. fruits   c. trip

CHAPTER 3

Consonant Blends

S

Blends

Unit 5 sn, sp, st
snack, snake, snail, space, spider, spin, star, stone, stop

Unit 6 sk, sm, sw
skate, ski, sky, small, smell, smile, swan, sweet, swim

Guess the words!

sn **sp** **st**

Listen & Blend Up

▶ TRACK 05-1

S- Blends

Listen > Point > Repeat

① **sn** **ack** → **sn** **ack**

② **sp** **ider** → **sp** **ider**

③ **st** **op** → **st** **op**

snack   **sp**ider   **st**op

Focus On ▶ TRACK 05-2

🔊 Listen > 🎵 Chant > ✏️ Highlight

1. sn

snack

snake

snail

2. sp

space

spider

spin

3. st

star

stone

stop

CHECK UP

Match Up ▶ TRACK 05-3

START GAME FINISH

👁 Look > 👂 Listen > Match

1

2

3

4 STOP

st

sn

sp

5

6

7

8 CHIPS

Color Up

START FINISH

Look > Say > Color

1 ♠

spider ✓ space

2 ♥

snack snake

3 ♦

star stop

4 ♣

snail spin

SIGHT WORD

Sight Word Fun

Look > Find > Color

★ Sight Word ★
many

Color the stars that have the word "many".

many

next

many

get

many

put

many

many

many

Sight Word Check

TRACK 05-4

Listen > Repeat > Circle

1

There are **many** ⭐.

There are **many** stars.

2

I see many .

I see many stones.

3

I have many .

I have many dresses.

4

I have many CHIPS at 🏠.

I have many snacks at home.

STORY BUILD UP

Reading Fun

Listen > Repeat > Put on the Stickers

I **stop** at **many** **stone**s.

I find a **snake** on a **stone**.

He eats **many** **spider**s.

There is a man in **space**.

He can **spin** in **space**.

He can see **many** **star**s.

Story Build Up

👁 Look > ❤ Put on the Stickers > 📖 Read

1

I stop at many stones.

I find a snake on a stone.

He eats many spiders .

2

There is a man in space .

He can spin in space.

He can see many stars.

REVIEW

🔊 ✅ Check Up 01 ▶ TRACK 05-6

1. Listen and check the right picture.

2. Listen and check the right word.

spin	spider	stone

📖 🖊 Check Up 02

1. Look and circle the right blend for the picture.

1 sp | sn

2 st | sp

3 st | sn

Well done!

2. Circle the right word to complete the sentence.

1

There are many ....

a. space   b. spin   c. stars

2

I see a black ....

a. spider   b. snail   c. star

3

I want to eat some ....

a. snacks   b. stones   c. snails

4

There is a man in ....

a. spider   b. snail   c. space

sk **sm** **sw**

Listen & Blend Up ▶ TRACK 06-1

S-Blends

Listen > Point > Repeat

① **sk** **ate** → **sk ate**

② **sm** **ile** → **sm ile**

③ **sw** **an** → **sw an**

skate smile swan

Focus On ▶ TRACK 06-2

🔊 Listen > 🎵 Chant > 🖍 Highlight

1 **sk**

skate

ski

sky

2 **sm**

small

smell

smile

3 **sw**

swan

sweet

swim

CHECK UP

Match Up ▶ TRACK 06-3

START GAME FINISH

👁 Look > 🔊 Listen > Match

1

2

sw

sm

sk

3

4

5

6

7

8

Color Up

START FINISH

Look > Say > Color

1 ♠ GAME

smile smell

2 ♥ GAME

sky ski

3 ♦ GAME

small swan

4 ♣ GAME

sweet swim

Sight Word Fun

Look > Find > Color

★ Sight Word ★
walk

Follow the word "walk" to get the sweets.

Mmm~I smell something sweet!

walk

walk

walk

walk

walk

walk

when

walk

next

go

get

put

Sight Word Check

▶ TRACK 06-4

🦻 Listen > 💬 Repeat > 🖌 Circle

1

I  for a ____ .

I go for a (walk.)

2

I ____ to see  .

I walk to see swans.

3

I ____ my  ____ .

I walk my small dog.

4

I ____ to the  .

I walk to the cliff.

STORY BUILD UP

Reading Fun

TRACK 06-5

Listen > Repeat > Put on the Stickers

We **walk** to a **small** lake.
We look up at the **sky**
when we **walk**.

My boy sees a **swan**.
He says, "**Swim**, **swan**, **swim**!"
My boy sees a **sweet**.
He says, "It **smells sweet**!"

Story Build Up

👁 Look > ❤ Put on the Stickers > 📖 Read

1

We walk to a small lake.
We look up at the sky
when we walk.

2

My boy sees a swan.
He says, "Swim, swan, swim!"
My boy sees a sweet.
He says, "It smells sweet!"

🦻✅ Check Up 01 ▶ TRACK 06-6

1. Listen and check the right picture.

2. Listen and check the right word.

swim	skate	sky

📖 🖊 Check Up 02

1. Look and circle the right blend for the picture.

1	2	3
sw sm	sk sm	sw sk

2. Circle the right word to complete the sentence.

1

"Swim, ..., swim!"

a. sky   b. swan   c. smile

2

I can .... food.

a. sky   b. swan   c. smell

3

There are many ....

a. sweets   b. small   c. sky

4

Look up at the ....!

a. skate   b. sky   c. smile

CHAPTER 4

Consonant Digraphs

Beginning

Digraphs

Unit 7 ch-, sh-
cheese, cherry, chin, chop, shake, shape, sheep, shirt

Unit 8 wh-, ph-, th-
whale, what, white, phone, phonics, photo, that, thin, think

1

2

3

4

5

6

7

8

9

10

11

12

13

A apple
B boy
C cake

14

15

16

17

Guess the words!

Listen & Blend Up ▶ TRACK 07-1

Beginning Digraphs

Listen > Point > Repeat

① ch eese → ch eese

② sh irt → sh irt

cheese

shirt

Focus On ▶ TRACK 07-2

🎧 Listen > 🎵 Chant > ✏️ Highlight

1 ch-

cheese　**cherry**　**chin**　**chop**

2 sh-

shake　**shape**　**sheep**　**shirt**

CHECK UP

Match Up

TRACK 07-3

START GAME FINISH

Look > Listen > Match

1

2

3

4

5

6

7

8

ch-

sh-

✨ Color Up ✨

START FINISH

👁 Look > 💬 Say > 🎨 Color

1 ♠ GAME

chin   chop

2 ♥ GAME

shape   shake

3 ♦ GAME

sheep   shirt

4 ♣ GAME

cheese   cherry

Sight Word Fun

START GAME FINISH

👁 Look > 🔍 Find > 🎨 Color

★ Sight Word ★
some

Color the shapes that have the same words on them.

some
chop

some
some

some
shape

some
sheep

some
some

some
some

some
some

some
some

Sight Word Check

▶ TRACK 07-4

🔊 Listen > 💬 Repeat > ⭕ Circle

1 I want (some) .

I want (some) cheese.

2 I  up some .

I chop up some cheese.

3 There are some .

There are some sheep.

4 I  some  .

I need some new shirts.

Reading Fun

TRACK 07-5

Listen > Repeat > Put on the Stickers

There are some sheep.
They have some grass on their chins.

There are some cheeses.
I like the shapes.
I chop up the cheeses.
I eat them with some cherries.

Story Build Up

Look > **Put on the Stickers** > **Read**

1

There are some sheep.
They have some grass on their chins.

2

There are some cheeses.
I like the shapes.
I chop up the cheeses.
I eat them with some cherries.

REVIEW

Check Up 01 ▶ TRACK 07-6

1. Listen and check the right picture.

2. Listen and check the right word.

| shake | shirt | shape |

Check Up 02

1. Look and circle the right digraph for the picture.

1 ch | sh

2 ch | sh

3 ch | sh

Well done!

2. Circle the right word to complete the sentence.

1

I .... up some cheeses.

   a. cherry   b. shake   c. chop

2

.... eat grass.

   a. Shirt   b. Sheep   c. Cheese

3

There are many ....

   a. shapes   b. chop   c. shake

4

I want to eat some ....

   a. chin   b. cherries   c. shape

UNIT 8

wh- ph- th-

Listen & Blend Up

TRACK 08-1

Beginning Digraphs

Listen > Point > Repeat

1. wh + ale → wh ale
2. ph + one → ph one
3. th + in → th in

whale

phone

thin

Focus On

▶ TRACK 08-2

🔊 Listen > 🎵 Chant > 🖍 Highlight

1 wh-	2 ph-	3 th-
 **wh**ale	**ph**one	**th**at
 **wh**at	 **ph**onics	 **th**in
 **wh**ite	**ph**oto	 **th**ink

CHECK UP

Match Up ▶ TRACK 08-3

START GAME FINISH

◉ Look > 🔊 Listen > 🖌 Match

1

2

3

4

ph-

th-

wh-

5

6

7

8

Color Up

START FINISH

Look > Say > Color

1 ♠

whale **white**

2 ♥

phone photo

3 ♦

thin think

4 ♣

that what

SIGHT WORD

Sight Word Fun

START GAME FINISH

Look > Find > Color

★ Sight Word ★
they

Color the phones that have the same words on them.

they
they

they they	they that	they they	they thin

they then	they they	thin they	they they	that they

Sight Word Check

TRACK 08-4

Listen > Repeat > Circle

1

	are	**(they?)**
What	**are**	**(they?)**

2

They	**are**	.
They	**are**	**whales.**

3

They	**are**	.
They	**are**	**thin.**

4

They	**have**	.
They	**have**	**phones.**

Reading Fun

TRACK 08-5

Listen > Repeat > Put on the Stickers

What is this?
This is a **white phone**.

What is **that**?
That is a **photo**.

What are **they**?
They are **whale**s.

Story Build Up

Look > **Put on the Stickers** > **Read**

1

What is this?
This is a white phone.

2

What is that?
That is a photo.

3

What are they?
They are whales.

REVIEW

🎧 ✅ Check Up 01 ▶ TRACK 08-6

1. Listen and check the right picture.

2. Listen and check the right word.

thin	phone	phonics

📖 🔴 Check Up 02

1. Look and circle the right digraph for the picture.

ph | **th**

wh | **ph**

th | **wh**

2. Circle the right word to complete the sentence.

1

.... is this?

a. White   b. What   c. That

2

Look! It is a white ....

a. whale   b. what   c. that

3

ABC~ I like .... !

a. phonics   b. thin   c. what

4

I like the color ....

a. phonics   b. thin   c. white

CHAPTER 5

Consonant Digraphs

Ending Digraphs

Unit 9 -ch, -sh
beach, bench, each, lunch, cash, dish, fish, wish

Unit 10 -ck, -th, -ng
duck, kick, neck, cloth, smooth, with, long, ring, wing

Guess the words!

-ch   -sh

Listen & Blend Up ▶ TRACK 09-1

Ending Digraphs

Listen > Point > Repeat

1 bea ch → bea ch

2 di sh → di sh

beach   dish

Focus On ▶ TRACK 09-2

🔊 Listen > 🎵 Chant > ✏️ Highlight

1 -ch

beach ✏ bench   each   lunch

2 -sh

cash   dish   fish   wish

CHECK UP

Match Up ▶ TRACK 09-3

START GAME FINISH

👁 Look > 👂 Listen > 🎯 Match

1

2

-ch

3

-sh

4

5

6

7

8

Color Up

START FINISH

Look > Say > Color

1 GAME

dish **cash**

2 GAME

lunch **each**

3 GAME

fish **wish**

4 GAME

bench **beach**

SIGHT WORD

Sight Word Fun

START GAME FINISH

Look > Find > Color

★ Sight Word ★
let's

Find and color the puzzle parts that have the word "let's" on them.

many   some

put

let's   let's   let's

let's   let's

let's

when   some

next   get

Sight Word Check

▶ TRACK 09-4

Listen > Repeat > Circle

1 (Let's)  to the  .

(Let's) go to the beach.

2 Let's  some  .

Let's eat some lunch.

3 Let's make a  .

Let's make a wish.

4 Let's  on a  .

Let's sit on a bench.

STORY BUILD UP

🔊 Listen > 💬 Repeat > ❤️ Put on the Stickers

Let's go to the beach.

We sit on a bench.

"I want my lunch."

"I have some cash.

Let's eat some dishes."

"I want to eat a fish dish."

Story Build Up

Look > Put on the Stickers > Read

1

Let's go to the beach.
We sit on a bench.

2

"I want my lunch."
"I have some cash.

3

Let's eat some dishes."
"I want to eat a fish dish."

🦻 ✅ Check Up 01 ▶ TRACK 09-6

1. Listen and check the right picture.

2. Listen and check the right word.

wish	dish	fish

📖 🎨 Check Up 02

1. Look and circle the right digraph for the picture.

1	2	3
-ch -sh	-ch -sh	-ch -sh

2. Circle the right word to complete the sentence.

1

I make a _____.

a. fish   b. each   c. wish

2

_____ sit on a bench.

a. Let's   b. See   c. Some

3

I want to eat a _____ dish.

a. wish   b. cash   c. fish

4

Let's eat some _____.

a. each   b. lunch   c. beach

UNIT **10**

-ck -th -ng

Listen & Blend Up

TRACK 10-1

Ending Digraphs

Listen > Point > Repeat

① **du** **ck** → **du ck**

② **clo** **th** → **clo th**

③ **wi** **ng** → **wi ng**

duck

cloth

wing

Focus On

▶ TRACK 10-2

🔊 Listen > 🎵 Chant > ✏️ Highlight

1 -ck

duck

kick

neck

2 -th

cloth

smooth

with

3 -ng

long

ring

wing

Match Up

TRACK 10-3

START   GAME   FINISH

◉ Look > 🔊 Listen > 🎨 Match

1

2

3

4

-th

-ck

-ng

5

6

7

8

Color Up

START FINISH

◉ Look > 💬 Say > Color

1 ♠ GAME

neck kick

2 ♥ GAME

smooth cloth

3 ♦ GAME

with wing

4 ♣ GAME

long ring

Sight Word Fun

START GAME FINISH

👁 Look > 🔍 Find > 🖍 Color

★ Sight Word ★
too

Color the balloons that have the word "too" on them.

get

too

too

too

too

put

too

too

too

too

too

Sight Word Check

TRACK 10-4

Listen > Repeat > Circle

1

He [ ] my [ ], (too.)

He kicks my block, (too.)

2

I want to [ ] like a [ ], too.

I want to swim like a duck, too.

3

I want to eat [ ], too.

I want to eat fish, too.

4

My dress is too [ ].

My dress is too long.

STORY BUILD UP

TRACK 10-5

Listen > Repeat > Put on the Stickers

There is a **duck** with **long wings**.

He has a **long neck**, **too**.

The **duck** sees a **white cloth**.

There is a **smooth ring** in it.

He puts the **ring** on a **wing**.

It is **too** small.

He **kick**s it under a tree.

Story Build Up

Look > Put on the Stickers > Read

1

There is a duck with long wings.
He has a long neck, too.

2

The duck sees a white cloth.
There is a smooth ring in it.

3

He puts the ring on a wing.
It is too small.
He kicks it under a tree.

REVIEW

Check Up 01 · TRACK 10-6

1. Listen and check the right picture.

2. Listen and check the right word.

| with | wing | long |

Check Up 02

1. Look and circle the right digraph for the picture.

1 -th · -ng

2 -ng · -ck

3 -th · -ck

2. Circle the right word to complete the sentence.

1
A duck has two _____.

a. kick   b. wings   c. rings

2
I am _____ my family.

a. long   b. wing   c. with

3
Look at the yellow _____.

a. ducks   b. kick   c. smooth

4
A giraffe has a long _____.

a. neck   b. cloth   c. wing

FINAL REVIEW 01

TRACK 11-1

1. Listen and circle the right picture.

a

b

c

2. Listen and circle the right blend for the word.

a

cl   **cr**

b

gl   **gr**

c

sm   **sn**

d

sp   **st**

For answers, go to p.47 in the workbook!

Well done!

3. Look and complete the word.

a
_ _ ink

b
ben_ _

c
_ _ ame

d
_ _ ide

4. Read the sentence and circle the right word.

a
I am a block black fly.

b
I see green grape grass.

c
I find a snail snake on a stone.

d
I want to eat a cash fish dish.

FINAL REVIEW 02

TRACK 11-2

1. Listen and circle the right picture.

a

b

c

2. Listen and circle the right blend for the word.
(or digraph)

a

bl   br

b

sm   sw

c

sh   ch

d

ng   wh

Well done!

3. Look and complete the word.

a

_ _ _obe

b

_ _ _ess

c

smoo_ _

d

_ _ _ale

4. Read the sentence and circle the right word.

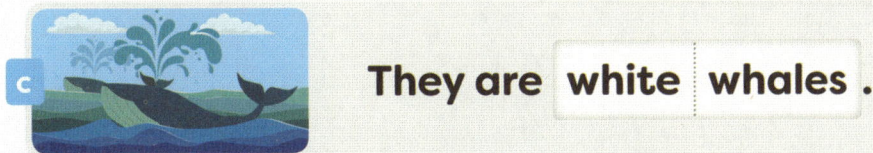

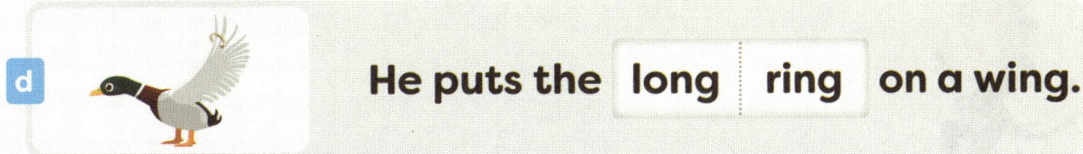

a

I put cream | cross on the bread.

b

"Swim, swan | sweet , swim!"

c

They are white | whales .

d

He puts the long | ring on a wing.

MEMO

Unit 01 pp20-21

flag

block

black

fly

next

clock

Unit 02 pp30-31

glass

plug

plate

sleep

glows

when

Unit 03 pp42-43

bride

cream

put

bread

cross

dress

Unit 04 pp52-53

grape   **frog**   **green**

friend   **get**   **trip**

Unit 05 pp64-65

spiders   **space**   **snake**

many   **spin**   **stop**

Unit 06 pp74-75

small   **smells**   **walk**   **swan**

sky   **Swim**   **sweet**

Unit 07   pp86-87

cheeses

shapes

cherries

sheep   chins   some   chop

Unit 08   pp96-97

What   they   that

phone   photo   whales

Unit 09 pp108-109

cash

Let's

lunch

fish

dishes

bench

Unit 10 pp118-119

duck

too

cloth

long

ring

kicks

smooth

AMAZING PHONICS

神奇的
自然拼读

发音·单词·句子·故事

韩国钥匙英语学习方法研究所 / 著

Vol. **4**

ADVANCED
VOWELS
& SILENT LETTERS

ZHEJIANG UNIVERSITY PRESS
浙江大学出版社

Nice to meet you.
What is your name?

My name is...

- -

AMAZING PHONICS
Vol.4 Advanced Vowels & Silent Letters

CONTENTS

FUN

Reading Fun
Match Up
Blend Up
Color Up
Stickers
Chants

EASY

Comprehensible Input
Simple Lesson Plans
Repeated Activities
Simple Activities
Step by Step

INDEPENDENT

Self-Perfection
Self-Correction
Individual Work
Hands-On Work

Hello, I am Jay!

I want to be a magician when I grow up.

Can you help me make something amazing happen?

Amazing Phonics Vol.4
Advanced Vowels &
Silent Letters

Vol.1 Short Vowel Sounds

Vol.2 Long Vowel Sounds

Vol.3 Consonant Blends & Digraphs

Vol.4 Advanced Vowels & Silent Letters

Hello, I am Curi!

I am very curious.
If you follow me,
we will have
so much fun!

Welcome to *Amazing Phonics*!

Amazing Phonics introduces a fun, easy, and effective way
to start your phonics journey.

Phonics is a method for teaching reading and writing of the English language by developing children's phonemic awareness.
Amazing Phonics Vol.4 teaches advanced vowels and silent letters. Advanced vowels include r-controlled vowels, diphthongs; a combination of two adjacent vowel sounds within the same syllable and spellings. Also by learning about silent letters, children can understand spellings better.

Amazing Phonics also focuses on "the way of learning". Children perfect themselves by repeating their work. They work toward mastery of the task. This repetition leads not only to mastery of the task, but also to a heightened ability to concentrate and an increased sense of accomplishment. So, if children are given enough time to practise, they can perfect their skills while feeling that they are learning well.

We hope every child can experience the joy of learning with *Amazing Phonics*. Have fun learning, everyone!

Features of *Amazing Phonics*

A truely amazing experience!

Amazing Phonics Vol. 4
Advanced Vowels & Silent Letters

R-Controlled Vowels	Diphthongs	Diphthongs & Spellings	Spellings	Silent Letters
Unit 1 ar, ir	**Unit 3** au, aw	**Unit 5** ou, ow	**Unit 7** air, are, ear	**Unit 9** kn, wr, mb
Unit 2 er, or, ur	**Unit 4** oi, oy	**Unit 6** al, wa	**Unit 8** ear, eer, ere	**Unit 10** g, h, t

1 ★ Books ★

Student Book

Pronunciation & Chant Videos

Step by Step Day by Day

Sight Word Fun One Step Closer to Reading

Now I can read phonics & sight words in the story!

I get more confident! Everything is so easy! Now I am ready for MORE!

Yay!

Workbook (My Writing Note)

I can write the **words & sentences** I learned!

I am so confident.
I can make my own sentences.
It is so much fun!

Features of *Amazing Phonics*

✨ Videos ✨

Fun phonics lectures with Mr. David, the magician!

I can understand the pronunciation better!

Guess the words!
Time to meet the words and become friends with them.

I love my phonics chants!
I want to sing them again and again.
It is easy and so much fun!

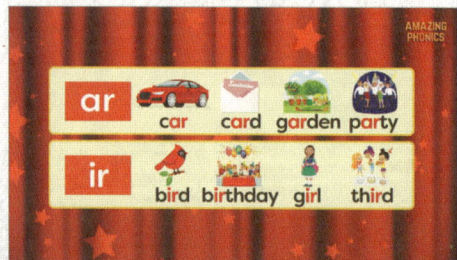

Pronunciation & Chant Videos Are Included with the Book
Full Lectures Are Available at

2 ★ Multimedia ★

Applet

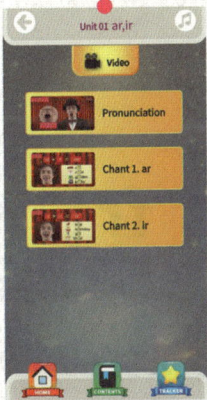
Video

Match Up

Story Building

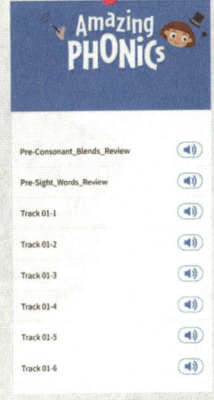
Word Quiz

MP3

I want to do it again and again!
I am perfecting myself by repeating the work.
I feel so confident! Now I can read more!

Pre-Learning
Cosonant Blends Review

MP3

★ Listen and circle the right blend for the picture. ★

1   bl   fl   ⊂cl⊃

2   br   bl   pl

3   gr   dr   fr

4   sn   st   sp

★ Color by Sight Word ★

want　want　want　want

this

this　this

want　this　this

can

come

this　this

can　can

come　come

can

this

want

want

want

come

this

this　this　this

this　this

want

want　this

is　is

big

big

this

want

big　big

is　is

is

this

this　this

big

this

want

this

this

this

want

want　want　want

1. is 🔴   2. can 🟠   3. this 🟡

4. big 🔵   5. want 🟣   6. come 🟢

CHAPTER 1

Advanced Vowels

R-controlled Vowels

Unit 1 ar, ir
car, card, garden, party, bird, birthday, girl, third

Unit 2 er, or, ur
dinner, finger, water, actor, fork, pork, burn, surf, turn

Guess the words!

UNIT **1**

ar   **ir**

Listen & Blend Up ▶ TRACK 01-1

R-Controlled Vowels

Listen > Point > Repeat

1 **ar** .... **car**

2 **ir** .... **girl**

car

girl

Focus On

▶ TRACK 01-2

🔊 Listen > 🎵 Chant > ✏️ Highlight

1 ar ♪

car **card** **garden** **party**

2 ir ♪

bird **birthday** **girl** **third**

CHECK UP

Match Up

START GAME FINISH

Look > Listen > Match

1
2
3
4

ar

ir

5
6
7
8

Color Up

START · GAME · FINISH

👁 Look > 💬 Say > 🎨 Color

1
card
party

2
bird
girl

3
car
bird

4
third
garden

5
birthday
garden

6
girl
car

7
card
party

8
birthday
third

SIGHT WORD

Sight Word Fun

START GAME FINISH

◉ Look > 🔍 Find > 🎨 Color

★ Sight Word ★
will

Find and color the cars that have the word "will" on them.

ICECOLD

will

well

will

will

will

wall

well

wall

will

will

Sight Word Check

▶ TRACK 01-4

🦻 Listen > 💬 Repeat > ⭕ Circle

1

I (will)  to the .

I (will) go to the party.

2

It will be my .

It will be my car.

3

My  will be like this.

My garden will be like this.

4

I will give her the .

I will give her the card.

STORY BUILD UP

Reading Fun

TRACK 01-5

Listen > Repeat > Put on the Stickers

I will go to a birthday party.
The birthday girl is my friend.
It is her third birthday.

The party will be in a garden.
I will give her a big birthday card.
We will go to the party by car.

Story Build Up

◉ Look > ♥ Put on the Stickers > 📖 Read

1

I will go to a [birthday] party.

The birthday [girl] is my friend.

It is her [third] birthday.

2

The party will be in a [garden].

I [will] give her a big birthday card.

We will go to the [party] by car.

REVIEW

Check Up 01 ▶ TRACK 01-6

1. Listen and check the right picture.

2. Listen and check the right word.

girl	bird	third

Check Up 02

1. Look and circle the right word for the picture.

1
thild
thard
third

2
cal
car
cir

3
bird
bard
bild

4
gardon
girden
garden

2. Read the sentence. Look in the word bank.
Write the right word for each sentence.

Word Bank

1. car   2. third

3. party   4. bird

*You can use each word only once.

1   It is my baby's .... birthday.

2   I have a yellow ....

3   My .... can sing very well.

4   It is my baby's birthday ....

UNIT **2**

er **or** **ur**

Listen & Blend Up ▶ TRACK 02-1

R-Controlled Vowels

> 🎧 Listen > 👆 Point > 👄 Repeat

❶ **er** ········· **fing**er

❷ **or** ········· **f**or**k**

❸ **ur** ········· **t**ur**n**

fing**er**

fork

turn

Focus On ▶ TRACK 02-2

🔊 Listen > 🍎 Chant > ✏️ Highlight

1 er 🎵

dinner

finger

water

2 or 🎵

actor

fork

pork

3 ur 🎵

burn

surf

turn

Match Up

TRACK 02-3

START · GAME · FINISH

Look > Listen > Match

1

2

3

4

or

ur

er

5

6

7

8

Color Up

START GAME FINISH

Look > Say > Color

1

pork
fork

2

burn
surf

3

water
finger

4

finger
dinner

5

pork
water

6

burn
turn

7

actor
dinner

8

actor
turn

Sight Word Fun

START · GAME · FINISH

Look > Find > Color

★ Sight Word ★
and

Color the letters in the word "and" different colors.

and

Find and circle the word "and".

and   and

and   will   and

on   and   you

Sight Word Check

Listen > Repeat > Circle

1

I like  (and)  .

I like turkey (and) pork.

2

One and two !

One and two forks!

3

Wash it with SOAP and .

Wash it with soap and water.

4

Let's have and go .

Let's have dinner and go surfing.

STORY BUILD UP

Reading Fun

TRACK 02-5

Listen > Repeat > Put on the Stickers

"It's dinner time!
Stop surfing and get your dinner!"
"Wow! There are turkey and pork!
Can I have my fork?"

"Go wash your hands.
Turn on the tap and wash your
fingers with soap and water."

Story Build Up

👁 Look > ❤ Put on the Stickers > 📖 Read

1

"It's dinner time! Stop surfing and get your dinner!"

"Wow! There are turkey and pork! Can I have my fork ?"

2

"Go wash your hands. Turn on the tap and wash your fingers with soap and water ."

REVIEW

🦻 ✅ Check Up 01 ▶ TRACK 02-6

1. Listen and check the right picture.

2. Listen and check the right word.

pork	fork	actor

📖 🅐 Check Up 02

1. Look and circle the right word for the picture.

1
wator
water
watur

2
pork
perk
purk

3
dinner
dinnor
dinnur

4
actur
acter
actor

**2. Read the sentence. Look in the word bank.
Write the right word for each sentence.**

Word Bank

1. Dinner　　2. Turn

3. fingers　　4. pork

*You can use each word only once.

1 I like turkey and ....

2 .... is ready!

3 .... on the tap and wash your hands.

4 I have ten ....

CHAPTER 2

Advanced Vowels
Diphthongs

Unit 3 au, aw
author, autumn, Laura, Paul, awesome, awful, prawn, saw

Unit 4 oi, oy
coin, oink, noise, point, boy, joy, soy, toy

Guess the words!

au

aw

Listen & Blend Up ▶ TRACK 03-1

Diphthongs

🔊 Listen > 👆 Point > 🎲 Repeat

❶ **au** .... **Laura**

❷ **aw** .... **prawn**

Laura

prawn

Focus On

▶ TRACK 03-2

🎧 Listen > 🍅 Chant > 🖊 Highlight

1  **au**

author   **autumn**   **Laura**   **Paul**

2  **aw**

awesome   **awful**   **prawn**   **saw**

Match Up

▶ TRACK 03-3

START GAME FINISH

👁 Look > 👂 Listen > 🖌 Match

1 Paul

2

3

4

aw   **au**

5 My name is Laura

6

7

8

Color Up

START GAME FINISH

👁 Look > 💬 Say > 🎨 Color

1
Paul
Laura

2
author
autumn

3
awful
awesome

4
saw
Paul

5
awesome
prawn

6
author
Laura

7
autumn
awful

8
prawn
saw

Sight Word Fun

Look > Find > Color

★ Sight Word ★
about

Find and color the leaves that have the word "about" on them.

about

about

about

about

and

and

about

about

about

and

about

Sight Word Check

TRACK 03-4

Listen > Repeat > Circle

1

is **about** to start.

Autumn is **about** to start.

2

I know all about ____.

I know all about Laura.

3

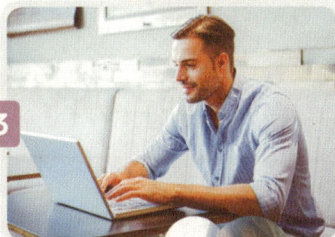

I write about an ____ man.

I write about an awesome man.

4

I think about ____.

I think about Paul.

STORY BUILD UP

Reading Fun

TRACK 03-5

Listen > Repeat > Put on the Stickers

Laura and Paul are friends.
They want to be authors.

Laura loves the autumn.
She writes about
an awesome autumn.

Paul sees a prawn.
He writes about it.

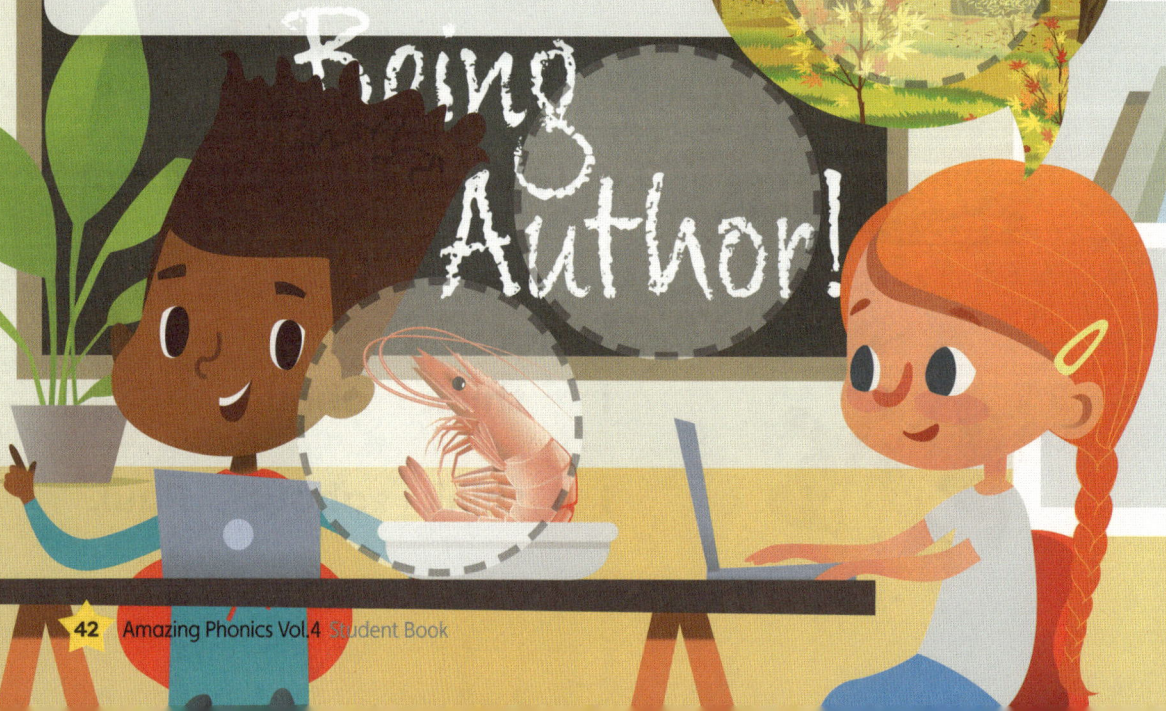

Being Author!

✨ Story Build Up

◉ Look > ♥ Put on the Stickers > 📖 Read

1

Laura and Paul are friends.

They want to be authors.

2

Laura loves the autumn.
She writes about an awesome autumn.

3

Paul sees a prawn.

He writes about it.

Check Up 01 ▶ TRACK 03-6

1. Listen and check the right picture.

2. Listen and check the right word.

autumn	Laura	author

Check Up 02

1. Look and circle the right word for the picture.

1
- Paul
- Pawl
- Parl

2
- arful
- auful
- awful

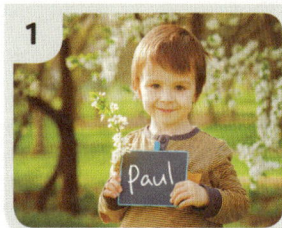

3
- artumn
- awtumn
- autumn

4
- prawn
- praun
- prarn

**2. Read the sentence. Look in the word bank.
Write the right word for each sentence.**

Word Bank

1. Laura
2. autumn
3. awesome
4. about

*You can use each word only once.

1 I write .... autumn.

2 .... and Paul are friends.

3 Look at the .... car!

4 Paul loves the ....

Listen & Blend Up

TRACK 04-1

Diphthongs

Listen > Point > Repeat

① oi .... coin

② oy .... boy

coin

boy

MP3 & Video & Game & Quiz

Focus On ▶ TRACK 04-2

Listen > Chant > Highlight

1  oi

coin **oink** **noise** **point**

2  oy

boy **joy** **soy** **toy**

CHECK UP

Match Up

TRACK 04-3

START GAME FINISH

Look > Listen > Match

1	2	3	4

oi   oy

5	6	7	8

Color Up

START GAME FINISH

👁 Look > 💬 Say > 🎨 Color

1

noise
oink

2

boy
soy

3

toy
joy

4

coin
oink

5

boy
soy

6

point
noise

7

point
coin

8

joy
toy

Sight Word Fun

START GAME FINISH

Look > Find > Color

★ Sight Word ★
enjoy

Find and color the coins that have the word "enjoy" on them.

point

enjoy

toy

enjoy

enjoy

oink

enjoy

bean

enjoy

enjoy

Sight Word Check

▶ TRACK 04-4

🎧 Listen > 💬 Repeat > ⭕ Circle

1

I (enjoy) playing with 🧸 pigs.

I (enjoy) playing with toy pigs.

2

I enjoy making .

I enjoy making noise.

3

I enjoy eating 🫛 beans.

I enjoy eating soy beans.

4

He enjoys 🥗 .

He enjoys lunch.

Reading Fun

TRACK 04-5

Listen > Repeat > Put on the Stickers

My **boy** has a **toy** pig.

He **enjoy**s making a **noise** with it.

The **toy** says, "**oink, oink**."

My **boy enjoy**s playing with it.

He **point**s at the pig's nose.

He says, "It looks like a **coin**!"

oink!

Story Build Up

⦿ Look > ❤ Put on the Stickers > 📖 Read

1

My (boy) has a toy pig.
He enjoys making a (noise) with it.
The toy says, "(oink), oink."

2

My boy (enjoys) playing with it.
He (points) at the pig's nose.
He says, "It looks like a (coin)!"

REVIEW

Check Up 01 ▶ TRACK 04-6

1. Listen and check the right picture.

2. Listen and check the right word.

oink　　point　　coin

Check Up 02

1. Look and circle the right word for the picture.

1
soi
soy
saw

2
point
poynt
paunt

3
coyn
coin
caun

4
baw
boi
boy

2. Read the sentence. Look in the word bank.
Write the right word for each sentence.

Word Bank

1. oink
2. toy
3. noise
4. boy

*You can use each word only once.

1 I play with my ....

2 What is the ....?

3 A pig says " ...."!

4 Look at the ....

CHAPTER 3

Advanced Vowels

Diphthongs & Spellings

Unit 5 ou, ow
around, cloud, house, mountain, cow, brown, flower, town

Unit 6 al, wa
always, call, tall, talk, wand, was, wall, waffle

1 2 3 4

5 6 7 8

9 10 11 12

13 14 15 16

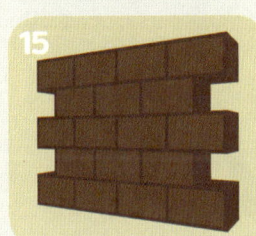

Guess the words!

UNIT 5

 ou

 ow

Listen & Blend Up ▶ TRACK 05-1

Diphthongs

Listen > Point > Repeat

1 **ou** .... **cloud**

2 **ow** .... **cow**

cloud   cow

Focus On

▶ TRACK 05-2

Listen > Chant > Highlight

1 ou

around   **cloud**   **house**   **mountain**

2 ow

cow   **brown**   **flower**   **town**

CHECK UP

Match Up

▶ TRACK 05-3

⏻ START 🎮 GAME ⏹ FINISH

👁 Look ＞ Listen ＞ Match

1

2

3

4

ow   **ou**

5

6

7

8

Color Up

START GAME FINISH

👁 Look > 💬 Say > 🎨 Color

1 house cloud

2  cow town

3  mountain around

4 brown flower

5  brown flower

6  cloud around

7  cow town

8  mountain house

Sight Word Fun

START GAME FINISH

👁 Look > 🔍 Find > 🎨 Color

★ Sight Word ★
down

Color the letters in the word "down" different colors.

down

Find and circle the word "down".

(down)   up

down   down   up

and   down   down

Sight Word Check

▶ TRACK 05-4

🎧 Listen ＞ 💬 Repeat ＞ ⭕ Circle

1

I go (down) the  .

I go (down) the mountain.

2

It   is   downtown.

It   is   downtown.

3

"Come   down,  ."

"Come   down,   cow."

4

Put   down   the  .

Put   down   the   flowers.

STORY BUILD UP

There is a small **town** up
in the **mountain**s.
I have a small **house**
in the **town**.

Look!

Let's walk **around** my
house now. Look **down**.
You can see **flower**s on the
ground. Look up.
You can see big **cloud**s,
too.

Story Build Up

Look > **Put on the Stickers** > **Read**

1

There is a small ⟨ town ⟩ up in the
⟨ mountains ⟩.
I have a small ⟨ house ⟩ in the
town.

2

Let's walk ⟨ around ⟩ my ⟨ house ⟩
now. Look down. You can see
⟨ flowers ⟩ on the ground.
Look up.
You can see big ⟨ clouds ⟩, too.

👂 ✅ Check Up 01 ▶ TRACK 05-6

1. Listen and check the right picture.

2. Listen and check the right word.

flower   **around**   **cloud**

📖 🅰 Check Up 02

1. Look and circle the right word for the picture.

1
hause
howse
house

2
cau
cow
cou

3
braun
broun
brown

4
mountain
mowntain
mauntain

**2. Read the sentence. Look in the word bank.
Write the right word for each sentence.**

Word Bank

1. around   2. flowers

3. town   4. clouds

*You can use each word only once.

1 I live in a small ....

2 I like red ....

3 There are some .... in the sky.

4 I walk .... my house.

UNIT 6 al wa

Listen & Blend Up ▶ TRACK 06-1

Spellings

🎧 Listen ＞ 👆 Point ＞ 👄 Repeat

1 al ·········· **tall**

2 wa ·········· **wand**

tall

wand

MP3 & Video & Game & Quiz

Focus On ▶ TRACK 06-2

🔊 Listen > 💿 Chant > ✏️ Highlight

1 al 🎵

always

call

tall

talk

2 wa 🎵

*Wall can be an 'al' word and a 'wa' word

wand

was

wall*

waffle

CHECK UP

Match Up

▶ TRACK 06-3

START GAME FINISH

👁 Look > 👂 Listen > 👆 Match

| 1 | 2 | 3 | 4 |

wa   **al**

| 5 | 6 | 7 | 8 |

Color Up

START　GAME　FINISH

👁 Look > 👄 Say > 🎨 Color

1

call

talk

2

call

wall

3

wand

was

4

tall

talk

5

wall

tall

6

waffle

always

7

wand

waffle

8

always

was

Sight Word Fun

Look > Find > Color

★ Sight Word ★
because

Color the waffle pieces that have the word "because" on them.

because

well

always

because

because

because

waffle

because

tall

smell

because

Sight Word Check

TRACK 06-4

Listen > Repeat > Circle

1

(Because) he is .

(Because) he is tall.

2

Because I was .

Because I was talking.

3

I  you because I like it.

I always call you because I like it.

4

I want a 🧇 because I smell it.

I want a waffle because I smell it.

STORY BUILD UP

🔊 Listen ＞ 💬 Repeat ＞ ❤ Put on the Stickers

I watched things over the **wall**.
Because I was **tall**.

I **always call** you.
Because I like **talk**ing.

I want to eat food now.
Because I smell **waffle**s.

Story Build Up

👁 Look > ❤ Put on the Stickers > 📖 Read

1

I watched things over the wall.
Because I was tall.

2

I always call you.
Because I like talking.

3

I want to eat food now.
Because I smell waffles.

REVIEW

Check Up 01 ▶ TRACK 06-6

1. Listen and check the right picture.

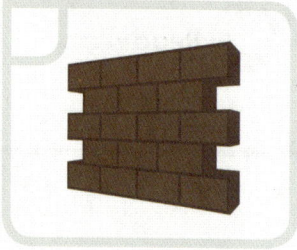

2. Listen and check the right word.

| was | waffle | wand |

Check Up 02

1. Look and circle the right word for the picture.

1.

carr
call
wall

2.

wand
was
waffle

3.

tall
talk
walk

4.

wand
waffle
wall

**2. Read the sentence. Look in the word bank.
Write the right word for each sentence.**

Word Bank

1. waffles
2. call
3. wand
4. tall

*You can use each word only once.

1 I like to eat ....

2 He is very ....

3 I have a magic ....

4 I will .... you.

CHAPTER 4

Advanced Vowels Spellings

Unit 7 air, are, ear
chair, hair, stair, hare, square, stare, bear, pear, wear

Unit 8 ear, eer, ere
ear, hear, near, cheer, deer, steer, adhere, here, sphere

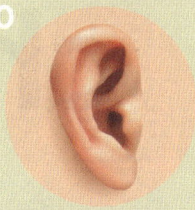

Guess the words!

UNIT 7

air are ear

Listen & Blend Up

▶ TRACK 07-1

Spellings

Listen > Point > Repeat

① **air** ········· **chair**

② **are** ········· **square**

③ **ear** ········· **bear**

chair

square

bear

Focus On ▶ TRACK 07-2

🎧 Listen > 🎵 Chant > ✏️ Highlight

1 air 🎵

chair

hair

stair

2 are 🎵

hare

square

stare

3 ear 🎵

bear

pear

wear

CHECK UP

Match Up

▶ TRACK 07-3

⏻ START 🎮 GAME ⏹ FINISH

◉ Look > 👂 Listen > 🖌 Match

1  **2**  **3**  **4**

are	ear	air

5  **6**  **7**  **8**

Color Up

START GAME FINISH

Look > Say > Color

1

~~bear~~
pear

2

chair
stare

3

hair
hare

4

hair
square

5

pear
wear

6

stare
stair

7

chair
bear

8

hare
wear

✦ Sight Word Fun

◉ Look 〉 🔍 Find 〉 🎨 Color

★ Sight Word ★
her

Color the balloons that have the word "her" on them.

her

her

her

and

her

will

her

her

her

her

her

her

Sight Word Check

▶ TRACK 07-4

🦻 Listen > 💬 Repeat > ⭕ Circle

1

Look   at   (her)  .

Look   at   (her)   hair.

2

She    her   coat.

She   wears   her   coat.

3

It   is   her  .

It   is   her   chair.

4

A  eats   her 🍐 .

A   bear   eats   her   pear.

STORY BUILD UP

Reading Fun

▶ TRACK 07-5

🔊 Listen > 💬 Repeat > ❤️ Put on the Stickers

I come up the **stairs**.
And sit on a **chair**.

I **stare** at a **hare**.
I like **her** **hair**.

There is a **bear** next to **her**.
He eats a **pear**.

Story Build Up

Look > Put on the Stickers > Read

1

I come up the [stairs].
And sit on a [chair].

2

I [stare] at a hare.
I like her [hair].

3

There is a [bear] next to [her].
He eats a [pear].

REVIEW

Check Up 01 TRACK 07-6

1. Listen and check the right picture.

2. Listen and check the right word.

| bear | pear | wear |

Check Up 02

1. Look and circle the right word for the picture.

1
hair
hare
hear

2
bare
bear
bair

3
stare
staire
stear

4
chare
chair
chear

2. Read the sentence. Look in the word bank. Write the right word for each sentence.

Word Bank

1. bear
2. chair
3. hair
4. square

*You can use each word only once.

1 I see a big brown ....

2 I want to sit on a ....

3 It is a ....

4 You have long ....

 **ear**  **eer**  **ere**

Listen & Blend Up ▶ TRACK 08-1

 **Spellings**

👂 Listen ❯ 👆 Point ❯ 💬 Repeat

① **ear** ·········· **ear**

② **eer** ·········· **deer**

③ **ere** ·········· **here**

 **ear**

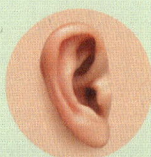 **deer**

 **here**

DAY 1

Focus On ▶ TRACK 08-2

🔊 Listen > 🎵 Chant > ✏️ Highlight

1 ear 🎵

2 eer 🎵

3 ere 🎵

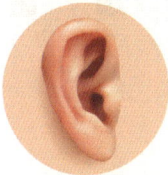

ear

cheer

adhere

hear

deer

here

near

steer

sphere

CHECK UP

Match Up

▶ TRACK 08-3

START GAME FINISH

👁 Look > 🎧 Listen > Match

1
2
3
4

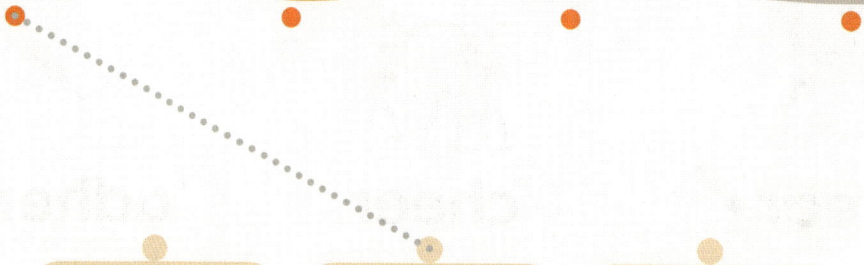

| ere | eer | ear |

5
6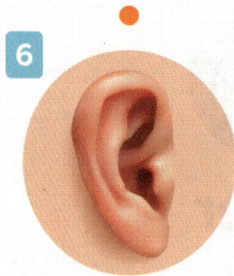
7
8

✨ Color Up ✨

START   GAME   FINISH

👁 Look > 💬 Say > 〰 Color

1

sphere

 adhere

2

hear

near

3

steer

cheer

4

here

sphere

5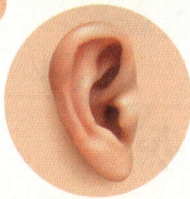

ear

hear

6

steer

deer

7

near

ear

8

deer

here

SIGHT WORD

Sight Word Fun

START GAME FINISH

Look > Find > Color

★ Sight Word ★
something

Find and color the puzzle parts that have the word "something" on them.

will

and

put

something

something

something

something

something

something

about

some

thing

get

Sight Word Check

TRACK 08-4

Listen > Repeat > Circle

1

I  (something.)

I hear (something.)

2

Something is  me.

Something is near me.

3

I need something  .

I need something here.

4

Something is in my  .

Something is in my ear.

STORY BUILD UP

Reading Fun

▶ TRACK 08-5

Listen > Repeat > Put on the Stickers

I **hear** a noise in my **ear**.
Something is **near** me.

Is it a cow?
No, it is **something** small.

A baby **deer**! I **cheer**.
I love **deer**.

Story Build Up

Look > Put on the Stickers > Read

1

I [hear] a noise in my [ear].
Something is [near] me.

2

Is it a cow?
No, it is [something] small!

3

A baby deer! I [cheer].
I love [deer].

REVIEW

🎧 ✅ Check Up 01 ▶ TRACK 08-6

1. Listen and check the right picture.

2. Listen and check the right word.

ear   hear   near

📖 🅰 Check Up 02

1. Look and circle the right word for the picture.

1 	heer hear here	2 	chear cheer chere
3 	dear deer dere	4 	are eer ear

2. Read the sentence. Look in the word bank. Write the right word for each sentence.

Word Bank

1. here
2. deer
3. hear
4. ears

*You can use each word only once.

1 I .... a noise.

2 I have two ....

3 We are ....

4 A .... is near me.

CHAPTER 5

Silent Letters

Silent Letters

Unit 9 kn, wr, mb
knee, knife, knock, wrap, wrist, write, climb, lamb, thumb

Unit 10 g, h, t
design, eight, sigh, hour, ghost, school, castle, listen, watch

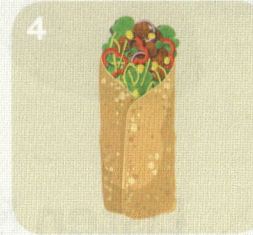

Guess the words!

UNIT 9

kn   wr   mb

Listen & Blend Up

▶ TRACK 09-1

Listen > Point > Repeat

① **kn** ·········· **knee**

② **wr** ·········· **write**

③ **mb** ·········· **lamb**

knee

write

lamb

MP3 & Video & Game & Quiz

DAY 1

Focus On ▶ TRACK 09-2

Listen > Chant > Highlight

1 kn ♪

knee

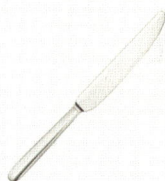
knife

knock

2 wr ♪

wrap

wrist

write

3 mb ♪

climb

lamb

thumb

CHECK UP

Match Up

▶ TRACK 09-3

START GAME FINISH

◉ Look > 👂 Listen > 🎯 Match

1

2

3

4

wr	mb	kn

5

6

7

8

Color Up

START GAME FINISH

Look > Say > Color

1
wrist
write

2
lamb
climb

3
wrap
write

4
knee
knife

5
thumb
knock

6
knock
knee

7
wrist
wrap

8
lamb
thumb

Sight Word Fun

Look > Find > Color

★ Sight Word ★
use

Find and color the lambs that have the word "use" on them.

use

use

well

and

use

use

will

Sight Word Check

TRACK 09-4

Listen > Repeat > Circle

I can (use) a 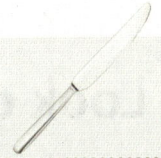 .

I can (use) a knife.

Use a pen to  .

Use a pen to write.

I use my  to  .

I use my wrist to knock.

I use my  to  .

I use my knees to walk.

STORY BUILD UP

Reading Fun

TRACK 09-5

Listen > Repeat > Put on the Stickers

Look at my **knee**s.

I **use** my **knee**s to walk.

Look at my **wrist**.

I **use** a pen to **write**.

Look at my **thumb**.

I **use** a **knife** to eat.

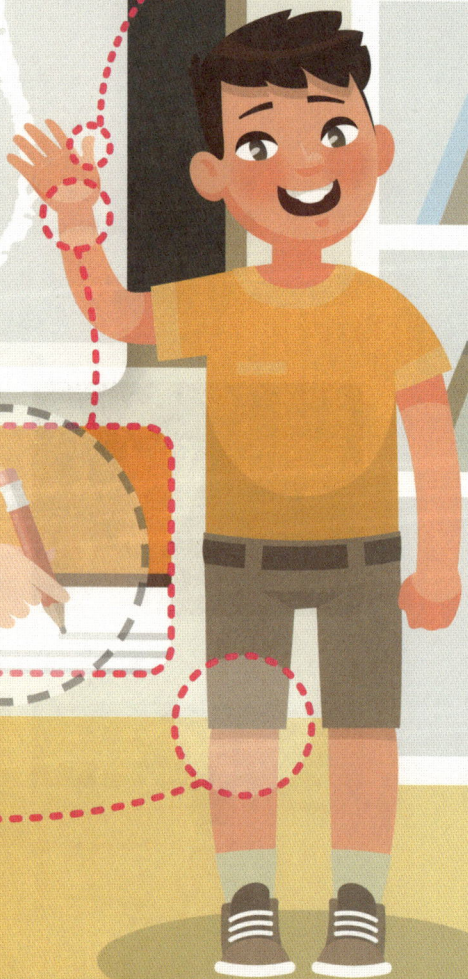

Story Build Up

Look > Put on the Stickers > Read

1

Look at my knees .
I use my knees to walk.

2

Look at my wrist .
I use a pen to write .

3

Look at my thumb .
I use a knife to eat.

REVIEW

Check Up 01 ▶ TRACK 09-6

1. Listen and check the right picture.

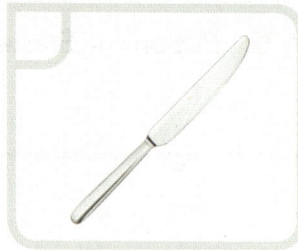

2. Listen and check the right word.

| climb | lamb | thumb |

Check Up 02

1. Look and circle the right word for the picture.

1	lamb
	lam
	lab

2	knock
	knoc
	knok

3	clib
	clim
	climb

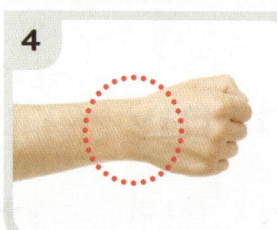

4	wrist
	wist
	rist

2. Read the sentence. Look in the word bank. Write the right word for each sentence.

Word Bank

1. knife   2. knees

3. climb   4. lambs

*You can use each word only once.

1 I have two ....

2 I see many .... in the grass.

3 I can .... up the mountain.

4 I see a fork and a ....

UNIT **10**

Listen & Blend Up

▶ TRACK 10-1

Silent Letters

🔊 Listen > 👆 Point > 💬 Repeat

❶ **g(h)** ········· **eight**

❷ **h** ········· **ghost**

❸ **t** ········· **castle**

eight

ghost

castle

Focus On ▶ TRACK 10-2

🔊 Listen > 🎵 Chant > 🖍️ Highlight

1 g

design

eight＊

*'gh' is silent.

sigh＊

2 h

hour

ghost

school

3 t

castle

listen

watch

CHECK UP

Match Up ▶ TRACK 10-3

START GAME FINISH

👁 Look > 👂 Listen > Match

1

2

3

4

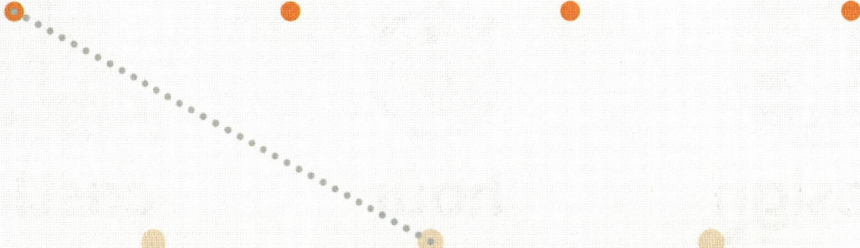

h   t   g

5

6

7

8

Color Up

👁 Look > 💬 Say > 🎨 Color

START GAME FINISH

1

~~school~~
sigh

2

ghost
hour

3

castle
listen

4

design
eight

5

ghost
hour

6

watch
listen

7

design
eight

8

watch
castle

Sight Word Fun

START   GAME   FINISH

Look > Find > Color

★ Sight Word ★
your

Color the letters in the word "your" different colors.

your

Find and circle the word "your".

your   your

and   your   will

your   will   your

Sight Word Check

▶ TRACK 10-4

🔊 Listen > 💬 Repeat > ⭕ Circle

1

Let   me   see   ⭕(your)      .

Let   me   see   ⭕(your)   watch.

2

I   like   your   .

I   like   your   design.

3

Is   it   your   ?

Is   it   your   castle?

4

Can   I   use   your      ?

Can   I   use   your   watch?

STORY BUILD UP

Reading Fun

TRACK 10-5

🔊 Listen > 💬 Repeat > ❤️ Put on the Stickers

What is **your** **school**?
My **school** is a **design school**.

What time do you go to **school**?
I go to **school** at **eight** o' clock.

Do you like **your** **school**?
Yes, I **listen** to many things.

Brand Design

Package Des

Story Build Up

👁 Look > ❤ Put on the Stickers > 📖 Read

1

What is your school?
My school is a design school.

2

What time do you go to school ?
I go to school at eight o' clock.

3

Do you like your school?
Yes, I listen to many things.

REVIEW

🔊 ✅ Check Up 01 ▶ TRACK 10-6

1. Listen and check the right picture.

2. Listen and check the right word.

| design | eight | sigh |

📖 🖊 Check Up 02

1. Look and circle the right word for the picture.

1
shool
school
scool

2
wauch
watch
wach

3
gost
ghost
goust

4
desain
desin
design

2. Read the sentence. Look in the word bank. Write the right word for each sentence.

Word Bank

1. eight
2. castle
3. ghost
4. watch

*You can use each word only once.

1 I go to school at .... o'clock.

2 There is a .... here.

3 I see a big ....

4 I need a new ....

FINAL REVIEW 01

TRACK 11-1

1. Listen and circle the right picture.

a

b

c

2. Listen and circle the right word.

a coin toy

b steer stair

c autumn awful

d deer here

Well done!

3. Look and complete the word.

a g_ost

b pa_ty

c ch_ir

d bo_

4. Read the sentence and circle the right word.

a Do you like your | scool | school ?

b There are turkey and | pork | fork .

c My boy has a | soy | toy | pig.

d I smell | waffles | flowers .

FINAL REVIEW 02

1. Listen and circle the right picture.

TRACK 11-2

a

b

c

2. Listen and circle the right word.

a

burn   dinner

b

bear   hare

c

sphere   hear

d

author   awesome

Well done!

3. Look and complete the word.

a aro_nd

b no_se

c clim_

d pe_r

4. Read the sentence and circle the right word.

a I come up the | chairs | stairs | .

b You can see big | around | clouds | .

c It is her third | birthday | garden | .

d Laura loves the | author | autumn | .

MEMO

图书在版编目（CIP）数据

神奇的自然拼读：全8册/韩国钥匙英语学习方法研究所著 . -- 杭州：
浙江大学出版社，2023.3

ISBN 978-7-308-23493-1

Ⅰ . ①神… Ⅱ . ①韩… Ⅲ . ①英语 - 儿童读物 Ⅳ . ① H319.4

中国版本图书馆 CIP 数据核字（2023）第 019615 号

浙江省版权局著作权合同登记图字：11-2022-229 号

神奇的自然拼读（全 8 册）

韩国钥匙英语学习方法研究所　著

特约策划	穆　强
责任编辑	罗人智
责任校对	卢　川
责任印制	范洪法
封面设计	红杉林文化
出版发行	浙江大学出版社
	（杭州市天目山路 148 号　邮政编码 310007）
	（网址：http://www.zjupress.com）
排　　版	西风文化工作室
印　　刷	北京雅图新世纪印刷科技有限公司
开　　本	787mm×1092mm　1/16
印　　张	47
字　　数	380 千
版 印 次	2023 年 3 月第 1 版　2023 年 3 月第 1 次印刷
书　　号	ISBN 978-7-308-23493-1
定　　价	188.00 元（全 8 册）

版权所有　翻印必究　印装差错　负责调换

浙江大学出版社市场运营中心联系方式（0571）88925591；http://zjdxcbs.tmall.com.

Unit 01 pp20-21

party   garden   will   girl

third   birthday

Unit 02 pp30-31

water   turkey   dinner

fingers   surfing   fork   Turn

Unit 03 pp42-43

autumn awesome authors

about Laura prawn Paul

Unit 04 pp52-53

points coin enjoys boy

oink noise

Unit 05 pp64-65

clouds house flowers town

house around mountains

Unit 06 pp74-75

talking

waffles

always

Because   was   wall

Unit 07 pp86-87

stare   pear   hair   stairs

chair   bear   her

Unit 08 pp96-97

ear   cheer   deer   hear

something   near

Unit 09 pp108-109

knife   write   use   knees

thumb   wrist

Unit 10 pp118-119

school   design   your

listen   eight